To John
with gratitude
+ affection —

Hugh

TSAR PAUL
AND THE
QUESTION OF MADNESS

TSAR PAUL
AND THE
QUESTION OF MADNESS

An Essay in History and Psychology

Hugh Ragsdale

Contributions to the Study of World History, Number 13

GREENWOOD PRESS
New York • Westport, Connecticut • London

Library of Congress Cataloging-in-Publication Data

Ragsdale, Hugh.
   Tsar Paul and the question of madness : an essay in history and
psychology / Hugh Ragsdale.
      p.   cm. — (Contributions to the study of world history, ISSN
0885-9159 ; no. 13)
   Bibliography: p.
   Includes index.
   ISBN 0-313-26608-5 (lib. bdg. : alk. paper)
   1. Paul I, Emperor of Russia, 1754-1801—Mental health.   2. Soviet
Union—Kings and rulers—Biography.   3. Soviet Union—History—Paul
I, Emperor of Russia, 1754-1801.   I. Title.   II. Series.
DK186.2.R34   1988
947′.071′0924—dc19   88-24677
[B]

British Library Cataloguing in Publication Data is available.

Library of Congress Catalog Card Number: 88-24677
ISBN: 0-313-26608-5
ISSN: 0885-9159

First published in 1988

Greenwood Press, Inc.
88 Post Road West, Westport, Connecticut 06881

Printed in the United States of America

The paper used in this book complies with the
Permanent Paper Standard issued by the National
Information Standards Organization (Z39.48-1984).

10 9 8 7 6 5 4 3 2 1

"All our lives long we are engaged in the process of accommodating ourselves to our surroundings: living is nothing else than this process of accommodation. When we fail a little, we are stupid. When we fail flagrantly, we are mad."
--Samuel Butler, *The Way of All Flesh*

"[Paul] devised each day ways to frighten others, yet he himself was the most frightened of all."
--Karamzin, *Memoir on Ancient and Modern Russia*

FOR

D. O. P.

N. P. P.

P. D.

M. O. M.

CONTENTS

PREFACE

Having worked for a time on the diplomacy of Russia in Europe during the early period of the Napoleonic wars, I have again and again run into the ill-famed and ill-fated personality of Paul I and his reputed madness. In an age when historians have resorted more and more to psychohistorical study, it seemed to me natural to undertake such a study of Paul, to deal with the disputed question of his mental condition. This book, then, has three aims.

The first is to describe the mentality of Paul in the context of the two most important influences which formed it, the thought of the European Enlightenment and the culture of the Russian society of his time.

The second is to examine that long-standing controversy in the historiography of Russia: was Paul really mad? His assassins claimed that he was, and they used his alleged madness--and the threat that it presumably posed to the well-being of the state--to excuse their rather extreme remedy of regicide.[1]

---

1. The memoirs of the assassins and of others are in *Tsareubiistvo 11 marta 1801 goda: zapiski uchastnikov i sovremennikov*, 2nd ed. (St. Petersburg: n.p., 1908).

There are different schools of thought in the controversy.[2] On the one hand, it is clear that, quite apart from the assertions of his assassins, whose viewpoint has always been subject to the gravest suspicions, others of Paul's contemporaries had the most serious doubts about his mental condition. The Austrian ambassador at the court of Catherine II, Count Louis Cobenzl, reported that Paul was entirely unpredictable and unstable.[3] Both Paul's childhood tutor, S. A. Poroshin, and his faithful civil servant, F. V. Rostopchin, were at times in despair over his behavior, and both predicted that he would make himself hated. Rostopchin added that Paul lacked the capacity for self-control.[4]

Later the British ambassador, Sir Charles Whitworth, reported to his court explicitly what the others--perhaps out of fear of retribution--were merely implying, that Paul was unambiguously out of his mind.[5] The French *chargé d'affaires* concurred.[6]

The great majority of historians have agreed with these damning opinions of Paul's mental condition. According to S. F. Platonov, "when he ascended the throne at the age of forty-two, Paul was a broken man, physically, mentally and spiritually." Kazimierz Waliszewski concluded that Paul "was the victim of morbid tendencies which inevitably resulted from . . . an abnor-

---

2. In fact, there are three previous psychological studies of Paul: Pierre Morane, *Paul I de Russie, avant l'avènement, 1754-1796* (Paris: Plon-Nourrit, 1907); Pavel I. Kovalevskii, *Imperator Petr III, Imperator Pavel I: psikhiatricheskie eskizy iz istorii* (St. Petersburg: Akinfiev, 1909); Vladimir F. Chizh, "Imperator Pavel I: psikhologicheskii analiz," *Voprosy filosofii i psikhologii,* 1907, passim. None of these works can be considered strong from the viewpoint of psychology/psychiatry; but both Morane and Chizh have done admirably conscientious work as biographers, and they are both cited relatively frequently here. For further comment on these and other works, see my remarks in Hugh Ragsdale, ed., *Paul I: A Reassessment of His Life and Reign* (Pittsburgh: University of Pittsburgh Center for International Studies, 1979), "Introduction."

3. Roderick E. McGrew, "A Political Portrait of Paul I from the Austrian and English Diplomatic Archives," *Jahrbücher für Geschichte Osteuropas* 18:506-507 (1970).

4. Chizh, "Imperator Pavel I," 3:274. *Arkhiv kniazia Vorontsova,* 40 vols. (Moscow: Universitetskaia tipografiia, 1870-1895), 8:76; 34:257-258.

5. Whitworth to Grenville, mid-March 1800; Public Record Office, FO 65/46.

6. Morane, *Paul I de Russie,* p. 372.

mal constitution of mind." Geoffrey Bruun refers to Paul as the "pathologically unbalanced son" of Catherine II.[7]

Now, it may be objected that it is not to the works of these authors that the present-day historian turns for authoritative opinion on the subject, and that is correct. Still, Waliszewski and Bruun in particular are widely read, and we can find much the same opinion in works from which the specialist cannot so readily withhold his respect. Nikolai K. Schilder, in a substantial biography that remains one of the standard works on Paul, found his statecraft deplorable and portrayed it by and large as a mockery of good sense.[8] Even Kliuchevskii, in many ways so favorably disposed to Paul, wrote that he was "morally abnormal" and that he refused to submit to the conventional constraints of human society.[9] There is substantial disagreement in the historical assessment both of Paul's policies and of his personality, but the idea that his alleged madness was a mere fabrication of the memoirists who assassinated him is untenable.

On the other side of the ledger is a body of very different opinion, and the difference derives in great part from the different selection of source materials on which it is based. This is the opinion of those historians who have turned their attention away from the well-worn accounts of the memoirists to the policies of Paul as recorded in the archives. They have found a Paul of quite a different quality.

A good example is the diplomatic and military history of the reign by Dmitrii A. Miliutin.[10] Miliutin found Paul's foreign policy to be constructive, consistent, rational, and purposeful, and though Miliutin missed some important documentation and consequently made some relatively serious errors, still his conclusions are, in my opinion, not far wide of the mark.

The study that has contributed more than any other both to revise the traditional pejorative judgments on Paul and at the

7. Sergei F. Platonov, *A History of Russia* (Bloomington: Indiana University Press, 1964), p. 304. Kazimierz Waliszewski, *Paul the First of Russia* (Philadelphia: J. B. Lippincott, 1913), p. 478. Geoffrey Bruun, *Europe and the French Imperium, 1799-1815* (New York: Harper, 1938), p. 40.

8. N. K. Schilder, *Imperator Pavel I: istoriko-biografitcheskii ocherk* (St. Petersburg: Suvorin, 1901).

9. V. O. Kliuchevskii, *Sochineniia*, 8 vols. (Moscow: Gospolitizdat, 1956-1959), 5:189-190, 439-440.

10. Dmitrii A. Miliutin, *Istoriia voiny 1799 goda mezhdu Rossiei i Frantsiei v tsarstvovanie imperatora Pavla I*, 5 vols. (St. Petersburg: Imperatorskaia Akademiia nauk, 1852-1853).

same time to inspire a generally revisionist reexamination of the matter is M. V. Klochkov's close and detailed analysis of the administrative business of the reign.[11] Klochkov's work describes administrative reforms inspired by exemplary dedication to rationalism, legality, and order. Paul was concerned to harness the spoiled nobility to do its duty. He was sensitive to the welfare of the common people. He streamlined an army grown fat, and he made the wheels of government turn markedly more efficiently. He appears in fact in many ways to be a model prince. The mind whose work is reflected in the documents that Klochkov reviewed was not conceivably that of a madman.

More or less in the tradition of Klochkov is a series of studies published recently by American historians who are also more heavily indebted to freshly exploited archival materials than to the older published sources. My own published research is among these studies, and the bulk of them I have collected and edited in a volume that reexamines Paul's personality and government. I have found, as my colleagues in this enterprise have found, that there is often a clear and rational design apparent in Paul's work.[12]

When I consider the particular problem of Paul's mental condition, however, I find that the evidence does not fall unambiguously on the side of the revisionists' works, including my own. It seems to me that Paul's mentality was a kind that is reflected in the formalities of bureaucratic procedure in a fashion that is so flattering as to be misleading. My opinion is that neither the Paul of the memoirists nor the Paul of the archival records is the whole Paul. Hence the question remains: What was the nature of his mental condition? Having written this work on the subject, I have naturally developed an opinion about it. But I have found the answer to be far from simple, and I do not presume to present it to the reader persuasively until he has followed me through the evidence that has led me to it.

---

11. M. V. Klochkov, *Ocherki pravitel'stvennoi deiatel'nosti vremeni Pavla I* (St. Petersburg: Senatskaia tipografiia, 1916).

12. Ragsdale, *Paul I.* In addition to the materials in this volume, there are other significant items of recent American scholarship. See my *Détente in the Napoleonic Era: Bonaparte and the Russians* (Lawrence: Regents Press of Kansas, 1980) and "Russia, Prussia, and Europe in the Policy of Paul I," *Jahrbücher für Geschichte Osteuropas* 31:81-118 (1983). An especially important item testifying to the clear and constructive nature of Paul's foreign policy in an area often neglected is Muriel Atkin, "The Pragmatic Diplomacy of Paul I: Russia's Relations with Asia, 1796-1801," *Slavic Review* 38:60-74 (1979). For a view of Paul more traditional and less revisionist than is usual in recent scholarship, see McGrew, "A Political Portrait of Paul I."

The third aim of this book is methodological. How is psychology/psychiatry to be used judiciously and appropriately in the study of history, and what variety of it lends itself to such use?

I began this study some years ago when enthusiasm for what is called, for better or worse, psychohistory was in full cry. The very prevalence of interest in the subject influenced both my selection of the topic and my outlook on it. I began the study, therefore, in the favored mode of psychohistorical science, if that is the right word, that of Freudian psychoanalysis. I was never, however, content to use the canons of psychoanalysis in history without considering their relative reliability, and I found very early that I had much work to do in order to satisfy myself on that question. At the same time, I have reminded myself stubbornly that there are other varieties of psychological inquiry and that I must be disposed to consider how productive these are in the study of history. I have found several approaches to the subject useful or interesting in one way or another, and especially three: the clinical apparatus of classifying mental illness in our own time (the *Diagnostic and Statistical Manual* of the American Psychiatric Association), a much cruder apparatus of the same kind from the late eighteenth century, and modern non-Freudian theories of personality.

As the study progressed, the usefulness of these first two approaches, the clinical terminology of the eighteenth century and that of the twentieth, increasingly asserted their value, and they are consequently represented here in a fashion intrinsic to the question of Paul's mental condition. Moreover, these two approaches have gradually supplanted that of Freudian psychohistory--and for two fundamental reasons. First, even assuming the entire soundness of Freud's theory in diagnoses pertinent to Paul, the theory failed to offer valuable suggestions of insight into his dynamics of personality. Second, and more seriously, when those elements of psychoanalytic theory pertinent to the kind of personality that Paul was found to have were examined in the light of clinical and experimental support for them, they were found to be wanting in soundness.

Hence, as the study progressed, it turned out that while traditional Freudian psychohistory had little of interest to say about Paul, the use of Paul as a test case spoke with unmistakable significance to the question of the reliability of Freudian theory in the study of history. It appeared in the end that the apparatus of Freudian psychohistory was simply not intrinsic to the question of Paul's mental condition, and hence it has been, in a sense, condemned here to the Appendices. I wish to emphasize as clearly as possible, however, that I do not consider it for that reason unimportant. On the contrary, it seems to me vastly important. We have had countless examples of this style of psychohistory parading its pontifical conclusions on issues great and small while its practitioners never pause to raise questions of empirical evidence or relative reliability.[13] And we have had significant statements of historical science examining and criticizing this form of the study of history.[14] What I have done here is to attempt to use those parts of the theory pertinent to Paul while evaluating them step by step through clinical and experimental literature. I hope that the results will be found more concrete and persuasive than the findings of efforts to deal with the problem in a more abstract form.

Two of the three subjects of this book, the question whether Paul was mad and the question what kind of twentieth-century Western psychology can lead us soundly through an eighteenth-century Russian subject, stray a good deal from the conventional pathway of the historian's work. I have frankly found them to be more awkward and taxing than I imagined at the outset, and for the sake of presenting my conclusions as clearly and cogently as possible, I have chosen to lay out the logical progress through the subject in a stubbornly elementary fashion exactly as it developed in my own mind. This procedure has what I find almost inadvertently to be another advantage: it preserves a kind of narrative mystery about a problem teasingly opaque until in the end enough evidence has been brought to bear on it to render it plausibly comprehensible.

Chapter 1 is a description of the salient features of the personality of the grand prince. Chapter 2 is a rather detailed examination of his education. Paul's education was unusually important for a number of reasons. It was designed with special care, and he took it especially seriously. It was characteristic of the eighteenth century to invest enormous faith in the efficacy of education. Moreover, his education lasted, in a sense, an unusually long time; or, to put the matter another way, it was only in the fourth decade of his life that he was able to practice the profession to which he had been educated. I have relied heavily

---

13. See Appendix B especially.

14. See especially Jacques Barzun, *Clio and the Doctors: Psycho-History, Quanto-History* (Chicago: University of Chicago Press, 1974), and David Stannard, *Shrinking History: On Freud and the Failure of Psychohistory* (Oxford: Oxford University Press, 1980).

here on translating several documents crucial to Paul's mind-set.

Chapter 3 is a summary of his reign. I have purposely made it brief, as it is the part of the story told here that is best known, and the reader can easily find additional detail, both in the older historical literature and in the recent American research cited in the notes.

Chapter 4 is an exploration of a hitherto unknown aspect of the assassination. There is evidence that the conspiracy that took Paul's life was much more ambitious than we have previously realized, that it incorporated plans to defame his reputation as a means of excusing the deed which the conspirators had in any event determined on.

Chapters 5 and 6 compare Paul's thinking and his policies with those of other absolute sovereigns of the time and describe how cases of mental illness were defined and treated in royal personages elsewhere.

Chapter 7 is an examination of the question of his mental condition by the standards of twentieth-century psychological and psychiatric literature. The applicability of Freudian and other personality theories is the subject of the Appendices.

Not without more than a little help from our friends do such books as this one appear.

To Forrest and Ellen McDonald I am indebted for editorial and practical advice, especially in chapter 5, for assistance in preparation of the manuscript, but above all for helping me to worry about it. Rod McGrew and I have shared an interest in the subject for years. He has read and commented on the manuscript and responded to all of my requests for consultation. John Lukacs has generously taken a lively interest in the work and has given me the benefit of his own impressive knowledge of history, no part of which seems far from his wide-ranging interests. Walter Pintner first heard excerpts of the book in a lecture that I gave at the Institute of History of the Academy of Sciences in Moscow, and his moral and other support have been encouraging. I have also benefited by the comments of Sam Baron and Al Rieber. Ed Streit and Mike Mendle have been remarkably patient in helping with some of the more exotic problems of word processing, especially in the match-up of old and outmoded systems with newer PCs, and Guy Hubbs and Don Muir have also responded to questions of this kind. My Soviet colleagues and friends--Aleksei Leont'evich Narochnitskii, Nikolai Nikolaevich Bolkhovitinov, Valerii Nikolaevich Ponomarev, Natan Iakovlevich Eidel'man, and Zhenia, Larisa, and

Masha Shiffers--have all had more influence on my Russian education than they could easily understand. Kate Ragsdale and Eleanor Streit read proof patiently and conscientiously. Anna Jacobs and Paula Dennis explained to me the mysteries of the contemporary technology of proportional font, and David Klemmack and Mike Rhiney put the necessary machinery at my disposal and showed me how to use it. The Graduate School and the Research Grants Committee of the University of Alabama supported this work with generous stipends. Grants which I received from the Fulbright Committee, the International Research Exchanges Board, the American Council of Learned Societies, and the American Philosophical Society for work in diplomatic history were indirectly instrumental in the progress of this book as well. Cynthia Harris and David L. Young of Greenwood Press have been unusually attentive and helpful.

We all know, of course, who is responsible for whatever inadequacies remain here.

With the exception of a few familiar Anglicized forms, Russian words and names are transliterated by a modified Library of Congress system.

TSAR PAUL
AND THE
QUESTION OF MADNESS

1

THE GRAND PRINCE: DEVELOPMENT OF PERSONALITY

The childhood of Grand Duke Paul Petrovich has been characterized in a nutshell by one of his biographers. "Few princes have made such a painful beginning in life as the son of Catherine II, Paul Petrovich. He grew up in a family devoured by hate, among a tumult of vulgar passions and degrading quarrels, in an atmosphere of spies and informers. [There was] a void of tenderness around the infant. While still a child, he witnessed a hideous and bloody spectacle: the murder of his father. His mother, usurper of the throne, punished him for the fact that the malcontents of the new reign rallied around his name; . . . she distrusted him and attempted to discredit him. He discredited himself by his [own] eccentricities."[1]

If this summary introduction strays a trifle in the direction of caricature, still there is much truth in it. In 1745, a petty German princess, Sophie of Anhalt-Zerbst, married the heir to the Russian throne, the future Peter III. History knows the bride as Catherine II or Catherine the Great, while Peter III is

---

1. Pierre Morane, *Paul I de Russie, avant l'avènement, 1754-1796* (Paris: Plon-Nourrit, 1907), p. i.

remembered as a hopeless idiosyncratic and one of those transient mock-martyrs who dominate the dynastic history of mideighteenth-century Russia. The marriage was doomed to disaster from the beginning both by conflicts of taste and temperament as well as by the contrasts of ability that distinguished Catherine from Peter. It was this family conflict itself that produced the first significant issue in the controversial biography of their son, the heir to the Russian throne.

Paul's very legitimacy is disputed in two different versions. The one that is well known observes that Catherine and Peter were married for nine years (1745-1754) without any progeny, that Catherine began to take lovers, and that Paul, born during Catherine's affair with Sergei Vasil'evich Saltykov, was the son of Saltykov, not of Peter III. The merits of the story cannot be resolved: there is little evidence to work with, archives do not record conceptions, and persons who are the subjects of such stories have their own reasons for telling what they want to be believed. Much of the support for this version of Paul's paternity comes from Catherine's memoirs, which excuse her various infidelities on the ground that Peter III never consummated the marriage. Again we cannot know if that was true. Circumstantial evidence, however, tends to support Catherine's account. If Paul was not Peter's son, then Peter never sired any progeny, legitimate or otherwise, though he dabbled in ostensibly amorous affairs of his own. His mistress, Elizabeth Vorontsova, reportedly accused him of impotence in the course of a drunken public quarrel, and she later married Alexander Ivanovich Polianskii and produced a son by him in 1774.[2] Catherine, on the other hand, had two more children (Anna, December 1758, who died soon after birth, and Alexei Grigorovich Bobrinskii, April 1762-1813), as well as two or more miscarriages.

The second version of Paul's illegitimacy is not well known, but it is not incompatible with the first. It is that Catherine's child of 1754 was stillborn, that Empress Elizabeth, in her passion for an heir, made a secret of the fact, kept Catherine insensate with alcohol, and rushed into the nearby Finnish countryside where she found and appropriated a newborn baby. In order to secure the secret, it was then necessary to transport to Siberia the whole village from which the baby was taken. There the story was uncovered by the Decembrist revolutionaries after 1825, and it made its way to Alexander

---

2. Ibid., p. 28.

Herzen's press in London, where it was first published in 1862.[3] The evidence supporting this story is shadowy in the extreme. In fact, this story is one more in an obscure succession of scandals in Romanov family history which are not likely to be elucidated satisfactorily by historians. Paul knew nothing of this story--as it first came to light in 1825--and yet it illustrates the difficulty of reconstructing his biography fully and reliably.

The first version of his illegitimacy he eventually discovered. When he rushed to his mother's deathbed, he sealed her cabinet and her papers. He discovered there, among other things, her memoirs, which contain the story implying that Saltykov was Paul's father. Paul therefore had to come to terms with the possiblity that he was not, so to speak, his father's son. He chose, however, to regard himself as the real son of Peter III.

With or without a disputed paternity, children born heir to an imperial throne get a special upbringing, which may be fortunate or otherwise. In Paul's case, it was otherwise. Elizabeth, having waited nine anxious years for an heir, took Paul from his mother the instant he was born, moved him into her apartments, and raised him under her own supervision. He was not someone's son--he was the ward of the state, maintained in virtual isolation from his parents. This situation reportedly bothered Catherine a good deal and Peter not at all.

Elizabeth guarded Paul, according to Catherine's memoirs, from all interference by his mother. He was surrounded by nurses and given every kind of excessive care. He was kept in a hot room in a cradle covered with black fox furs, a heavy satin quilt, and a pink velvet blanket. Catherine feared that such measures would spoil his health, but there was nothing that she could do about it. Catherine alleged that she first saw Paul forty days after his birth and that she was allowed to visit him only three times during the first six months of his life. Only toward the end of Elizabeth's reign, when Paul was seven years old, could Catherine see him once a week.

Catherine has sometimes been blamed for neglecting or abusing Paul: she is often held responsible for the bad relations

---

3. Natan Iakovlevich Eidel'man, "Obratnoe providenie; istoricheskii ocherk," *Novyi mir*, 1970, No. 5, pp. 226-241. This legend describes Paul as a "chukhonets," a somewhat pejorative slang word for Finn. I once asked an old Kuban Cossack, a veteran of World War I and of the Tsaritsyn campaign of the Russian civil war, if he knew the story of Paul as *chukhonets*. He answered in a single word: "*konechno* (of course)."

that later developed between them.[4] It seems more likely, however, that the abnormal relationship between Catherine and her son in his infancy was in great part the product of Elizabeth's policy. At age eleven, Paul himself remarked that he had been accustomed to seeing Elizabeth only once or twice a year but that he saw his mother "rather frequently" after she took over the throne.[5] On the other hand, if it was initially Elizabeth's regime that made the development of normal maternal and filial affection impossible, Catherine would later make significant contributions of her own.

Elizabeth died in January 1762, and it was the reign of her successor, Peter III, which precipitated the most serious problem of Paul's life prior to his reign. Peter was politically frivolous. He had been raised a Lutheran in Germany, and he mindlessly offended the Russian nobility by parading his scorn for the Russian Orthodox Church. He offended the officers' corps of the Russian army by his uncritical admiration and imitation of the Prussian army of Frederick the Great. Catherine wrote in her memoirs that she had long found the crown of Russia more attractive than her husband and that she lay plans to take the throne from him. In fact, she conducted herself with consummate prudence and cunning. She exhibited piety and respect for Russian institutions and the traditions of the country. Equally important, she selected her lovers shrewdly. She contracted a liaison with Grigorii Orlov, a member of the crucial guards' corps, which had made and unmade Russian sovereigns in the eighteenth century. Catherine's plans developed and culminated in the palace revolution of 28 June 1762. A few days later, Peter III died mysteriously in a careful captivity. Catherine reported at various times that he had died of apoplexy, diarrhea, and excessive drinking. In fact, he was strangled. It is possible that Catherine did not, in the most literal and documentary sense, give the order for his murder. It is not possible that the people who did it, the Orlov brothers, failed to understand the benefit and security which she would share with them in disposing of Peter. At the time of the coup and the murder of his father, Paul was eight years old. We can surmise that these events frightened him, but, unfortunately, we do not know his precise reaction.

---

4. For example, George P. Gooch, *Catherine the Great and Other Studies* (London: Longmans, Green, 1954).

5. Semen Andreevich Poroshin, *Zapiski*, 2nd ed. (St. Petersburg: Balashev, 1882), col. 613.

Two years later, in July 1764, a disgruntled army officer named Mirovich tried for some unfathomable reason to liberate a dynastic relic from a preceding generation: Ivan VI. Poor Ivan, in the second year of his life, had served for thirteen months (1741-1742) as nominal ruler of Russia. One of those endemic coups had overthrown him, and he had been placed under strong guard in a fortress. In his confinement, he experienced neither sunlight nor conversation, and by 1764, at age twenty-five, he had become through environmental deprivation an idiot, a human vegetable. In July 1764, his guards did what they had been instructed to do should anyone try to liberate him: they killed him.[6] This time we know Paul's reaction. He was reported to have been "excited" and to have slept very badly the night after Mirovich's execution.[7]

From the time of her seizure of the Russian throne, Catherine's possession of it became an apple of discord between herself and her son Paul. Catherine's claim to the throne of Russia had not a shred of legitimacy. She was, after all, not a Romanov, not even a Russian.

Paul, on the other hand, was officially a Romanov whatever the truth of his paternity. The Russian law of succession obtaining at the time of Catherine's coup was that decreed by Peter I in 1722. It gave the Russian sovereign the right to choose his or her own heir. When Peter III ascended the throne in 1762, he announced that an heir *would be* designated, though he never named one. The natural choice would have been his putative son Paul, but that choice was not made. When Catherine followed Peter to the throne soon afterward, she did officially designate Paul as heir. Thus in a fashion full of irony and confusion, Paul derived an allegedly legitimate right to the Russian throne from a sovereign who seized and occupied it illegitimately. Still, the situation was accepted at the time, and there is no reason to question the force of Paul's claims. It was precisely the force of those claims, established by Catherine herself, which aggravated her own insecurity on the throne.

Count Nikita Ivanovich Panin was both the governor/guardian of Grand Prince Paul and the chief counselor of

---

6. Peter had visited and interviewed Ivan VI, possibly with a view of naming Ivan as his heir. The visit, however, showed the poor pretender to be in no shape for such a role. Hedwig Fleischhacker, "Porträt Peters III," *Jahrbücher für Geschichte Osteuropas* 5:178 (1957). Sergei M. Solov'ev, *Istoriia Rossii s drevneishikh vremen*, 15 vols. (Moscow: Mysl', 1959-1966), 13:78.

7. Poroshin, *Zapiski*, col. 14.

Catherine at the time of the coup. The success of her seizure of the throne owed much to Panin's influence and cooperation. He had supported her palace revolt, however, on the supposition that she would govern as regent for Paul until the time of his majority, and he clearly favored such an arrangement. Catherine stubbornly resisted the idea and governed as empress in her own right. From that time, a split was established between mother and sovereign on the one hand and son and heir on the other.

The legitimate claims of Paul were a standing threat to Catherine, as her own illegitimate power was a threat to him. The seriousness of the threat is abundantly illustrated by the fates of Peter III and Ivan VI. The policies of any sovereign will generate some unpopularity and opposition, and in any relationship such as that between Paul and Catherine, it was only natural that xenophobic and misogynist Russians discontent with the government of an illegitimate foreign woman would turn their hopes onto a legitimate native man, an heir raised in Russia by Russians. This situation was one of Catherine's most serious political problems, and as Paul approached maturity, it was the most acute problem of his life.

It was both symptom and cause of this dynastic tangle that from early childhood, Paul was conspicuously popular among the Russian people. According to foreign diplomats, the population was rather demonstrative in its expression of affection for him. For example, when Paul was first formally presented to the Russian army in the maneuvers of 1765, the troops cheered him enthusiastically. Moreover, the Russian public evidently understood instinctively the threat which was posed to Paul by virtue of his being his mother's rival in a situation in which two former rivals had not survived. It felt some concern for his safety. Before both of his foreign trips as grand prince, the first to Berlin in 1776 and the second to Vienna and Paris in 1781-1782, crowds gathered to see him off. They lavished affection on him, and, in both cases, they expressed some apprehension of misfortunes lying in wait for him along the way. In the second instance, according to the Prussian ambassador, it made Catherine feel insecure, and she increased the size of the guard at the Winter Palace.[8]

Paul's popularity was especially conspicuous in Moscow. From the time of Peter I, who created his "window on the West" in the place that bore his name, the capital has migrated back

---

8. Morane, *Paul I de Russie*, pp. 167, 217.

and forth between Russia's two greatest cities, Moscow and St. Petersburg--later Petrograd, later Leningrad, the "cradle of the revolution"--establishing between them something of a rivalry that continues even in Soviet times. Whichever of the two is not serving as the official capital at any particular time becomes the opposition capital, the capital of disgruntled dissent, a kind of contrary capital. So it was in Catherine's time, and the expression of this discontent often took the form of demonstrations partial to Paul. Thus, when Paul and Catherine traveled to Moscow early in 1775 to celebrate the end of the Turkish war, it was reported that there was a nuance of chill in the reception which the people gave Catherine but that they received Paul warmly. Somewhat later in the spring, Paul drilled a regiment of troops in Moscow, and crowds gathered about him and kissed his boots. On her way back from New Russia in 1787, Catherine invited her grandsons Alexander and Constantine to meet her in Moscow. When the parents demanded permission to accompany their sons, Catherine refused, according to the French *chargé d'affaires*, because she was afraid to expose Paul to his popularity among the public there.[9]

There is other evidence that Moscow was the site of special tension for mother and son, and that has to do with his health. He was a distinctly sickly child. He suffered from digestive troubles, diarrhea, and vomiting, he was very likely hyperkinetic, and he had frequent fevers. He slept badly, and he was tense and nervous. Catherine was conspicuously solicitous and concerned about his health. She visited him regularly when he was ill. She did even more. In 1768, in the wake of the death of Panin's fiancée, Sheremeteva, from smallpox, she called on the English Dr. Thomas Dimsdale (1712-1800) to inoculate herself and Paul. (She took care to get the full approval of the Senate for Paul's inoculation.) In spite of Paul's sickly childhood, however, Dr. Dimsdale found him at age fifteen to be in excellent health. Moreover, it is clear that as an adult, his physical health was quite robust. He pursued a rigorous daily routine, rising early for military drill and spending most of the day in vigorous activity. He was remarkably free of illness during his extensive foreign travels, though his wife, Mariia Fedorovna, was frequently sick during the trip of 1781-1782. We know very little of adult illness in Paul.

But in Moscow, the scene of his most conspicuous popularity, the scene of popular conflict over rights to the Russian throne, the youthful grand prince was regularly sick. He ac-

---

9. Ibid., pp. 50, 134-136, 313.

companied Catherine to Moscow for her coronation in August 1762, and he promptly developed a fever there.[10] In October 1762, he was still ill of the fever, and reportedly, of swollen legs as well.[11] He returned with Catherine to Moscow for the opening of the great Legislative Commission in 1767, and again he fell ill. On this occasion, she planned a further trip down the Volga to examine unfamiliar parts of her dominions, and when it happened that Paul was too ill to accompany her, she left him in Moscow in the care of the Orlovs, i.e., in the city of his greatest popularity and of her own unpopularity, and in the hands of his father's assassins.[12] Yet, later, as emperor, he would positively enjoy his visits to Moscow and did not experience any of the health problems that had so bedeviled his childhood there.

There was another old Russian tradition that aggravated distrust between Catherine and Paul, the tradition of the "little father tsar." The idea is that the tsar is his people's protector, benign and loving. If he does not so behave, then, according to Russian folklore, he is not the real tsar, or, as the revolutionaries of 1905 put it, "he is not our tsar." This peculiar popular outlook has had a singular influence on the Russian tradition of revolution. In modern times, the Russian masses have revolted chiefly in the name of superior legitimacy: they have rebelled in times of discontent in search of the real tsar whose absence is responsible for their plight.[13]

Paul, of course, fit into this tradition remarkably plausibly. He was accepted as clearly legitimate. He was reputed to be generous to the common people and demanding of the nobility. His mother, on the other hand, was an illegitimate foreign woman whose claims yielded distinctly to his own by both the standards of folk myth and those of law. She was increasingly perceived as the corrupt and pampered creature of the nobility. Even in historical literature, the period is remembered as the golden age of the Russian nobility.

In such circumstances, both petty conspiracies and grand revolts against Catherine's government were likely, and, in fact, they were not rare. A plot in the Preobrazhensky Guards in

---

10. N. K. Schilder, *Imperator Pavel Pervyi: istoriko-biograficheskii ocherk* (St. Petersburg: Suvorin, 1901), p. 35.

11. Morane, *Paul I de Russie*, p. 37.

12. Schilder, *Imperator Pavel Pervyi*, p. 66; Morane, *Paul I de Russie*, p. 50.

13. For amplification, see Daniel Field, *Rebels in the Name of the Tsar* (Boston: Houghton, Mifflin, 1976).

July 1772 resulted in the banishment of several persons to Siberia. In October 1773, the Holstein diplomat in Russian service, Caspar von Saldern, was discovered plotting in favor of Paul. In 1786, Prince Eugene of Württemberg, the brother of Mariia Fedorovna who had been received at the Russian court, entered into secret relations with Gustav III of Sweden to support a revolution in favor of Paul, evidently in hope of occupying a decisive position in the ministry of the new monarch. Somewhat more important was a clique of young journalists, who, having become disillusioned of their original expectations of Catherine's allegedly enlightened government, rallied behind Paul and began a systematic criticism of Catherine's policy. Most important was the formidable rebellion mounted in 1773-1774 by Emelian Pugachev, a Cossack leader and pretender who, drawing directly on the resentment of the common people, declared himself to be Peter III and announced a campaign to assert his own rights and those of his "dear son Paul" to the Russian throne. Developments such as these served as constant reminders of the conflict that divided empress and heir and continued to poison relations between them.

It is obvious that the circumstances into which Paul was born were not auspicious. We need to consider now something of the disposition and temperament which he brought to the problems that he faced. Our best source on Paul's behavior in childhood is the reportage of one of his tutors, Semen Andreevich Poroshin, who was engaged by Panin to teach history and mathematics to Paul. From September 1764 to January 1766, his diary gives us a detailed and intimate portrait of the grand prince at age ten to eleven, and that portrait suggests that Paul's temperament contributed as significantly to his difficulties as did his environment.

He was headstrong and willful. One day one of his servants (a "Kammerdiener") asked him what kaftan he wanted to wear. Paul said that he wanted "the green velvet one." When the servant objected that it was old and worn, Paul grew angry and said that he wanted it anyway. At this point, Poroshin intervened and suggested that it was not necessary to be so stubborn, that it was all right to change one's mind. Paul reconsidered, agreed, and decided to order a new kaftan. Poroshin observed that it was possible to correct in Paul some of his faults and to incline him to recognize good behavior but that it was necessary to know how to approach him.[14]

14. Poroshin, *Zapiski*, col. 61.

One of the most conspicuous qualities which Poroshin remarked in the grand prince was impatience. "His Highness has the terrible custom of hurrying everything: he hurries to get up, he hurries to eat, he hurries to lie down to sleep. An hour or more before we usually sit down to lunch . . . he sends . . . to Nikita Ivanovich [Panin] to ask to have lunch a bit early."15 Thus he was always tense and in a frenzy. His attention was not long held by anything, and his behavior was relentlessly anticipatory. The matter at hand soon bored him, and he looked constantly ahead to the next one, of which he also soon tired; and so keeping him content required providing him a constant parade of novelty to keep him in a state of excitement.

He grew bored at a great state dinner one evening and began to cry. Poroshin consulted Panin, who asked Poroshin to explain to Paul how undignified his behavior was. Similarly, on another occasion, Paul and Panin were talking with several ministers of state at a formal reception in Catherine's presence when Paul grew bored and asked to be taken home. Panin responded that they must remain until the empress was ready to dismiss them. Paul then began to misbehave. Panin punished him by requiring that no one in the household talk to him until he apologized. The next day, he apologized contritely. On this occasion, he earnestly sought Poroshin's advice about how to avoid such behavior in the future. He listened attentively, embraced Poroshin, and assured him that he would do better in the future.16

A few days later, Paul visited Catherine, and, as he related to Poroshin, Catherine asked him confidentially if he knew why Panin was in such an ill temper. Paul said that he did not know. Catherine suggested that it was perhaps because Paul had embarrassed him several days previously. She asked him not to do so again.17 Paul began to cry as he related the story to Poroshin.

At dinner one evening, nearly everyone present had finished eating when someone asked for butter and cheese. Paul grew angry and asked why butter and cheese had not already been brought. He then suggested that the servants were stealing them. He was rebuked by Panin, who explained to him in

---

15. Ibid., col. 166.

16. Ibid., cols. 240, 241.

17. Ibid., col. 246.

French, which the servants did not understand, how offensive his accusation was. Paul then apologized.[18]

The restlessness which characterized his behavior during the day also plagued his sleep. Almost every night, Poroshin said, Paul talked in an audible delirium during his sleep, sometimes in French, sometimes in Russian. If he had had a happy day, his talk was calm and happy. Otherwise, it was angry and ugly. If anything threatening or exciting had happened during the day, he would be unable to sleep at all.

He had a distinct sense of his own importance and a sensitive pride that was easily offended. At age ten, he complained bitterly that the audience in the theater applauded before he did. He asked Catherine to "send away"--*vyslat' von*, a habitual practice of his both at his own "little court" and later as emperor at the court of St. Petersburg--persons in the theater who did not take their cue to applaud from him.

In his regard for people, he was very impressionable, but his feelings were very volatile. Conversations favorable to persons absent--or unfavorable to them--would determine Paul's attitude toward them when he next met them. He was notoriously suspicious, as he himself would later admit. Poroshin noted that it was easy to be liked by Paul but hard to continue in his favor.[19]

He easily became irate when disappointed. When he could not have the dish that he wanted for a meal, he was furious. On such occasions, Panin reproached him clearly, waited for Paul to calm down, then explained his misconduct carefully and deliberately.

Some of the notorious passions of Paul's adulthood were prefigured clearly in his childhood. For example, Poroshin read to him once a story of the Maltese knights, and it so stimulated his imagination that several days later he was still playing games in which he fancied himself a knight of the order.[20] Moreover, it is obvious that his military mania was already developed in his childhood, and this is perhaps the more surprising since Panin regarded the military preoccupations of Peter III as excessive and unbalanced and did all that he could to discourage a similar interest in the heir. Paul was forbidden to play with guns, for example, or with toy soldiers, but it was more or less requisite that the heir review military maneuvers

---

18. Ibid., col. 268.

19. Ibid., col. 96.

20. Ibid., cols. 267-268.

occasionally. In July 1765, he attended such maneuvers in the capacity of a colonel of a regiment of cuirassiers, and it made an enormous impression on him. Poroshin reports that Paul simply lost his interest in study and that for some time thereafter he could think only of military affairs.[21] Of course, Nikita Panin's brother, General Peter Panin, was a frequent visitor in the household, and on such visits there was a great deal of conversation about military affairs at dinner.

Poroshin has been accused by most of Paul's biographers of bending over backwards to give a flattering view of his student. Yet even Poroshin could not hide from himself the more problematic and repugnant features of the character of the grand prince. The particulars are recorded on nearly every page of his diary. One of the constants repeated over and over again in the struggle to mold the character of the future sovereign was the admonition to control himself (*preodoliat' sebia*). A deficit of self-control and a rush to manifest whatever access of emotion he felt was one of his fundamental characteristics. (Still, he controlled himself sufficiently to avoid challenging Catherine directly.) Even Poroshin became discouraged at times, and on one occasion, he prophesied Paul's future ominously and accurately: "With the best intentions in the world, you will make yourself hated, Monseigneur."[22]

V. F. Chizh, in reviewing Poroshin's notes, points out somewhat heavy-handedly that "the child is father to the man," though it is Russian proverbs that he cites to do so: "As in the cradle, so in the grave"; "Only the grave straightens out the hunch-backed."[23] Of course, that is to read history backwards; it is not strictly fair to the subject. Still, it is hard to ignore, considering the observations of Poroshin, the close analogies in the behavior of Paul as child and as adult.

There is one other item preserved by Poroshin, but rarely mentioned by Paul's biographers, that deserves attention. It is a short "memoir of [Paul's] life from 1755-1761 [i.e., from age two to seven] written down in his own words by S. A. Poroshin in 1764-1765."[24] The bulk of this memoir of approximately twenty pages consists of isolated memories, unconnected and incoherent. There are mistakes, and there are obscurities, things im-

21. Ibid., cols. 329, 338, 341, 342-343, 345.

22. Ibid., col. 89.

23. V. F. Chizh, "Imperator Pavel Pervyi; psikhologicheskii analiz," *Voprosy filosofii i psikhologii*, 1907, p. 240.

24. Poroshin, *Zapiski*, col. 602-614.

possible to understand, even if they are worth trying to understand.   On the whole, it is a disappointing document which would require a really dedicated scholastic to make strict sense of, and yet there are in it a few items of interest.

Many of the memories are military.   Paul remembered being shown a battle plan, a model fortress, and a map of the conquests of Russia containing the inscription "the peoples are jealous of you; they often think of you and repeat: you are joy, you are love, the hope of all joys."   He remembered being forbidden to play with the weapons of the Preobrazhensky grenadiers. One of his observations is sophisticated to the point of precocity: he had been visiting Empress Elizabeth, and he had said to her of the new field commander whom she had sent in 1759 to expedite the campaign against Prussia--and who had failed to do so--"Petr Semenovich [Saltykov] went to make peace and did not make peace; and now, of course, he is making neither war nor peace."

But some of the memories are purely personal.   Paul remembered only one person who was a playmate, Savelii Danilovich Titov (?), and he said that he was very glad to see someone of his own size.   He remembered especially tenderly both the birth and the death of his sister, Anna.   Most interestingly, he recalled that in 1758, the "cowardice attacked" (*trusost' napala*): someone slammed a door, and Paul hid under a table and then threw himself at the feet of Panin.

The significance of the military memories does not require elaboration.   There are suggestions of grandiosity in the inscription on the map of Russia's conquests. We may infer that he felt a deprivation of playmates or peers. As for the observation about cowardice, the terms *boiazlivyi* and *boiazlivost'*, fearful and fearfulness, figure prominently in all of the biographical studies of him.

In January 1766, Panin dismissed Poroshin.   There are two probable causes.   Poroshin seems to have developed affection for the fiancée of Panin, Anna Petrovna Sheremeteva.   In addition, he had read excerpts of his diary on Paul to Paul himself, first exacting the promise of secrecy.[25] Subsequently, however, Paul evidently mentioned it.   In any event, the diary came to Panin's attention, and he obviously did not approve of it. After Poroshin, we have no more such careful record of the life of Paul.

---

25. Ibid., col. 448.

The bulk of what we know about Paul's adulthood before his reign and apart from his public conflict with Catherine has to do with two subjects, his education and his family life. His education requires an extensive examination and is reserved for the next chapter. The duties of family life are of exceptional importance for the sovereign of a hereditary monarchy, and that family life is subject to special attention and scrutiny. For that reason, perhaps, it tells us a good deal about Paul.

There are strong suggestions, but no entirely definite evidence, that Paul was deliberately introduced to, tutored in, sexual matters when he was a young man, perhaps with a view of taking no chances on the important business of providing future heirs to the throne. He may have had children by the Kammerfrau of the empress, Iureva. He supposedly had a son known as Semen Velikii by a widow Czartoryska. There are reports in the French diplomatic correspondence that he had liaisons with ladies-in-waiting such as Mme. Bruce or Mme. Talitsin.[26] In any event, it seems clear that although there is no evidence from any period of his life of strong sexual appetites, yet he was not a perfect ingénu. He was conspicuously successful in his imperial sexual duty: he produced an abundant proliferation of children of both sexes, including four male heirs and the next two sovereigns.

In 1773, Catherine invited the Landgravina of Hesse-Darmstadt to visit St. Petersburg with her three daughters, and Paul was given the freedom to choose a bride from the three. He picked Wilhelmina, the second. She was reputed to be aloof and reserved, but Catherine thought that Paul had made the best choice. In his public exposure during the wedding festivities, he made a good impression. He was reported to be attractive, courteous, full of religious sentiments, pleasant, and charming.

The marriage filled Paul with happiness. Wilhelmina, who took the Russian name Nataliia Alekseevna, was clever and respectful of Catherine. Catherine was delighted with this whole turn of events and especially with the reconciliation that it occasioned between herself and Paul, a reconciliation that she gratefully attributed to Nataliia.

But the idyll did not last long. Marriage symbolized Paul's attainment of maturity, and soon thereafter he was granted his long-standing wish to be initiated into the political

---

26. Chizh, "Imperator Pavel Pervyi," pp. 629, 646; Morane, *Paul I de Russie*, pp. 64-65; Isabel de Madariaga, *Russia in the Age of Catherine the Great* (New Haven, Conn.: Yale University Press, 1981), p. 257.

processes of St. Petersburg. The initiation was, however, to be gradual, cautious, and modest. Paul had demanded participation in politics; Catherine began by instructing him in politics. She ordered one of her secretaries to read to him from important state papers twice a week. Before this procedure had long endured, Paul demanded flatly participation in the councils of state. Catherine courteously but firmly refused, saying that it was yet premature. Paul was twenty years old at the time, and he reacted by writing his first policy paper, which was a strong indictment of the principles of Catherine's policy. It made her angry, and it destroyed any chance of his early entry into real politics. From the time of her refusal, he was evidently afflicted with feelings of persecution.[27]

To make matters worse, some weeks after the wedding (September 1773), news of the Pugachev rebellion reached St. Petersburg, thus reminding Russian society of the dubious claim of Catherine to the throne. Catherine also decided about this time to diminish the influence of Nikita I. Panin. After the wedding, he was covered with honors and retired from his position as *Oberhofmeister* of Paul's household. Nikolai Ivanovich Saltykov was appointed in his place. Someone then suggested that Saltykov was probably sent as a spy, and relations between the two royal households soured again.

All of these developments together portended a new estrangement, but there was another contributing factor: Nataliia. Catherine's initial delight with her daughter-in-law soon wore thin. Nataliia was sick a great deal because, Catherine alleged, she did everything to excess. Paul himself remained content with his marriage. He was genuinely devoted to his wife and apparently blind to her sins, but his happiness was interrupted by a tragic childbirth. In April 1776, Nataliia died after horrible suffering, and the child died, too. Perhaps to assuage his sorrow, Catherine informed Paul that Nataliia had betrayed him, that she had become the lover of his friend A. K. Razumovskii. Paul did not at first believe the story, but Catherine produced correspondence to prove it.

These events made the arrangement of a new marriage the order of the day. Frederick the Great, eager to oblige

---

27. E. S. Shumigorskii, *Imperator Pavel Pervyi: zhizn' i tsarstvovanie* (St. Petersburg: Smirnov, 1907), pp. 30-31; Morane, *Paul I de Russie*, pp. 124-125; Catherine's letter of refusal is in *Sbornik imperatorskago russkago istoricheskago obshchestva*, 148 vols. (St. Petersburg: Stasiulevich, 1867-1916), 42:356 (hereafter *Sbornik IRIO*). Paul's policy paper is important and will be examined in detail in the next chapter.

Catherine and put her in his debt in matters of this kind, assisted.   He arranged to break the engagement of Sophia Dorothea of Württemberg to a prince of Hesse-Darmstadt and to have her engaged to Paul instead. Paul traveled to Berlin with a suite to complete the formalities. He was impressed by Berlin and remembered the visit fondly all his life. He had long since become an ardent admirer of Frederick and Prussia. He was pleased with his new fiancée, too. They returned to St. Petersburg, and the wedding took place in September 1776. Sophia Dorothea adopted the Russian name Mariia Fedorovna. She remained grateful to Frederick and was constantly his partisan at the Russian court.

Another reconciliation with Catherine occurred, effected partly by Catherine's arrangement of the new marriage and Paul's satisfaction with its results. During his trip to Berlin, he and Catherine had corresponded amiably. Catherine was pleased with his new bride, and Paul drew up a list of recommendations to Mariia Fedorovna on adapting to her new land and getting along with Catherine.

This marriage was more durable and more important than the first. Mariia Fedorovna had grown up in Montbéliard on the German frontier of the French Enlightenment, in an atmosphere heavy with the reveries of Rousseau. It was under the inspiration in particular of her father, Prince Frederick Eugene, that the parading of the Rousseauist idyll, full of the romance of peasant wisdom and virtue and the sentimentality of German *Schönseligkeit*, was carried to an extreme. The French elements in her education consisted especially of manners, music, dancing, needlework, and painting, as well as literature. At the same time she was taught a good deal of German reserve and distrust of the "levity of French manners and morals," of the decline of French family life, of a society in which women were regarded, in the opinion of these Germans, as playthings. Mariia Fedorovna was encouraged to believe that "in a woman family virtues are valued above all."[28] She imbibed all of the heavy moralism of the age. Her mother, Princess Dorothea, gave her lessons in the form of "Advice of a good mother to her daughter," and Mariia Fedorovna's notebooks were filled with such essays as "The Advantages of Friendship," "On the Choice of Friends," "Of the

---

28. E. S. Shumigorskii, *Imperatritsa Mariia Fedorovna, 1759-1828* (St. Petersburg: Skorokhod, 1892), 1:24-25. The other planned volumes of this biography were never published.

Vices That Corrupt Friendship," and "The Rudeness of a Friend Is Better Than the Flattering Embrace of an Enemy."

She sought a pastoral simplicity and especially a feminine naiveté that was distinctly alien to the worldly salons of metropolitan France, and she composed verse in that spirit:

> Il n'est pas honnête, et pour beaucoup de causes,
> Qu'une femme étude et sache tant de choses.
> Former aux bonnes moeurs l'esprit de ses enfans,
> Faire aller son ménage, avoir l'oeil sur les gens
> Et régler la dépense avec économie:
> Doit être son étude et sa philosophie.[29]

Mariia Fedorovna made an excellent first impression in St. Petersburg in general and on Catherine in particular. She was appreciated there as a kind of charming innocent, a natural product of the idyllic romanticism of the age, and she was, in some respects, an ideal spouse for Paul. She sympathized instinctively with the injustice to which he had been subjected, and she and Paul found a harmonious rapport and a genuine affection. She "perceived in Paul very quickly that there was something of a permanent void" as a consequence of his being held so far from the duties which he had inherited, and she attempted to divert him from his frustration by filling the void with *affaires de ménage*.[30]

She had certain weaknesses, too, which, in the long run, would tell against her. According to the sophisticated--and dated--judgment of the French emissary Corbéron, "her spirit and her character are not of the sort to develop in the place that she occupies. A narrow range of ideas and of knowledge will always restrict her to mediocrity, and nothing discloses on her part what some keener observers want to take for her political address. Princess of Württemberg, grand duchess, empress, she will always be a woman and nothing more."[31] Catherine eventually came to agree with some of this sentiment, as she wrote to Baron Grimm, "She reads much, including perhaps things which she does not understand."[32]

Mariia Fedorovna established a regular routine for the family at Pavlovsk. She busied herself with the ménage and

---

29. Ibid., p. 26.

30. Morane, *Paul I de Russie*, p. 189.

31. Shumigorskii, *Mariia Fedorovna*, pp. 101-102.

32. *Sbornik IRIO*, 23:659.

with books and arranged life at the young court in a quiet and even monotonous fashion. The marriage was a happy one, it did not soon yield to infidelity, and it did produce male children: Alexander in December 1777 and Constantine in May 1779. The birth of the children, however, spoiled the relations between the parents and the grandmother, for Catherine did not hesitate to do with Paul's children just what she had so bitterly complained of Elizabeth's doing with Paul: she took the boys away from their parents in order to establish their upbringing under her own auspices, and this development considerably aggravated the already bad relations between parents and grandmother.

Conflict over the children provided part of the motivation for the extended tour of Europe which Paul and Mariia Fedorovna took in 1781-1782, but there were other considerations as well. Paul wished to divert himself, to distance himself from the source of his most serious frustration and political conflict. Mariia Fedorovna wished to visit her parents in Württemberg. They both wished to see some of the fabled sites in Europe which they had never seen. Mariia Fedorovna's one reservation was her hesitation to be absent from the children for so long.

On Catherine's part, she was equally glad to be rid of daily conflicts over both personal and political matters. In addition, she was just in the process of working a major change in her foreign policy, a shift of favor from Prussia to Austria. It was the fate of the southern provinces of Russia and the Ottoman Empire that was at stake, an area in which the Austrian alliance was significantly more useful than the Prussian alliance. Joseph II had visited Catherine in 1780 to discuss the matter, and Catherine was eager not only to cement the alliance, but also to commit her heir to it if possible. If that were possible, it was, at best, difficult, for Paul remained as attached as ever to the image of Frederick II of Prussia.

One of Paul's courtiers, Nikolai Repnin, approached Catherine's favorite, Prince Grigorii Potemkin, about the prospect of the tour. Potemkin recommended that Paul petition Catherine. Catherine feigned a reluctant consent, which she was in fact only too glad to give. Much to Paul's distress, Catherine insisted on excluding Berlin from the itinerary, and not all of Paul's heated protests sufficed to make her change her mind.

The couple went first to Austria. Joseph met them at the frontier and accompanied them to Vienna. He spared nothing to make a favorable impression on his guests. He invited Mariia

Fedorovna's parents to visit at the same time, and they did. Every form of splendor and favor was lavished upon both couples. Paul had planned to spend only one or two weeks in Vienna, but he stayed more than a month. The visit was a qualified success. Paul formed a good impression of Joseph and of his capital and government, but he retained the most serious reservations about the wisdom of an Austrian alliance for Russia.

From Vienna, they went south to Venice, Rome, Naples, and Florence. At Naples, Paul saw the Chateau Santa Elena, the old prison where a former itinerant heir of the Russian throne had lived in refuge/exile before being taken home by his father, Peter I, to a formidable fate which he did not survive. In Tuscany, they were entertained by Joseph II's brother Leopold, one of the most enlightened princes of the age.

In Paris, they met Benjamin Franklin, who described Paul as "lively and active, with a sensible, spirited countenance."[33] Pierre Beaumarchais read to them from his "Marriage of Figaro." Among their more lasting impressions was a visit to the Duke de Condé at Chantilly, and they would do a good deal later on their own estates in imitation of what they admired at Chantilly. In the summer of 1782, they visited the parents of Mariia Fedorovna at Montbéliard and returned to St. Petersburg through Switzerland and Vienna.

Paul made a particularly lively and favorable impression in France both by his knowledge of the French language and of contemporary French literature. It was, the French said, as if he had been born and educated in France. More consequential, from the political point of view, was the impression that he left in Vienna. Joseph courted Paul assiduously, observed him carefully, and forwarded his impressions to his brother Leopold of Tuscany, where Paul's arrival was imminently expected. "The Grand Duke and the Grand Duchess join to uncommon talents and an extensive knowledge a great desire to see and to learn, and at the same time to succeed and to please sincerely throughout all of Europe, and as one can count on their discretion and honesty, nothing will please them more than to show them everything without artifice and affectation, to speak to them with the greatest frankness." Joseph said that they might be received rather familiarly, that they liked to keep a regular schedule, and that they grew tired if they were entertained late

---

33. Benjamin Franklin, *Autobiographical Writings*, Carl van Doren, ed. (New York: Viking Press, 1945), p. 553.

at night. He observed that they were curious about learned men and women and people of distinction in general.[34]

Leopold responded with impressions of his own, and they were similar to Joseph's. "The Comte du Nord [Paul's incognito] . . . has, in addition to much intelligence (*esprit*) . . . and talent for reflection, the capacity to grasp ideas accurately . . . and to see at once all of their implications. One sees in all his conversation that he wishes the good (*le bien*). I believe that with him it is necessary to act openly and plainly (*rondement*), sincerely, and straightforwardly (*avec droiture*), in order not to make him distrustful and suspicious. . . . I believe him very firm, resolute, and decided when he has taken a position and certainly not a man to let himself be guided by anyone. In general, it seems that he is not fond of foreigners and that he will be rather severe and given to order [and] subordination."[35]

Leopold and Joseph understood much about Paul. They found in him something of a kindred, enlightened spirit. They were perhaps too much in harmony with him to see as deeply into him as their family's archantagonist, Frederick of Prussia, had seen on Paul's Berlin visit of 1776. Frederick was older, more battle-scarred, a seasoned curmudgeon, and a caustic cynic who, in spite of all of the saccharine moral piety of the age, had never been denied enrollment in the ranks of the Enlightened. He foresaw the problems of Paul with startling clarity. "He seemed proud, haughty, and violent, which made those who know Russia apprehend that he would have no little trouble maintaining himself on the throne, or in governing a people rude and primitive (*dure et féroce*) and spoiled by the lax government of several empresses; he would have to fear a fate like that of his unfortunate father."[36]

Back in St. Petersburg, Paul's familiar problems quickly reappeared. He had spoken his mind freely throughout his travels about his distaste for his mother's policies and her system of favorites, and he had made no secret of his Prussophile sympathies, which the trip had done nothing to alter. He had traveled with a considerable suite, and members of his entourage had carried on correspondence with friends at home in which they

34. *Joseph II und Leopold von Toskana: Ihr Briefwechsel*, 2 vols., Alfred von Arneth, ed. (Vienna: Braumüller, 1872), 1:332-339.

35. Ibid., 116.

36. Frederick II, *Oeuvres historiques*, 7 vols. (Berlin: Decker, 1846-1847), 6:122.

were foolish enough to forget the ancient custom of "perlustration," the opening and scanning of correspondence. Some of them made unflattering references to Catherine and her policy and spoke hopefully of a party of "right-thinking" people. Catherine was furious. One of these correspondents was subsequently arrested, others were exiled, and Paul was severely reprimanded.

This whole affair cast a pall over the young court. For a month after his return from Europe, Paul evidently was afraid to pay a visit to Panin, much to the latter's distress. Then Panin fell seriously ill, and Paul and Mariia Fedorovna rushed to his bedside with an apology and an explanation. They were reconciled, and Panin died.

Paul was at this time (1783) twenty-eight years old. His mentor was gone. His friend A. K. Razumovskii had alienated himself by seducing Nataliia Alekseevna. Another friend and confidant, A. B. Kurakin, was in trouble with Catherine for writing critical letters from Europe the year before. Paul was largely isolated in the country that he was destined to rule. The next few years were to be extremely trying for him, and this phase of his life was characterized largely by withdrawal to his estates at Pavlovsk and Gatchina.

Pavlovsk was a peaceful country idyll, preeminently the domain of Mariia Fedorovna. Gatchina, on the other hand, required more construction and refurbishing, and it was Paul's preferred site for the exercise of his taste for military drill. In the 1780s, the couple busied themselves on the two estates, as Catherine observed, like "good masters of the parish."[37] They aspired to establish an interesting social life, and they were reported to entertain all visitors lavishly, but Catherine made their social life problematic. Though she had often visited Gatchina in particular before she made a present of it to Paul in 1783, she never visited there afterwards. In addition, she made it plain that she did not approve of visits by prominent courtiers or by ministers credited to her court. As a consequence, few people visited, and those few came prudently and rarely. Princess Dashkova said that she avoided Gatchina because the empress knew all that took place there and that it was best to avoid being asked unpleasant questions about it. "I visited their highnesses

---

37. S. Kaznakov, "Pavlovskaia Gatchina," *Starye gody*, July–Sept. 1914 (special issue titled "Gatchina pri Pavle Petroviche, tsesareviche i imperatore"), p. 103.

[at Gatchina] only on holidays when the whole court visited them."[38]

In the absence, then, of the style of social life to which they aspired, the royal couple was left in considerable solitude, and they filled their time in a variety of ways. Paul practiced his habitual military exercises. He maintained at Gatchina an army of 2,000 men, and he was up early every morning for drill. Mariia Fedorovna read, managed the household, and designed Gatchina to be a modest replica of Chantilly. They were both fond of picnics. In the evenings, they played chess or parlor games, and there was a great deal of theater, chiefly light French plays.

In the early 1790s, mainly in 1793, Paul departed significantly from the usual routine and gave himself wholeheartedly for a time to the reform and renaissance of the town, as opposed to his own estate, of Gatchina. He ordered a wooden church built for both Catholic and Lutheran services and established regulations for the use of the church for different services at different times. He founded a hospital. He established for the local children a school without any restrictions of sex or social class as well as an orphanage for children of the military. He had glass, chinaware, and textile works and a brick kiln built. He issued a police "Instruction" to maintain good order in the town and to control prices in the local market. He regulated the rent regimes and established measures of poor relief for the local peasants. Finally, he had a mill and a fabric factory built, both of which functioned as concessions to foreigners.[39]

Apart from this flurry of activity of 1793, life at Gatchina continued in the traditional mode. The French ambassador, the Comte de Ségur, found life there in the late 1780s altogether charming. "[The family] circle, although numerous enough, seemed, especially in the country, more an amiable company than an oppressive court. Never did a private family offer with more ease, grace, and simplicity the hospitality of its home; dinners, balls, spectacles, and celebrations, everything there is marked with the stamp of the noblest decency, the best tone, and the most delicate taste. The grand duchess, dignified, affa-

---

38. Ibid., p. 105.

39. S. V. Rozhdestvenskii, *Stoletie goroda Gatchiny, 1796-1896* (Gatchina: Gatchinskoe dvortsovoe upravlenie, 1896), pp. 9-38.

ble, and natural, beautiful without coquetry, amiable without pretence, gives the impression of virtue adorned."[40]

Not all observers were of this opinion. The Princess of Sachsen-Coburg visited Gatchina in 1795 and came away with a very different impression. It had none of the relaxed style of the court of St. Petersburg. Everything there was stretched and strained. Paul was clever and could be charming if he wanted to be, but he was "distinguished by incomprehensible strangeness and foolishness," especially by the wish to arrange everything about himself in the old Prussian form. His estate was covered by military barriers and by sentinels who challenged passers-by, and the soldiers "were dressed in ancient Prussian uniforms which disfigured them and made them seem un-Russian." Going to Gatchina, she said, was like entering a foreign land.[41]

The alternating roles of lord of the manor and imperial drill sergeant did not altogether satisfy Paul. It was in the mid-1780s that he wrote to a friend plaintively, "I am already thirty years old, and I have nothing to do."[42] He busied himself increasingly with trifles, especially with military mania. He continued to dissent from Catherine's policy, as is evidenced chiefly by the treasonous correspondence which he carried on with the court of Prussia through the diplomatic service. In 1789, Count Peter Panin died, and at the same time, the French Revolution began, chasing numbers of French émigrés to the distant asylum of St. Petersburg. It is generally agreed that the developments of the revolution and the arrival of the émigrés excited Paul a good deal, more even than it alarmed the rest of Russian society. We have already observed the fearfulness (*boiazlivost'*) of his childhood and his distinct penchant for good order. The revolution may have aggravated Paul's fears and encouraged his search for the emotional asylum of an assured social and political order.

It was in these disconcerting circumstances that the Nelidova affair occurred. Catherine Ivanovna Nelidova was a graduate of the Smolny Institute for noblewomen and a member of Mariia Fedorovna's entourage. Toward the middle of the 1780s, she became a favorite companion of Paul and was soon rumored to be his mistress, which is unlikely. Their close rela-

40. Louis Philippe, Comte de Ségur, *Mémoires*, 2 vols. (Paris: Firmin-Didot, 1859), 1:106-107.

41. *Russkii arkhiv*, 1869, 7: col. 1102.

42. Shumigorskii, *Mariia Fedorovna*, p. 270.

tionship did not initially disturb Mariia Fedorovna, but eventually, platonic relations or not, jealousy did its work, and when the tensions of the young court became extreme, Nelidova modestly retired to Smolny. At length, however, Mariia Fedorovna discovered in her a sympathetic and unaffected character and an essential ally in the struggle to reason with and to exert a constructive influence on the increasingly willful Paul. They thereupon became inseparable companions. The entire affair is one of the more revealing episodes in Paul's biography.

Chizh observes that "only a strong moralist will condemn Paul Petrovich for growing bored in the company of his wife: in her company many were bored."[43] But it seems that Paul's affection for Nelidova did not supplant his affection for Mariia Fedorovna except when Mariia Fedorovna tried to combat it. One of the elements said to lie at the basis of his friendship with Nelidova was the force of mysticism so conspicuous in that age. It was the era of Mesmer (1734-1815), Cagliostro (1743-1795), and Swedenborg (1688-1772). As Morane explains, "the Grand Duke Paul was one of the first in Russia to react against rationalism and to abandon himself to the mystical current that after the great trial of 1812 and 1813 took possession of Emperor Alexander I and Russian society with such force."[44]

As for the nature of the affair between Paul and Nelidova, Morane judges it to have been platonic: "The love that the son of Catherine vowed to Mlle. Nelidoff was a refined love which addressed itself to the soul, that made no pretension . . . with respect to the senses and that resigned itself to live on Platonism. . . . Paul and Mlle. Nelidoff felt the invincible need to spiritualize their love, to sublimate it, to attribute to it a religious character. They exchanged books of piety; they prayed together. . . . In their love letters, it is entirely a question of God, of heaven and of the infinite."[45]

In fact, their correspondence bears out this opinion. Paul gave her many gifts, and she habitually objected. On one such occasion, she wrote to him typically, "You know, Sire, that while I appreciate the friendship which you have offered me for such a long time, I have felt this sentiment [of friendship] alone, and that your gifts have always caused me more pain than pleasure. Permit me, then, to beg you not to oblige me to receive the

---

43. Chizh, "Imperator Pavel Pervyi," p. 638.

44. Morane, *Paul I de Russie*, p. 345.

45. Ibid., pp. 348-349.

one that I take the liberty of returning."[46]   On one of Nelidova's birthdays, Paul evidently sought to circumvent this kind of objection, so he gave 2,000 serfs, not to Nelidova, but to her mother. Nelidova was nevertheless embarrassed, and she wrote to ask him to reduce the gift by half.[47] Paul also sent a great many small items, including cookies.

One of Nelidova's constant roles in relation to Paul was that of interceding in the interests of persons about to be punished or disgraced. Early in his reign, Paul was considering abolishing the military decoration of St. George, which Catherine had established, and evidently largely because it was Catherine who had established it. Nelidova begged him to change his mind, reminding him of the services and merits of those who had received the award.[48] Their correspondence is full of letters in which she petitioned for forgiveness for persons who had committed various offenses important or otherwise.[49]

A conduct so simple and disinterested as that of Nelidova was obviously somewhat unusual at the court. The court physician, Rogerson, found it quite remarkable. "This young woman conducts herself in such a fashion as to awaken surprise and respect: she appears at court dinners now and then, but she does not want to meddle in anything, although nothing would be denied her."[50] Not everyone, however, took such a benign view of Nelidova, and when, in the early stages of the affair, the gossip at court reached Catherine's ears, she rebuked Paul for an indecent relationship. The irony of such a reproach from a woman of Catherine's moral standards cannot have been lost on him, and he wrote to Catherine an anguished protest of innocence. "I wish to say something to you, Madame, not as my Sovereign and my Mother, something that my conscience dictates to me before God and before men; it is to justify an innocent who might suffer, at least indirectly, for me. I have seen malice appoint itself as judge and give false interpretations to a relationship uniquely of friendship that has been formed between Mlle. Nelidova and me. I swear on the subject of our relationship before the tribunal where we shall all appear that our

46. *Osmnadtsatyi vek*, 4 vols., Petr Bartenev, ed. (Moscow: n.p., 1869), 3:424.

47. Ibid., p. 427.

48. Ibid., p. 425.

49. Ibid., pp. 437-438, 439.

50. *Arkhiv kniazia Vorontsova*, 40 vols., Petr Bartenev, ed. (Moscow: Universitetskaia tipografiia, 1870-1895), 30:84.

consciences can do so without any reproach. . . . If I could cer-
tify it at the price of my blood, I would do it . . . in taking my life.
I swear . . . that we have been united by a tender and sacred
friendship, but [one] innocent and pure. I call God to witness to
it." He appealed to Catherine to do what she could to undo the
evil gossip about Nelidova.[51]

On the other hand, however pure and innocent, exalted,
and high-minded the liaison may have been, it was one of passion and intimacy, even if platonic. As Paul departed for the
Swedish front in 1784, he wrote to Nelidova, "Know that dying I
will think of you."[52] As she was interceding for some unfortunate, she opened her letter, "What are you doing, my heart?
(*Que voulez-vous, mon coeur?*)"[53] In October of 1797 (probably),
she wrote that she had received a letter from Paul every day for
a week.[54]

In spite of this degree of intimacy between the two of
them, once the rapprochement of Mariia Fedorovna and Nelidova
was formed, theirs was also a friendship of unshakable confidence and trust, and, for a time, there was a happy threesome.
Nelidova wrote to Paul on one of his travels that "[Mariia Fedorovna's] heart is sad far from you." Mariia Fedorovna wrote to
Nelidova in the summer of 1797, "Our dear Emperor has shown
me your letter . . . , he was much moved by it, and I am as well.
You are and you will be always our good, our true friend, and to
love you *is a blessing for us* (*est un bien pour nous*). Come join
us. . . . The pleasures of Gatchina lose their savor (*prix*) because
you are not here; it is what he [Paul] feels and he says, I say it
with him. . . ." And Paul added a postscript: "Come, we await
you. . . . I await you."[55]

Finally, perhaps the most interesting comment on the
Paul-Nelidova liaison is an undated letter from her to him. "I
thank you for everything, and above all for the pleasure that you
allow me of loving you with all my heart. They say that it is not
necessary to say to any man that one loves him a lot because
they are all more or less ingrates. But then are you a man to
me? I swear to you that I have never thought of you [as a
man] . . . ; it seems to me that you are my sister: because, with

51. *Osmnadtsatyi vek*, 3:445-446.

52. E. S. Shumigorskii, *Ekaterina Ivanovna Nelidova (1758-1839)* (St.
Petersburg: Obshchestvennaia pol'za, 1898), p. 21.

53. *Osmnadtsatyi vek*, 3:441.

54. Ibid., p. 437.

55. Ibid., p. 455. Emphasis in the original.

Your permission, I am not constantly concerned with the distance that God has placed between your grandeur and my modest station; but friendship only proceeds better in this fashion, although I feel with all the satisfaction of my soul that You are my master. Adieu, my good friend, may God keep You in health and happiness."[56]

Nelidova's obituary, 17 February 1839, in the *Severnaia pchela*, spoke of her "enlightened mind, ardent love of virtue (*dobro*) and truth, invincible tenacity (*tverdost*) . . . ; she lived by the words of the New Testament: 'Be as little children.'"[57]   Of course, whatever features she exemplified were qualities that Paul admired, and hence a knowledge of her character--and of their relationship--is a key to his.   Their inspired search for a state of sublimated and idyllic blessedness unmixed with the sordid compromises of the mundane was characteristic enough of the era, but it would be a difficult one to blend with the duties of Paul's inheritance.

We can now consider a kind of summary inventory of the character of Paul as grand prince.

His amusements were simple. He liked to play chess and caroms. He was never given to hunting and refused to participate in it when invited to do so by Ferdinand IV of Naples. On the other hand, he was devoted to horseback riding. Apart from riding and the military exercises associated with it, he had no taste for sports.

Similarly, he had no taste for luxury. His favorite food was *sosiski*, a kind of wieners. Joseph II remarked in Vienna that though the finest dishes were prepared for him, he ate only simple things, especially fresh fruit compote. He did not care for alcohol, and he drank mineral water by preference.

His cultural interests were limited. He showed no interest in science, though he lived in an age full of scientific excitement. He had no favorite authors. On the other hand, he was fond of the theatre, and he liked declaiming Racine and Corneille. His grand tour of 1781-1782 did excite in him some interest in the arts.

Morally, he was uncomplicated. He was pious and unusually honest. He never deceived anyone, and he seemed entirely incapable of dissimulating whatever he was thinking. Like

---

56. Ibid., p. 435.

57. Ibid., p. 457-459.

Nelidova, he simply spoke what was on his mind whether it was tactful and prudent or not.

Socially, he was often far from graceful, though when he was in a good mood, all who met him agreed that he could be gracious and charming. He had a sense of humor, but he was given to suspicion. It has been observed that there was only one person in his entourage with whom he never broke, A. A. Bezborodko (the reasons will be explored later). In spite of his frequent difficulty in getting along with others, he was not usually a loner. During most of his life, he distinctly did not like to be alone and actively sought the company of others.

There is every sign that fearfulness was one of his primary characteristics, that he was tormented by a diffuse and generic insecurity that was not always focused on anything in particular. There were, of course, good reasons to be fearful during much of his life on account of his conflict with Catherine and the fate of his predecessors. Perhaps there is a connection between his fearfulness and his frightful inability to control himself in the face of provocations that typically upset him. The most characteristic kind of emotion that he displayed in public was wrath (*gnev*), a word that his biographers find indispensable. And he was certain that the best way to deal with human vices and shortcomings was by rigorous punishment. Chizh comments that Paul was distinguished by "Prussian severity and French fastidiousness (*prusskoe kapralstvo i frantsuzskaia utonchennost*)" and that his most important failing was weakness of the will.[58] Additional materials on his eduation and his conduct of policy as emperor will enable us to amplify and refine these assessments.

As the period of his reign approached, Paul had exhibited enough bizarre behavior to raise rather general doubts about his mental condition. Toward the end of the 1780s, as Shumigorskii puts it, "Little by little all the friends of Paul . . . began . . . to look on him as on a dear sick person in need of some supervision and care."[59] For example, both Mariia Fedorovna and Nelidova were in the habit of accompanying Paul during his daily military drills for the sake of restraining his violent outbreaks of wrath. Not long before Catherine's death, Mariia Fedorovna observed that Paul had become uncharacter-

---

58. Chizh, "Imperator Pavel Pervyi," pp. 231-232, 240, 250, 267, 277, 415, 425, 436, 449, 455, 612; Morane, *Paul I de Russie*, pp. 61, 224.

59. Shumigorskii, *Nelidova*, p. 20.

istically moody and aloof.   She begged Nelidova to try to bring
him out of his seclusion, which, she said, was depriving him of
all of his friends.   "There is no one," Mariia Fedorovna observed,
"who does not daily remark the disorder of his faculties."[60] This
authoritative opinion was neither unsympathetic nor isolated.
F. V. Rostopchin, a courtier in whom Paul had at this time special faith, found Paul's behavior equally distressing.   "It is impossible to observe what the grand prince does without shuddering and pity. [It is] as if he seeks out every means of making
himself hated.   He is obsessed with the idea that people do not
respect him and that they scorn him.   Proceeding from that
[assumption], he fusses over everything and gives orders indis-
criminately.   Having four marine battalions of 1600 men and
three squadrons of horse, he imagines with these forces to imitate the deceased king of Prussia.   On Wednesdays, he holds
maneuvers, and every day he is present for the changing of the
guard and also for punishments, when they take place.   The
slightest tardiness, the slightest contradiction put him beside
himself, and he is inflamed with rage. It is remarkable that he is
never aware of his own mistakes and continues to be angry with
those whom he has offended.   He pronounces sentences on everyone: now he sends away a whole detachment because it lost
an order sent yesterday; now he orders that Count Zinoviev be
told that he must show more respect to persons enjoying Paul's
favor; or Gurev, that he must not forget the Marshals of the
Household, that he will teach them how to serve . . . he is de-
stroying himself and contriving the means of making himself
hated. . . .   He threatened to beat Bush, the gardener at
Tsarskoe Selo, with a stick . . . Countess Shuvalova, arriving
somewhat late [for a formal function] was . . . told that she must
hurry for Paul because she had always carried out all that
Prince Potemkin had told her to do." Finally, Rostopchin said,
as Poroshin had observed earlier, Paul lacked the capacity to restrain and control himself.

The foreign diplomats echoed these alarming views. The
English ambassador, Sir Charles Whitworth, described Paul as
characterized by an "acrimony of disposition which already renders the Great Duke an Object dreadful to those who look for-

---

60. Kazimierz Waliszewski, *Paul the First of Russia* (Philadelphia: J.
B. Lippincott, 1913), p. 381.

61. *Arkhiv kniazia Vorontsova,* 8:76; 34:257-258.

ward to a future Reign."[62]   The Austrian ambassador, Louis
Cobenzl, agreed: "One absolutely does not know what to count
on with the Grand Duke, he changes his language and his sentiments almost every moment. . . . There is no one among the
Russians who might have the least notion what to expect of the
Grand Duke in internal affairs . . . with a Prince of his character,
one cannot count on the stability of his sentiments."[63]

The French emissary at St. Petersburg went further:
"They are going so far as to say that his mind is deranged."[64]

In these circumstances, Catherine evidently felt, after
brooding over the matter for a long time, that she was obliged to
consider dispossessing Paul of the throne. She turned first for
help to Mariia Fedorovna, who, horrified, told Paul. Catherine
thought next of Alexander, and she tried to persuade Alexander's mentors, Nikita Ivanovich Saltykov and César La Harpe, to
take up the matter with him. Both refused, so she approached
him herself. Alexander consented, it seems, to cooperate with
Catherine, but he also established documentary evidence that
he favored his father's succession. It was widely rumored that a
decree dispossessing Paul would be published on 1 January
1797.   In November 1796, before the matter was resolved,
Catherine died. When the news of her death reached Paul, he
gave orders that the papers be sealed. If there was a decree in
them dispossessing him, it was destroyed.

---

62. Roderick E. McGrew, "A Portrait of Paul I from the Austrian and
English Diplomatic Archives," *Jahrbücher für Geschichte Osteuropas* 18:506-
507 (1970).

63. Ibid.

64. Morane, *Paul I de Russie*, p. 372.

2

PAUL'S EDUCATION
AND VALUES

Reading eighteenth-century literature will quickly demonstrate that the age had a genuinely fantastic faith in the moral efficacy of education. Locke, in so many ways the progenitor of the age, wrote in his influential *Some Thoughts Concerning Education* (1693): "Of all the Men we meet with, nine Parts of ten are what they are, good or evil, useful or not, by their Education. 'Tis that which makes the great Difference in Mankind."[1] Helvétius believed that variation in the quality of education was the exclusive cause of the variation in the quality of men: "If I could demonstrate that man is but the product of his education, I should have undoubtedly revealed a great truth to the nations. They would then know that they hold within their own hands the instrument of greatness and happiness, and that to be happy and powerful is only a matter of perfecting the science of education."[2] Of course the education of princes

---

1. John Locke, *Some Thoughts Concerning Education* (Cambridge, Eng.: Cambridge University Press, 1898), p. 1.

2. As quoted in Leo Gershoy, *From Despotism to Revolution, 1763-1789* (New York: Harper and Row, 1944), p. 210.

was even more important, for obvious reasons, in particular because not their least crucial role was to be the chief educator of the societies that they governed.

The persons who educated Paul perfectly reflect this outlook. Hence to come to terms with the personality of Paul, we must examine the nature of his education.

Russian historiography has attributed many of the unfortunate aspects of Paul's character to the malign influence of his mentor, Nikita Ivanovich Panin, and to a lesser extent to that of his brother, General Peter Ivanovich Panin. The problem demands some consideration.[3]

Panin's reputation at the time consisted of two rather distinct elements. Among the foreign diplomats, in particular, it was agreed that he was a cultured, refined, well-educated aristocrat of the age, full of honor and integrity. On the other hand, he was procrastinating, slow, and more than a little lazy. In the words of Kobeko, "he loved a good table and elegant women and was in general inclined to pleasure (*udovol'stviia*)."[4] The French emissary characterized him typically somewhat later in his service as Catherine's minister: "M. Panin would be an able minister if his laziness allowed him to give to business the devotion that it demands."[5]

Panin was, in any event, a man of distinguished intellect and character, and his appointment to the duties of *Oberhofmeister* of the grand duke was probably a fortunate one. Paul did not, however, initially appreciate it. He seems to have felt content and secure under his previous perhaps lax supervision, and he dreaded the coming of Panin. In his own words, he was "indescribably afraid" of Panin.[6] In particular, he feared that Panin would dismiss most of the women by whom he was surrounded, as Panin in fact soon did. Slowly, however, Panin won Paul's confidence, and though conflicts between them oc-

---

3. The Russian literature will be cited where appropriate. The fullest and most authoritative account of this subject in English is David L. Ransel, *The Politics of Catherinian Russia: the Panin Party* (New Haven, Conn.: Yale University Press, 1975). I am much indebted to Ransel's work, as will appear.

4. Dmitrii F. Kobeko, *Tsesarevich Pavel Petrovich, 1754-1796* (St. Petersburg: n. p., 1881). p. 15.

5. *Recueil des instructions données aux ambassaduers et ministres de France depuis les traités de Westphalie jusqu'à la Révolution française*, 29 vols. (Paris: Commission des Archives nationales, 1884-1969), 9: *Russie 2*: 276.

6. Poroshin, *Zapiski*, col. 607.

curred and Panin sometimes had to resort to somewhat severe discipline, the relationship eventually developed into one of the closest that Paul was to experience. His dependence on Panin continued until the latter's death in 1783.

Panin received general instructions from Elizabeth on the discharge of his duties. It would be too much to expect Elizabeth Petrovna to have drawn up a carefully premeditated and grand academic scheme--she was given to more plebeian tastes. Nevertheless, the content of her instructions is interesting. She strongly emphasized traditional religious and moral teaching (instruction in *dobronravie*). She explicitly charged Panin to provide a constant supply of distinguished visitors about the grand prince and a steady stream of edifying conversation.[7] She exhorted him to spare Paul the saccharine flattery to which his position would obviously expose him. Panin was specifically encouraged to teach Paul respect for Elizabeth's father, Peter the Great, and for the Russian fatherland. Academic subjects, as might be expected, were left entirely to the discretion of Panin.[8]

The injunctions were appropriately reflected in the discharge of Panin's duties. But it would have been strange if a man of Panin's background had not brought some ideas of his own to Paul's education. In fact, he had much more definite ideas than the empress. During Panin's service at the Swedish court, the education of Prince Gustav had been the subject of lively conflict between the royal family and the estates. Panin was a close friend of Gustav's first tutor, Count Carl Gustav Tessin, and he knew the content of Count Tessin's educational plan. When the Riksdag supplanted Tessin by another tutor and another plan, Panin took an interest in the new developments in Gustav's education. He was also familiar with the precepts of Leibnitz, and he was generally well versed in the educational ideas of the age.[9] It is clear that he was qualified for the responsibilities of the job.

---

7. Panin carried out this charge conscientiously, as will be seen.

8. 24 June 1761; *Russkaia starina*, 1881, No. 1, pp. 18-21. In 1784, when Catherine drew up her instruction to Nikolai Ivanovich Saltykov on the education of Alexander Pavlovich and Constantine Pavlovich, she included more details about the academic dimensions of their education, but the spirit of her instruction is otherwise consonant with that of Elizabeth. See "Instruktsiia kniaziu Nikolaiu Ivanovichu Saltykovu pri naznachenii ego k vospitaniiu velikikh kniazei," in Catherine II, *Sochineniia*, 3 vols. (St. Petersburg: Imperatorskaia Akademiia nauk, 1849), 1:199-248.

9. Ransel, *The Panin Party*, pp. 204-207.

He had already, before his appointment as tutor, submitted his own educational plan to Elizabeth, the "Prospectus on
the Education of His Imperial Highness Paul Petrovich." Panin's
Prospectus is full of benign bombast of a sort that might be dismissed as courtier's rhetoric if it did not also occur consistently
in private communication between him and Paul.

The good monarch, Panin observed, showed concern for
his subjects. He must be "God-loving, just and kind . . . a good
ruler does not have and cannot have either genuine interest or
genuine glory apart from the advantage and the well-being of the
subject peoples entrusted to him by God." Therefore, moral and
religious training must be emphasized first.   The future
sovereign must be protected against spiritual corruption. According to Panin, the three principal human virtues were "a sensitive knowledge of one's Creator, His holy intention in creating
us, and our consequent devoted duty to Him. The first occurs
when the heart is already filled with love and obedience to
Him . . . ; the second comes from the sincere wish to fulfill [the
duties of] one's calling . . . ; the third, from the fervor and concern to make oneself competent to fulfill the duty of that calling.
The human condition itself prompts an understanding of the
first outlines of these three rules of life; our Orthodox Christianity illuminates them. . . .   This is why instruction in the Scriptures is the most important point of a good education."[10]

The man whom Panin eventually selected to be Paul's
tutor in religion was a most unusual person, Metropolitan Platon of Moscow, a Russian cleric thoroughly familiar with the
secular literature of the Western Enlightenment. As Ransel observes, "under his direction, Paul developed an unusually tolerant and yet deeply pious religious outlook."[11] Platon was fond of
associating with foreigners--by no means conventional behavior
of the Russian clergy--for what he could learn from them. He
never traveled abroad. He learned a good reading knowledge of
several European languages, and he was able to speak a passable French. Panin found him to have sound views and a "clear
head" and evidently enjoyed his company. He was, of course,
scrutinized and interviewed very carefully before being appointed
Paul's preceptor.

Platon began to tutor in August 1763. For approximately
two years, he gave three lessons a week of an hour each. He devised a rather personal form of catechism for his pupil.   The

---

10. *Russkaia starina*, 1882, No. 36, pp. 315-330.

11. Ransel, *The Panin Party*, pp. 208-209.

subject matter of the lessons is recorded in Platon's diary: the four gospels; divine providence; the difference between piety and sanctimony; the relationship of the Old and New Testaments; an analysis of the Nicene Creed; the obligations of the Orthodox sovereign; and divine and natural law.[12]

The remainder of the curriculum was modern.   Highest priority was given to mathematics, history, and modern languages.   After the fundamentals of these subjects were mastered, future plans included commerce, financial affairs, domestic and foreign policy, warfare, and manufacturing.   Military affairs were given a limited emphasis, as Panin himself had little taste for them and thought it important to shun the Prussophile tastes of Paul's father and to teach him to value peace.   Paul read Buffon, Voltaire, Racine, Fénelon, and most of the more acclaimed Western writers of his day.   Panin's plan was a statement of values and purposes, not a statement of educational philosophy.   It is as much as anything a statement of biases, those of the tutor.

The daily regimen established by Panin was rather fastidious.   He arranged dinner, dinner guests, and dinner conversation with considerable care.   There was much ado in the household about the question who came to dinner, and Paul sometimes complained about it.   The dinner company was generally adult; decorum at the table was rather severe; and the conversation was edifying and didactic.   Poroshin regularly recorded who "sat at table" and what the evening's "conversation was about."

The coup d'état that brought Catherine II to the throne considerably enhanced the influence of Panin.   He had despised the behavior and the policy of Peter III, and he had played a principal role in the conspiracy against him.   He emerged as Catherine's most intimate adviser, and he was the chief ornament of her administration.   In the early days of her rule, Catherine evidently felt, with reason, a sense of insecurity.   During the preceding generations, various sovereigns more legitimate than she had been deposed by palace revolutions.

---

12. When Platon asked Paul where the natural law resided, "Paul pointed to his head and said 'there.'" Platon also served to introduce Paul's wives to Russian Orthodoxy.   He was the religious tutor of Nataliia before her marriage and her confessor after marriage.   He trained Mariia Fedorovna in Orthodoxy as well, but by that date, Catherine had evidently grown jealous of his intimacy with the young court.   In any event, he was not selected to continue as the confessor after marriage.   K. A. Papmehl, *Metropolitan Platon of Moscow* (Newtonville, Mass.: Oriental Research Partners, 1983), pp. 13-14, 27-33, 94-95.

Panin had a good political head and a solid reputation. Hence Catherine needed him for the most basic of reasons, to stabilize her power.

It is true that she soon invited d'Alembert to serve as a tutor of Paul, but there is no evidence that she thereby intended to remove Panin from his responsibilities. Her invitation to d'Alembert asked him to come to Russia "pour contribuer à l'éducation de mon fils." The French ambassador understood this to mean that d'Alembert would teach mathematics to Paul under the direction of Panin.[13]

On the other hand, tension and conflict between Catherine and Panin were present from the beginning of her reign. Though he had enthusiastically endorsed the overthrow of Peter III, Panin wanted Catherine to become not sovereign of Russia, but regent for Paul. Catherine was fully aware of this, but she refused to renounce the throne. Panin thus came to be the champion of Paul's rights, and both he and Paul came to be suspect in Catherine's eyes. Eventually their influence was removed from court, and they witnessed the triumph in the councils of state of other advisers and new favorites. Paul grew notoriously indignant about the parvenu statesmen who occupied what he thought of as his rightful place in Russian politics. It was an attitude that he certainly shared with--and perhaps learned from--Panin.

Catherine's denial of Paul's claims was simply the first of Panin's disappointments in her. During the early months of her reign, Panin proposed that Catherine regularize her executive apparatus by establishing a central government institution known as the State Council. Historians have traditionally seen in the project a reflection of Panin's experience in Sweden, an effort to establish in Russia a constitutional monarch of the Swedish sort. His own explanation of his purpose was somewhat different from the historians' interpretation. He wished, he said, to avoid the more repugnant features of recent reigns. "If we take the reign of Elizaveta Petrovna, . . . Prince Trubetskoi was Procurator General by virtue of court favor, as an accidental personage; consequently he did not enforce the laws and good order, but could do and did everything and, we dare say, arbitrarily corrupted everything; in the later period he himself became the toady of favorites and minions.

"The reign deserves special attention: during it everything was subordinated to the present moment, to the wishes of the favorites, and to all the superficial and petty aspects of pub-

---

13. Ransel, *The Panin Party*, p. 202.

lic affairs. . . .   All the while the dignitaries and favorites knew no limit to their aspirations and designs, though governmental plans remained unattended; everything was thrown into confusion; the most important duties and offices were transformed into ranks and rewards for favorites and flatterers; favor and seniority became everywhere the basis for assignments; nothing was left to talent and merit.   The whims and favors of court intrigues enabled everyone to grab and take possession of the section of government he expected to be of greatest convenience in defeating his rival or for combining with others against a third."[14]

A common thesis about the Panin party maintains that it led a "gentry opposition" to Russian absolutism and wished to curtail Catherine's power through the establishment of Swedish forms of constitutional monarchy.   This argument has been authoritatively explored by David Ransel, who points out very substantial differences between Panin's proposal and the Swedish system of government.   The Swedish constitution of 1720 established clear limits on the monarch's power.   Panin's project was ambiguous where Catherine's power was concerned.   It is not clear that executive power would have been limited.   Ransel suggests that apart from the high purposes that Panin stated in his own preamble to the document--the wish to stabilize Russian government and to avoid the influence of cabals and favorites--he was concerned to sustain his own services and party at court by institutionalizing them.   Catherine appears to have been on the verge of implementing the project, which she actually signed, when she solicited the comments of other persons at court, some of them Panin's enemies (for example, the Vorontsovs).   Their commentary was quite critical, and she shelved the project indefinitely.   Ransel suggests that Catherine thought at this point in her reign that her situation was not sufficiently stable to permit her to dispense with Panin's enemies at court any more safely than she could dispense with him.   So the project failed; then later in the 1760s, when Panin's ascendance at court seemed secure, he appears to have neglected his previous proposal as if it were no longer important.[15]

On the other hand, as will appear later, Panin made a distinct effort on his deathbed to provide Paul with the blueprint

---

14. "The Memorandum of Count Nikita Panin, 28 December 1762," in Marc Raeff, ed., *Plans for Political Reform in Imperial Russia, 1730-1905* (Englewood Cliffs, N.J.: Prentice-Hall, 1966), pp. 53-68.

15. Ransel, *The Panin Party*, pp. 76-136.

of a constitution of sorts, and that fact would seem to suggest that his 1762 project was not a mere political maneuver.

Another common view of the brothers Panin holds that they turned Paul against Catherine and against Russia as well, that they taught him to scorn Russians and Russian culture and to admire only Europeans, especially Germans.[16] The Panins did admire much in the West, particularly its relative cultural and technical advancement. This is an old and familiar problem for the Russian mentality: how to adjust the evident material and cultural superiority of the West to the claims of Russian patriotism and self-respect. Nikita Panin was of the opinion that Sweden was more advanced than Russia. But what he admired most about the West was in Denmark, and that was the Danish aristocracy. He admired it for its devotion to the state and for the fact that court rank in Denmark, in his estimation, depended on real merit and service rather than on accidental or personal factors.

He admired the quite Russian government of Peter I for the same reasons.   Peter was, of course, a Westernizing monarch. Panin had grown up steeped in esteem for Peter. His mother's family had been close to the Menshikovs, and in his childhood he had obviously derived from this source an enormous respect for Peter. It was not, however, the vast importation of things Western that was the object of Panin's respect, but rather the Petrine political ethic, the devotion to duty, and the stubborn insistence on rewarding the court nobility on the basis of services performed for the fatherland rather than on antiquity of lineage or by capricious favoritism. In fact, it was the uncritical admiration and importation of things Western that Panin especially deplored in Peter III.[17]

If the Panins had been a source of rabid Russophobia, Catherine would hardly have left such an important charge of the state as Paul in their midst. Peter Panin's correspondence with Paul was full of patriotic expressions. He sometimes satirized Catherine's government, but he spoke with great respect of the deeds of the Russian army of old. There is no reason to think that the Panins poisoned Paul's regard either for his

---

16. See Petr S. Lebedev, *Grafy Nikita i Petr Paniny* (St. Petersburg: Obshchestvennaia pol'za, 1863), pp. 14-75, 85, and passim.

17. Ransel, *The Panin Party*, pp. 11, 27-29, 62-63, 202.   Chizh, "Imperator Pavel I," pp. 233-235.   Platon A. Geisman and Aleksandr N. Dubovskii, *Graf Petr Ivanovich Panin, 1721-1789: istoricheskii ocherk voennoi i gosudarstvennoi deiatel'nosti* (St. Petersburg: Vasil'iev, 1897), p. 90.

mother or for Russian culture. On the other hand, it is clear that they taught him to look critically at both.

The tension between Catherine and the Panin party was aggravated by another factor. As Morane explains, Nikita Ivanovich Panin "was in the eyes of the people the sole guarantee of the security of the grand duke," and consequently, to remove him from the office of *Oberhofmeister* of the heir would have been "to unleash tempests" of sedition or revolt.[18] Thus Paul remained in a tense and delicate environment where attitudes to his mother and her policy were markedly ambiguous.

What was the enduring legacy of the Panin party in Paul's outlook? It was clearly the strongest influence to which he was subjected. Nikita Panin had had high hopes for Catherine's reign. She regarded herself as a progressive, enlightened monarch, and she evidently aspired to rule accordingly. Panin subscribed to much the same outlook. During the 1760s, he attracted and patronized a group of idealistic young writers who shared his outlook and his hopes for Catherine's reign. Among them were A. P. Sumarokov, I. F. Bogdanovich, and Denis Fonvizin. They supported a foreign policy of peace and a domestic policy of internal development. They deplored the evil of court favoritism. Fonvizin may well have been the most articulate spokesman of the program for which the party stood. Nikita Panin especially cherished Fonvizin's play *The Brigadier* (1769), a bitter satire of the boorish, provincial Russian nobility. The play attacked the notion that rank at the Russian court was a sure sign of virtue in the individual occupying it, and it travestied the pompously Westernized provincial parvenus whom Panin so disdained.

By the end of the 1760s, the ascendance of the Panin party had largely run its course. The young journalists constituting the literary support of the party were increasingly disillusioned with Catherine and her policies. They were especially disconcerted by the fate of the Legislative Commission and by Catherine's appetite for aggrandizement in Poland and Turkey. Disappointed in the sovereign, they turned their hopes onto the heir. When Paul recovered in 1771 from a near-fatal attack of influenza, Fonvizin composed a "Discourse on the Recovery of His Imperial Majesty." He called Paul "the hope of the fatherland," the "sole precious source of our tranquillity."

All the best efforts of the party were now devoted to preparing in Paul the kind of personality and values appropriate to doing what Catherine had failed to accomplish: "They worked

18. Morane, *Paul I de Russie*, p. 52.

to instill in him the belief that he was a new Peter the Great, but one who would devote himself to realizing the constitutional program developed by the Panins. They did not conceal from Paul the despotic nature of Peter's rule. He had forced the challenge of Westernization on the elite, driven the nobles to get educated in the European spirit, and exhorted them to continue to learn from the West and to introduce into Russia the best of Western institutions. Yet the Panins impressed on Paul that although Peter had ruled despotically, his plan was to create conditions that would make despotism unnecessary. Hence, Paul could best make himself worthy of his great-grandfather's ambitions by implementing constitutional guarantees that would achieve these aims."[19]

Fonvizin's play *The Minor* (1782), a heavily didactic work, continued to preach the party's program. The chief exemplar of virtue was Starodum (Oldthink). He strutted about much as Paul did later, bristling militant virtue. He recited tiresome, repetitious homilies. He praised Peter I for his directness and lack of ceremony. "In those times the courtiers were soldiers, and not the soldiers courtiers." His remarks on the contemporary court were scathing.[20] He made it plain that the privileges of nobility entailed duty to the state, the duty to use one's talents patriotically and conscientiously in the cause of Russian state and society, after the fashion of the Petrine service ethic.

Shortly before the death of Nikita Panin in 1783, the brothers Panin and Denis Fonvizin assembled a series of papers which they recommended to Paul as something like the political legacy of his mentor. The first of these, written by Fonvizin in consultation with Panin, is a tract called "Discourse on Permanent State Laws," and it is a searing indictment of Catherine's court and government,[21] in place of which the Panins wished Paul to institute the contemporary ideal of the *Rechtsstaat*, a government not of men, but of law and of virtue.

"Supreme power is entrusted to the Sovereign for the sole benefit of his subjects. . . .   In fact, all the radiance of the throne is but an empty gleam (*blesk*) unless virtue sits on the

---

19. Ransel, *The Panin Party*, p. 268.

20. See Acts III and IV especially.

21. "Razsuzhdenie o nepremennykh Gosudarstvennykh Zakonakh," in Evgenii S. Shumigorskii, *Imperator Pavel I, zhizn' i tsarstvovanie* (St. Petersburg: V. D. Smirnov, 1907), Appendix, pp. 4-13. I have drawn on, without always following, Ronald Hingley's translation in Marc Raeff, ed., *Russian Intellectual History: An Anthology* (New York: Harcourt, Brace, 1966), pp. 96-105.

throne together with the Sovereign. . . . a Sovereign, like God and the earthly inheritor of His almighty power, cannot commemorate (*oznamenovat'*) either his might or merit except by establishing in his state fundamental, unalterable rules based on the general welfare and which he himself could not breach without ceasing to be sovereign.

"Without these rules, . . . without permanent state laws, neither the condition of the state nor that of the sovereign is stable. . . . Who can guarantee that a successor will not choose to destroy in a single hour everything that was established in all the previous reigns? . . . Where the caprice of a single person is the supreme law, there no stable common bond can exist; there is a state there, but not a fatherland; there are subjects but not citizens; there is no body politic of which the members are united by the knot of mutual rights and obligations." Interest governs all legislation, and people do not keep faith because no one keeps faith with them. And here they begin to describe the Russia of Catherine:

"In this situation . . . the senseless command of a powerful person is carried out unquestioningly with servile sycophancy. Anyone who can issues orders, but no one governs. . . . Subjects are enslaved to the Sovereign, and the Sovereign is usually enslaved to an unworthy *favorite*. I have called him unworthy because the title *favorite* is never applied to a worthy man who has offered real services to his fatherland but rather to a person who has attained high degree by the successful cunning of pleasing the sovereign. In such a perverse situation, the abuse of despotism reaches incredible lengths, and any distinction between what is the Sovereign's and what is the favorite's ceases. Everything depends on the whim of the latter. . . . The favorite's vices not only gain currency but are almost the sole means of obtaining preference. . . . No one intends to be deserving; everyone seeks to be promoted. . . . And who can stop the aspiration of vice when the idol of the very Sovereign [Potemkin], before the eyes of the whole world in the imperial palaces themselves, raises the banner of lawlessness and dishonor; when shamelessly indulging his lust, he openly mocks the holy bonds of kinship, the rules of honor, the duty of humanity, dares to flout the laws, both human and divine, before the face of the lawgiver?

"The good Sovereign is good for everyone, and all his favors have to do not with private advantages but with the general well-being. . . . The ruler is the first servant of the state. . . ."

The condition of Russia was a caricature of the Panins' ideal. "Now let us imagine a state which is larger in territory than any other state in the known world and which relative to its size is the least populated in the world, a state divided into more than thirty large provinces, and consisting, one may say, of only two cities, in one of which people live chiefly of necessity, in the other of which they live chiefly by their wish--a state frightful by virtue of its large and brave army, and whose situation is such that the loss of a single battle might some time destroy it entirely; a state whose strength and glory attract the attention of the whole world, and which a peasant, whose human appearance alone distinguishes him from swine [Pugachev], unled by anyone, can bring in the course of several hours, so to speak, to the very verge of ruin and collapse; a state which provides other lands with sovereigns and in which the throne itself depends on the opening of taverns for a bestial crowd of rowdies who safeguard the sovereign's person; a state where there are all political conditions of people but where none of them has any advantages and one differs from another only by empty appellation, a state governed by daily decrees, often contradicting each other, but lacking any stable code of laws. . . ."

And so Paul was called on to remedy the ills of Russia. "An enlightened and virtuous monarch, finding his empire and his own rights in such disharmony and disorder, begins his great service by the swift defense of the general security by means of immutable laws. In this important business, he must not lose sight of two important considerations: first, that the state demands of him quick healing of all the evils brought to it by the abuse of despotism; second, nothing can bring final ruin to the country so swiftly as the sudden and unprepared grant of those privileges which are enjoyed by the fortunately governed peoples of Europe. Attached herewith is a separate draft of what might be the first fundamental laws based on this consideration."

Nikita Panin's last effort to ensure Paul's proper approach to the political future came just a few days before his death, when he and Paul conferred on the nature of a constitutional project. Their plans called for a state council similar to the one that Panin had proposed to Catherine early in her reign. The council would comprise the heads of the departments of justice, revenue, finance, budget, commerce, navy, army, and foreign affairs. The state council was designed to coordinate and develop legislation. The chief judicial organ was to be the Senate, distinctly separate from the executive branch of government and elected by a narrowly restricted franchise of the upper nobility. The Senate would not only receive appeals, but have the power to review legislation as well. Branches of the Senate were to be established in the provinces to broaden the access of the people to judicial procedures.

This plan represents a considerable limitation of the hitherto autocratic prerogatives of the Russian monarch. The ruler's own power was to be limited both by a separate judicial authority in the Senate and by the required consultations with ministers, or department heads, in the state council. Presumably, this plan represents the high tide of the Panins' influence over their pupil, Paul.[22]

About the same time, evidently in order to leave as little room for Paul's error as possible, General Peter Panin spelled out further recommendations in some detail. He was concerned first to secure the age-old position of the Orthodox Church. He declared that the monarch must be forbidden by law to embrace any faith but the Russian Orthodox. On the other hand, he wished to permit the free practice of other faiths in Russia utterly without interference by the government. Members of other faiths, however, would be forbidden to proselytize among the Russian Orthodox.

On the need of a new law of succession, Peter Panin recommended that it be spelled out precisely, that male heirs be preferred to females, and that it be made quite clear in the laws what legal procedure was to be followed in the event of a royal minority or other incapacity of the sovereign. Similarly, in the event of the dying out of the dynasty, he recommended procedures for the election of a new one.

There followed a list of topics appropriate for further legislation: on the rights of the nobility, the clergy, the merchants, the peasants; on an appropriate law of inheritance for each of these classes; on the right of private property, dowry, divorce and its legal ramifications, and especially the rights of parents over children and the duties of children to parents; on the powers of the landlords over serfs and the obligations of the latter. He recommended the establishment of a stable monetary system and an auditing commission to examine the activity of the government. A regular structure should be delineated to bring complaints and petitions to the attention of the sovereign as well

---

22. This constitutional project came to light only recently. See David L. Ransel, "An Ambivalent Legacy: The Education of the Grand Duke Paul," in Ragsdale, *Paul I*, pp. 1-16; and M. M. Safonov, "Konstitutsionnyi proekt N. I. Panina--D. I. Fonvizina," *Vspomogatel'nye istoricheskie distsipliny* 6:261-280 (1974).

as a clear description of the jurisdiction and duties of each branch of the administration.[23]

General Panin also prepared two manifestoes which he thought might be useful for Paul to proclaim upon his accession to the throne. The first said that the Creator has been pleased to lead the heir miraculously through various threatening misfortunes and to preserve him for the throne. The new sovereign would take his cue in governing Russia from his forebear Peter the Great. It would be his object to root out of the empire the late corruption of morals and abuses of government.

The by now familiar series of pious principles was again rehearsed. Virtue was everywhere encouraged: "The entire reasonable world, and We ourselves, recognize the nobility as the first member of the state, as the support and defense of the Sovereign and the Fatherland from enemies without and from occasional villains within." The nobility was urged to take upon itself genuine state service, as in former days, and not merely to seek rank alone. Bribery and simony were deplored, as was the general lack of attention to educating the young. This document was a rehash of the old program. It was one of the more meandering, more rhetorical, and least well written of the Panins' political productions.

The second manifesto that Peter Panin recommended to Paul had to do with the succession.[24] It declared that autocracy was the timeless and immutable form of government in Russia. The right of inheritance of the Russian throne was to belong to the firstborn son of the first marriage of the reigning monarch, or, in the event of the death of the firstborn son, to his firstborn son and, after that, to his other sons,[25] in order of birth, "always preferring the male sex over the female." In the event of the deaths of all the male heirs of the firstborn son of the monarch, the succession rights should revert to the second son of the last ruling monarch and to his heirs; in the event of his or their deaths, to the third son; and thus through all the males of the first marriage of the last ruling monarch. After this the same principles would apply to the second marriage, then the third marriage, and so on. In the event that no males were available according to the prescribed order, the eldest female of the first marriage was to inherit the throne, and so on, in the prescribed

---

23. Shumigorskii, *Imperator Pavel I*, Appendix, pp. 13-20.

24. Ibid., pp. 32-35.

25. The wording here is not entirely clear.

order, until a male heir was produced.   At that point, male precedence was to be restored.

The Panins were evidently trying to control part of Russia's future after their own deaths.   Such was the program which they bequeathed to Paul, when, at age 28, he was left to carry on the precious legacy without the counsel of his mentor. It is interesting to examine the duration of this influence in his own convictions.

Among the more private and revealing sources of Paul's convictions are his student notebooks of the early 1770s.[26]   They reveal especially the moral teachings and convictions of his childhood.   A good example was his 14 June 1772 comment "On Pleasures."   There were, he said, two kinds of pleasure, spiritual (or moral) and physical.   The former was experienced "while doing good or listening to the story of some beautiful deed.   This pleasure is not so strong and momentary as the greater part of [physical pleasures]; one may call it a sweet and quiet happiness, the duration of which constitutes the delight (*naslazhdenie*) and happiness of all who realize it.   The physical pleasures . . . to tell the truth, are livelier and more impetuous (*poryvistee*) than the [spiritual], by their very nature."   Thus every clear-headed and well-meaning person should naturally prefer the superiority of the former, the spiritual pleasure.

On satisfaction (*dovolstvie*), Paul observed that it "is nothing more than the sweet feeling of joy which we experience upon fulfilling our obligations, both in respect to others and in respect to ourselves.   I use the expression 'fulfillment' (*udovletvorenie*), for sometimes, wishing, even with all our heart, to do something, we meet with an obstacle in inadequacy of means [which] deprives us of the possibility of doing what we want.   However, it is not this that usually stops us; on the contrary, we prevent ourselves, [by] not doing everything in our power, out of weakness or some other reason."   Thus, through lack of commitment, we deprive ourselves of much satisfaction.

On the conflict of reason and the passions, one of the most prominent themes of eighteenth-century thought, he was entirely typical of the age.   "Happy are the people who can reason in that decisive moment when the passions--the inevitable consequences of strong sensual impressions--struggle with reason and too often dominate it."

On sloth: "There is nothing more harmful than idleness both in itself and in its consequences.   It is the product of a

---

26. *Russkaia starina*, 1874, No. 9, pp. 667-683.

weak and lazy mind to which every serious occupation is averse."

An entry dated only 1772 is concerned with the role of law and the principles of government, and the phrasing of it suggests that a teacher had been relentlessly drilling the idea into his mind : "Réflections, qui me sont venus au sujet d'une expression qu'on m'a fait si souvent sonner aux oreilles, qui est: *les principles du Gouvernement.*" Power, Paul thought, derived originally from "physical force . . . in the state of nature." The strong conquered the weak and presumed to "give them the law." Later, men assembled in civilized society chose governors (*chefs*) and surrendered themselves voluntarily to their governors' directions. The governors, seeing no constraints on their power, committed excesses. Society then sought to set a limit to the power of the governors, and here was the origin of the laws. "C'est la base de ces loix (*sic*) appréciées à tel pays ou tel état qui [sert] comme de guide au pouvoir dirigeant et qu'on nomme *principe du Gouvernement.*"[27]

Paul developed a special admiration for the way in which Henry IV exemplified dedication to the proper principles of government. "Thanks to his labors, he was capable of judging and even of enlightening those who served him. . . .

"His mind, ardent and exalted, occupied with the affairs of [all of] Europe, did not neglect the smallest details. . . .

"In the conviction that nothing is more shameful for the sovereign than to be deceived, he wished to know--and did know--about everything."

He concerned himself with the state's finances, not with his own glory. His love for his people lightened his burdens. "The extravagant splendor of his court seemed to him a mockery of the people's poverty; he knew that he must give an example to others. Everything that was superfluous was curtailed. . . .

"He sent to their estates all the courtiers whose service did not support the court and who sought their fortune in the king's favors."

Too few princes exemplified the virtues of Henry. "Read history: the greater part of the kings spent their lives immersed in *pleasures*, not rooting out but only facilitating evil; in blind

---

27. "Reflections that have come to me on the subject of an expression which has often been made to sound in my ears, namely: *the principles of Government.*" "It is the foundation of these laws valued in this country or that state which serves as a guide to executive power and which we call *the principle of Government.*"

self-assurance, almost all of them forgot the . . . cardinal duties (*naznacheniia*) of the sovereign."

This is followed by a "personal note on Henry IV." Henry combined skillful policy with the greatest candor; simplicity of manners and style of living with the most elevated feelings; an inexhaustible supply of love of humanity with the courage of a soldier. Paul then reflected on the impact which such a ruler might have in Russia. "If there appeared among us at some time a reasonable (*blagorazumnyi*) sovereign who, confessing errors of [previous] policy, concerned himself to correct them . . . ," he would undertake to civilize the somewhat rude spirit of the Russian people, their unsociable manners, and would make them thereby the envy of all their neighbors.[28]

Paul's attitude toward the Russian people was somewhat ambivalent. On the one hand, he felt tender and paternal about the masses. On the other, he was resentful and contemptuous of the privileged classes, both for their lack of contribution to national affairs and for their toleration of his mother's government and her abuse of him. As he told Countess Rosenberg during one of his trips abroad, "if fate brings me to the throne, do not be astonished at what you see me do; you know my heart, but you do not know those people . . . , and I know what is necessary to manage them."[29] He is alleged to have expressed himself on one occasion even more definitely: "This perverted people wishes constantly to be ruled by women, in order that its masters be favorites and that all crimes go unpunished."[30]

In 1774, Paul made his first venture into politics. He wrote and submitted for his mother's consideration what amounts to a policy paper. Clearly Paul was eager by this time to be included in the councils of state. The paper may have been designed as a reminder to Catherine that it would be appropriate to recognize his political claims. It was entitled "Reflections on the State in General," but it had to do especially with military affairs. It was generally supposed to have represented some of the strong ideas of the Panins, and some of it was probably worked out in conversations and correspondence with Peter Panin. Paul's ideas as expressed in this document

---

28. The sense of the grammar, strictly speaking, is that the "hard spirit" and the "severe and unsociable manners" are characteristics of "errors of policy."

29. Nikolai K. Schilder, *Imperator Pavel I: istoriko-biograficheskii ocherk* (St. Petersburg: A. S. Suvorin, 1901), p. 426.

30. Chizh, "Imperator Pavel I," p. 594.

are strikingly theoretical and abstract, like much of the thinking of the Panins.[31]   Yet they have little resemblance to Nikita Panin's state council proposal of 1762.

"Our kingdom is now in a situation that requires peace (*pokoi*)." The Turkish war of five years, the Polish disturbances of the previous eleven years, and the Cossack rebellion on the Yaik were sufficient reason to think of peace, "for all these things drain the kingdom of people (*iznuriaet gosudarstvo liudmi*) and thereby diminish the tilling of the soil and devastate the land. Although this war [turned out] in our favor, we have at the same time suffered harvest failures and an ulcer which was of course a consequence of the war, internal disturbances, especially [difficulties] in recruiting. Now it remains only to hope for a long peace, which would give us complete rest, in order to . . . put things in order. . . . To achieve this, it is necessary to begin with the restoration of internal calm." Paul appealed for lower taxes and the end of recruiting levies. Thus the chief causes of dissatisfaction would be removed. "Our people is such that the smallest satisfaction makes it forget years of discontent and even calamity. But we have this time, relying on the obedience and naturally happy disposition of the people, taken everything and saved nothing." The patience of the people, he said, had been stretched to the breaking point, and the state would therefore be unprepared in the eventuality of any genuinely unexpected emergency. "The preservation of the kingdom is the preservation of the people: the preservation of the people is the preservation of the kingdom. The kingdom should be considered like a body: the sovereign is the head; the laws are the soul; morals are the heart; wealth and abundance are the health; the military forces are the arms and all the members which serve for protection; and religion is the law under which all is comprised."

Paul was engaged in an impassioned quest to find the principles appropriate to establish a harmonious equilibrium of state and society and to maintain them in that happy condition indefinitely.

"Supposing the military forces [to be like] the arms and the other limbs serving for defense, they should be, following this analogy, maintained exactly in that condition in which the

---

31. The full name of the memorandum was "Razsuzhdenie o gosudarstve voobshchee, otnositel'no chisla voisk, potrebnago dlia zashchity onago, i kasatel'no oborony vsiekh predielov." Lebedev, *Grafy Nikita i Petr Paniny*, pp. 185-199. Geisman and Dubovskii, *Graf Petr Ivanovich Panin*, pp. 88-98. "Velikii kniaz' Pavel Petrovich; perepiska v. k. Pavla Petrovicha s gr. Petrom Paninym," *Russkaia starina*, 1882, No. 33, pp. 403-418, 739-764.

members of a healthy body are [maintained]; that is, strong and powerful without excess, for if there is an excess [of power in one of the members], then, of course, it will damage the remaining members, taking from them, for its superfluous strength, nourishment (*soki*) necessary for the equal satisfaction of all the members."

A theme that recurs again and again in Paul's thought is a sensitive concern for the well-being of the Russian people and the Russian state. He had written a condemnation of the foreign policy of aggression and aggrandizement and an invidious comparison of Catherine's reign with an imagined reign of peace and prosperity. His conflict with Catherine was political as well as personal.

To remedy the deplorable state of affairs which he described, he set down rather explicit recommendations:

1. All offensive war should be repudiated and the entire armed force of the nation should be deployed for defense. A series of fortresses should be built along the borders. They should be supported by formations of the army drawn from the local population, which would naturally know the enemy on its part of the border well and which would fight more bravely for its own homes than for unfamiliar territory.

2. So that the defense of the nation would not be a burden on those who did not require it, the army should be deployed primarily on the borders and in force like that deployed against it on the other side of the borders: one army against Sweden, one against Austria and Prussia, one against Turkey, and one in Siberia. The remaining forces should be scattered through the kingdom and supported by the provinces in which they were quartered.

3. To compensate for populations inadequate to support sufficient forces in a border province, recruiting should be done in neighboring provinces.

4. Once the regiments were settled into permanent quarters, deceased and disabled soldiers should be replaced by new recruits drawn from the children of the soldiers themselves. The families of the soldiers were to be settled in military colonies with them. Thus the regiments would sustain themselves.[32]

5. Detailed manuals and instructions should be provided especially "to prescribe to all, beginning with the field marshal, ending with the common soldier, all that they must do"; thus each one could be held precisely responsible for his duties,

---

32. Alexander's later institution of the military colonies may have owed its origin to Paul's idea.

and the quality of the regiments ought to be maintained uniformly high.

6. By strictly subordinating everyone in the regiments to the manual of instructions, discontent caused by personal preferment and commanders' caprices would be avoided; and thus everyone would be more eager to serve and to serve well.

The document disappointed and angered Catherine. Far from preparing Paul's entrance into the councils of state, it postponed the occasion.

Much of the content of this document was repeated in Paul's letters to Peter Panin in 1778 and 1779. This correspondence, which sometimes contains word-for-word excerpts of the "Razsuzhdenie" of 1774, suggests that the Panins were not directly instrumental in the composition of the earlier document. Paul was inviting the reaction of Peter Panin to his ideas. In one instance, he formulated his arguments in a briefer and more schematic manner. Three things, he said, were necessary to the internal equilibrium of the state: the integrity of the empire depended upon the equal protection of all its borders; the peace and satisfaction of the provinces depended, in order to avoid impoverishing them, on the reasonable distribution of forces; and the equal contributions of the parts to the defense of the whole.[33] In the course of this correspondence, Paul made a rare and interesting comment on his father: "My deceased father came to the throne and took it upon himself to institute order . . . imprudence [neostorozhnost'], perhaps, was a part of his character, and thus he did many things which made painful impressions, which, together with the intrigues against his person, . . . destroyed him."[34]

Paul contrasted his own virtue with the vices of Catherine and sought strength in his own purity. In 1777, he wrote to a friend: "If I were in need of a party, then I would be able to hold my tongue about the disorders, in order to humor certain persons; but being what I am, I can have neither party nor interest except that of the State, and it is painful (dur), given my character, to see that things are going awry and above all that negligence and self-seeking views are the cause of it;--I prefer to be hated for doing good than loved for doing evil."[35] This was Paul's concise way of objecting to Catherine's "government of favorites." He hotly resented Potemkin and the others who owed

---

33. *Russkaia starina*, 1882, No. 33, pp. 406-417, 739-750.

34. Ibid., p. 748.

35. Paul to Baron Sacken, 4/15 Feb. 1779; *Sbornik IRIO*, 20: 412.

their occupancy of what he regarded as his rightful place in government to his mother's personal whim. The last line was possibly a reference to Catherine's pursuit of popularity, at least among the nobility; but it is also worth considering literally. So considered, it is an attitude that was to cost Paul dearly.

When Paul married the second time, he was concerned to avoid the indiscretions on the part of his new wife that had disturbed his first wife's relations with Catherine. He composed an "Instruction" (*Nastavlenie*) for the benefit of Mariia Fedorovna, a document intended to acquaint her with the customs and peculiarities of her new land, with the character of Catherine (and of himself), and with what was expected of her in her new role. This document, somewhat tedious in its conception, is vital to understanding the mentality of Paul.[36]

"1. Concerning religion, what it is necessary to observe in relation to church services, customs, etc." The princess is urged to take religion very seriously, to consider it carefully and conscientiously, and always to practice it piously.

"2. Concerning Her Majesty and the princess's conduct in relation to her. The princess, arriving alone in this little-known and distant land, will understand that her own advantage demands that she draw near Her Majesty and gain her trust, in order to enjoy in her a second mother and a person who will guide her in all her acts, without any personal interests (*vidov*) or aims. In relation to the empress, the princess must be attentive and gentle, must not express disappointment or complain of her to anyone at all; a face-to-face explanation will always be better. Thus [the princess] will spare herself many intrigues." Mariia Fedorovna was advised to speak entirely candidly with Catherine about anything on her mind.

"3. Concerning her desired behavior with me. I will not speak of love or affection, for these depend entirely on good fortune (*ot shchastlivoi sluchainosti*); but so far as friendship and trust are concerned, these things depend on ourselves. I do not doubt that the princess wishes to acquire these by her conduct, her genuine kindness (*serdechnoiu dobrotoiu*), and by her other virtues. . . . *It is appropriate for her above all to arm herself with*

---

36. Evgenii S. Shumigorskii, ed., "Instruktsiia Velikago Kniazia Pavla Petrovicha Kniagine Mariia Fedorovne (1776)," *Russkaia starina*, 1898, No. 93, pp. 247-261. I have made one alteration in the text. In the printed document, the text of the instruction is preceded by a list of "points of the instruction," which are like chapter titles. I have inserted each of these fourteen headings at the beginning of the appropriate chapter or paragraph.

patience and meekness in order to tolerate my ardor and volatile disposition and, equally, my impatience.[37] I would like her to accept indulgently all that I may sometimes express coldly (*sukho*) but with good intentions with respect to her way of life, dress, etc. . . . Since I have some knowledge of the situation here, then I may at times give her such advice or express such an opinion as may serve her well. I wish her to be on a completely friendly basis with me, not however transgressing decency, and to say candidly all that she does not like in me; never to place between me and her a third person [and] never to allow anyone to reproach me in a conversation with her, because that does not correspond to the distance that should be kept between a person of her rank and mine [on the one hand] and subjects [on the other].

"4. Concerning our public, and consequently indirectly the reputation of the princess even in other spheres." Russian society, Paul said, was more demanding than most in part because it was poorly educated, took first impressions more seriously, and sometimes concentrated its attention on trifling details. Therefore it would be best for the princess to formulate a plan of action which would serve as her defense; with this as a guide she would not do anything embarrassing. Above all it would be well for her not to devote more time to one person than to others, or at least not to allow [such favoritism] to be detected.

"5. Concerning our people (*narod*), which may be easily offended." The Russian masses (*narod*), like the Russian gentry (*publika*--upper-class opinion), is poorly educated and easily offended. Russians were inclined to be very respectful toward persons in authority, and they very much liked appropriate attention, but excessive kindness (*liubeznost'*) only provoked a surfeit of petitions, which were inconvenient. The people also liked to see religion piously observed.

"6. The Russian language and other necessary information on Russia." There would be many persons in the princess's entourage who did not speak either French or German; therefore she would have to communicate with them in Russian.

"7. Concerning her personal staff." It would be better to have Countess Rumiantsova (who was in charge of the princess's staff) deal with the servants in order to avoid many intrigues and many requests and many searches for weaknesses in the princess.

---

37. Emphasis added.

8.   They, the couple, will receive money every four months; thus, since there is a long time between receipts, it is necessary to manage the budget carefully so that they will not run out of money.   The money must be allocated to various anticipated expenses.   "The remaining sum must be deposited in savings (*vnesena v khranenie*): *this will be money for a rainy day* (*eto budet dengi na chernyi den'*)."[38]   The accounts for a given four-month period are to be presented and paid on the first or second day of the succeeding period, and they must be verified with care to see that they are correct.

With respect to the princess's wardrobe, Paul observed that it was currently quite ample and unlikely to need replenishment soon.   When it was necessary to make more purchases, they must never be bought on credit, but always from current funds.   All purchases should be made through a single person. If more than one purchaser were to be used, then all kinds of people would try to flatter her and abuse her trust and sell her material of low quality and for unfair prices.

"9.   Concerning the trust which she may confide in [Countess Rumiantsova]."   She was a worthy person, could be relied on, and would not abuse the princess's trust.   It would be well to consult with her early.   "But the princess should be warned not to resort to any familiarity with her in view of the possibility that Countess Rumiantsova might do something not worthy of the princess's approval [sic].   So long as relations with her are maintained with decorum, the princess may rebuke her, although gently.   Meanwhile, she should rely exclusively on Rumiantsova to deal with the staff."

There was nothing in which Paul invested quite so much faith as in proper rules and regularity of daily regimen, and some of his more important and revealing instructions to Mariia Fedorovna were directed to that subject.

"10.   Concerning [our] manner of life in general.   Our manner of life must be strictly regulated (*strogo opredelen*). . . . By subjecting ourselves (*podchiniaias v zhizni*) to well known rules, we protect ourselves from our own fantasies, which frequently become caprices, and . . . we give an example to other people who are obliged to subject themselves to the same rules." Particular days must be designated for receptions, lunches, and dinners, and all this should take place in a strongly ordered way, "without changes, because any change in these things appears in the eyes of the public as a caprice."   Thus it is necessary to establish two orders of etiquette: one for reception days

---

38. Emphasis added.

and holidays, the other for ordinary days. "Then [we] will in no way depart from protocol." If receptions sometimes prove monotonous, the princess should take comfort in the thought that she and her husband are doing their duty and that it will be doubly sweet to retire to the freedom of their own apartments when their duties are over.

"11. Concerning those persons whom we will see in society." Enough has been said about this above (evidently in the section on the Russian people). "I should remark only that we do not have the custom of seeing foreigners except on days appointed for receptions."

"12. Concerning [our] manner of life at home and the people in the domestic entourage. I said above that the exact fulfillment of the rules is one of the chief conditions which it is necessary to observe in life; I repeat this again, especially relative to the domestic regime (*obikhod*). As long as we hold to the established rules, we spare ourselves much, including tedium, one of the chief enemies of man--it does not have, so to speak, power over us. Therefore I consider it my duty to ask the princess to subject herself . . . to the established rules both in her manner of life and in regard to her duties in particular." She was advised to get up rather early, in order to have time to do her hair, to use an hour or two for her duties, and then to complete her toilette early, because "my own use of time is distributed such that, beginning at ten o'clock, when I am completely dressed, and until noon, I do not have a minute of free time. . . . I strongly request her to be ready at noon, and on Sundays and holidays at 10:30." After lunch Paul asked her to occupy herself with reading, music, and other things; in the course of her morning duties, he asked her to appoint an established time for the study of the Russian language and other subjects in order to acquire some understanding of the history, politics, and geography of the country.

In view of the fact that the princess would be extremely busy with her duties and her social life and would consequently not have much free time, she would probably want to spend a few minutes a day entirely alone, without even her service staff present. She should be warned, however, that to establish any circle of intimates about herself except that which is appointed for her would cause suspicion in the eyes of the public and give rise to gossip. "Concerning bedtime, *I beg the princess to submit to my custom of a regular schedule*, since in consideration of my health and my morning duties, I do not have the possibility, in spite of my young years, of staying up all night." Finally, she should not do anything, even in her own room, that might give rise to the suspicion of secretiveness.

"The following two points are considered especially important."

"13. Never interfere in any affair not directly concerning her, nor speak of any intrigues or gossip. . . . Thus the princess must treat everyone alike, without the slightest familiarity; this does not give flatterers and . . . obsequious people a chance to discuss with her, under the guise of devotion, their own intrigues, or to slander anyone."

14. The princess "must not accept from anyone except persons specially appointed for this [purpose], and especially not from the service staff, any kind of advice, however trivial, not to mention [advice] which in any way concerns me."

A note later appended to the Instructions indicates Mariia Fedorovna's opinion that they were not as necessary as Paul had supposed, that his anxieties about her conduct derived largely from the bad experience of the first marriage. Paul indicated that he agreed with this judgment. In spite of that, the Instructions remain an invaluable guide to Paul's mind. Paul betrayed here the same urge to establish inviolable order that was apparent in the *Razsuzhdenie* of 1774. Schedule, expense, etiquette, protocol--everything was to be put in strict order. He was seriously religious. He was, at least at this time, ready to be more considerate of Catherine. He knew and pointed out, in terms entirely consonant with the judgment of others, his own faults and peculiarities. He was obviously alarmed about the influence of court intrigues, as is indicated by his multiple warnings about them. At first thought, his sensitivity on this subject seems exaggerated, but this impression is easily diminished by reading in Catherine's own memoirs the experience of a young bride at the Russian court.

The last series of papers that are important for understanding Paul's values are those that he prepared prior to his departure for the army in 1788.[39] First there are letters between him and Mariia Fedorovna containing an agreement on the succession to the throne in the event of his death at the front or in the event of Catherine's death in his absence.[40] In the latter event, Mariia Fedorovna was to be the acting ruler of Russia un-

---

39. See Chapter 1 as well.

40. Mikhail I. Semevskii, ed., "Materialy k russkoi istorii XVIII veka (1788)," *Viestnik Evropy* 1:297-330 (1867).

til Paul's return to the capital. In the event of his death, the
succession was to pass to his eldest son, Alexander, and then to
his heirs, on the principle of primogeniture. This represented a
major change in the law of succession; as has been noted, Russian sovereigns since Peter I, according to a decree of 1722, were
entitled to choose their successors. The results had been
chaotic, the "era of palace revolutions," and Paul hoped to put
an end to dynastic confusion and political revolution. His recommended resolution of the problem was quite similar to the
Panins' proposals, though it was not so detailed or so militant.

Subsequently, Paul wrote his political testament.[41] It is
as important for his view of politics as is the Instruction to
Mariia Fedorovna for his views of the private life of the royal
couple. It is a detailed recitation of his political dedication, and
two things in his outlook are especially noteworthy: that the
application of proper principles could realize an unprecedented
degree of social harmony, political stability, and public prosperity; and that he had retreated a considerable distance from the
limitations on autocratic prerogative that he had accepted in
1783 under the tutelage of the Panins.

"1.   The object of every society is the happiness
(*blazhenstvo*)[42] of each and of all. Society cannot exist unless
the will of everyone is directed to a common goal. This is what a
government is for, any kind of government. The best is that
which most directly and most advantageously reaches its goal.
[In pursuit of this end] various kinds of government arise. The
larger the land, the more difficult the means of fulfilling [the goal
of happiness]; consequently the first care (*pervoe popechenie*)
must be to facilitate them (*oblegchat' ikh*). The simplest means
is to entrust power to a single person, but there are human in-
capacities (*neudobstvami chelovechestva*) inherent in it.

"2.   Having set forth the rules as to who shall govern the
land,[43] it is necessary to say that there is no better form of gov-

---

41. Ibid. I am indebted to Sergei Ignashev for checking my translation of this material.

42. This is a term which Paul used repeatedly in this document as
well as in others. It was also used by Bogdanovich in his 1773 poem dedicated to Paul, "Blazhenstvo narodov." Ippolit F. Bogdanovich, *Stikhotvoreniia
i poemy* (Leningrad: Sovetskii pisatel', 1957), pp. 187-194. Much of Bogdanovich's work closely reflected the outlook of the Panin party. See, for example, idem., "Pchely i shmel," pp. 169-170 and "Portret rossiiskogo
polkovodtsa," pp. 179-180.

43. In the document projecting the inheritance of the throne in the
event of Paul's death.

ernment than the autocratic, for it combines the force of the laws and the efficiency (*skorost'*) of the power of one person.

"3. For this reason, there must be a law [on succession to define] exactly who is to be the sovereign.

"4. Laws we have, but [it is necessary] to introduce order into their interpretation; not to make new laws, but to coordinate (*soobrazit'*) the old ones with the internal situation of the state.

"5. The laws are to be observed. It is necessary to keep an eye out for non-observance (*za nebliudeniem dolzhno smotret'*). The sovereign, being a [mere] man, cannot watch over everything, even if he is impartial"; thus governments are necessary, as well as different organs of government.

"6. The sovereign [has authority] over everything . . . and therefore to assist not only his mind but his conscience, he needs a council composed of persons entrusted with the different parts and kinds of affairs of state.

"7. Into the Council of State all matters from all branches [of government] enter." The Council of State should be the chief organ of government, and its membership should include the Chancellor of Justice, the Chancellor of Foreign Affairs, the Vice-Chancellor of Justice, the Vice-Chancellor of Foreign Affairs, the Minister of Defense, the Minister of the Navy, the Finance Minister, the Minister of Commerce, and the Minister of the State Treasury.

8. The most direct means of achieving the proper object, the well-being of society, is through affirmation of the laws. The first estate of the kingdom is the nobility. It is the main support of the state and the sovereign. It must be respected and not admit any superfluous or unworthy persons to its ranks. It has an equal interest with the sovereign in serving the state.

9. The second estate is the clergy, the holiness of whose duties is worthy of respect, and for this reason it deserves special attention and special observation (*prismotra*) to see that it teaches a proper understanding of God and not superstition.

10. The distinctive concern of the middle estate, which is a separate estate, is commerce and industry, and it should occupy itself such that shortages do not develop and that industry thrives and spreads and leads to an abundant life.

11. The remainder of society is comprised of the peasantry, whose condition is, by virtue of its labors, worthy of special respect. To deserve the respect of the fatherland, it must work better and provide a steady supply of agricultural products.

12. But a mere definition of the duties of these estates is not sufficient; it is necessary for them to fulfill their functions, which is not possible unless every member of every estate learns through education the scope of his obligations, of which the first is to serve the well-being of society. This cannot be achieved without education (*vospitanie*), from which an understanding of the law comes. Without this, the people are corrupt.

13. Thus the foundation of schools, "based on the rules of government," is necessary in order to teach everyone, according to his social station (estate), his appointed duties and how to fulfill them for the betterment of society.

14. Trade serves to enrich the land, to guide the people, and to polish their manners (*poliruet nravy*); it opens up new ways of thought and enhances the capacities of the state and the people.

15. Manufacturing and handicraft are the strength and thus the security of society, and it is necessary to nurture them, especially among us, where they are neglected.

16. On the liquor and salt monopolies. The latter is neglected, and its function must be improved; the former is founded on abuse because the crown monopoly has a corrupting influence on the people's morals. It is necessary to seek this source of revenue somewhere else, through encouraging other trades.

17. It is necessary to do something to change the condition of the "possessional" serfs attached to factories and mines.

18. Thus bending all parts to the object of the general well-being, the state peasants and the free peasants (*chernososhnye*) also deserve an improvement of their condition. The economic peasants (peasants living on monastery lands prior to confiscation of these lands by the state in 1762) must be left in their current condition, but the income from these lands should be spent either on monasteries or on charitable institutions; whatever remains should be used directly for state necessities. The court peasants should remain as they are, supporting the royal family.

19. State revenues belong to the state, not to the sovereign, and represent the wealth and well-being of the land. They are of two kinds: either from farming or from trade and industry. The former it is necessary to collect sparingly, for it comes from private persons. The latter must be encouraged, for

it is founded on labors and diligence, the eternal source of the power and strength of the land.[44]

20.   Both state and private debts lead to disturbance of the balance of exchange and thus, little by little, they must be eliminated, especially the latter, for they ruin private citizens; they come from luxury-loving and corruption of morals.

23.   Expenditures must be coordinated with revenues and with the needs of the state and must be allocated so as not to spoil the condition of the land: it is necessary to remember that a sudden emergency requiring a large expenditure may arise; for this reason a spare collection in the treasury must be maintained; but not too much, in order not to imbalance the normal course of exchange.

24.   Ordering things as described above cannot fail to produce moral and physical balance, leading "to general good faith" everywhere. Someone must oversee the situation, for the establishment of the peace and happiness (*blazhenstvo*) of each and all is the primary purpose of God's law.

25.   For the attainment and preservation of such an objective, it is necessary to establish the rule of general security, born of the convergence of everything toward a common end. Thus it is necessary to establish rural and urban police.

26.   The condition of the foreign affairs of a state "should correspond to the physical and moral stature of the state. . . . We do not have a great need for anyone's help. We are ourselves sufficiently strong if we want to use our strength.

"27.   We must take care with whom we maintain [foreign] relations and of what kind."   Circumstances between states change, and their relations change, too. Obligations must not have an inflexible character. Different circumstances give rise to

---

44. The idea here may be that the bulk of Russian industry (and trade?) is mingled with the state economy, thus that private citizens are not so threatened by taxing it; but it must be encouraged. Paul's thought is not very clear. There follows at this point a series of homilies on economic virtues, possibly inspired by the *Memoirs* of the Duc de Sully, one of Paul's favorite readings. The spirit of this whole document--but not the style--is close to that of Sully, who admired the principle "Que les bonnes moeurs & les bonnes lois se formen réciproquement." *Mémoires de Maximilien de Béthune, duc de Sully*, 10 vols. (London: n.p., 1778), 5:292. Sully favored authoritarian government and strove to bring the French nobility under the control of the crown. In the opinion of one student of the man, "All Sully's personal papers bear the imprint of a mind loving order and uniformity." David Buisseret, *Sully and the Growth of Centralized Government in France, 1598-1610* (London: Eyre and Spottiswoode, 1968), p. 194. Paul admired all these things and the man associated with them.

different needs. Personal relations or kinship should never be allowed to make us forget the direct interests of the state.

28. We should not allow anyone dominion over our freedom of action. We should not blindly follow someone else's interest. We should keep our neighbors in a state of balance, in order that "no one threaten the freedom of another; [but rather] observe impartially, and with conduct based on justice, prudence and firmness, respect and good faith toward [the Russian] State. . . . This is the basis of the political well-being of the State.

"29. Showing thus in what political purpose consists, now we must show how to attain this object. By good faith, founded above all on honor, in our conduct; by alliances in the north with powers who need us more" than we need them; and by unshakable military strength based on Russian numbers and good discipline.

"30. It is clearly evident that if morals and character (*nravy*) are needed for the internal well-being of the state, then they are as much needed for external security. They are the guarantee and the foundation of everything, and the attainment [of this condition] will lead the state to the . . . object of the happiness of each and of all."

31. The protection of the Russian land requires a large armed force, both offensive and defensive. But the scant population of this vast expanse of land makes such protection difficult. Thus the armed forces must be distributed on four frontiers and in the interior.

32. The State, being surrounded on many sides by seas, necessarily requires a fleet on each of these seas as much as it requires land forces. Schools for the fleet are also necessary.[45]

Here we have the vintage thought of Paul. He was concerned with comprehensive, systematic, neat approaches to achieve happiness for Russian society. He saw autocratic government as the best means of attaining it, but he thought that the autocratic government needed good laws. He thought that the nobility had a special responsibility in governing the state.

---

45. Claus Scharf has observed that there is astonishingly little concrete detail in Paul's plans for the reform of the state. He thinks that Paul's constitutional ideas were, in many respects, shared by both Catherine and Alexander. See his comments in "Staatsauffassung und Regierungsprogramm eines aufgeklärten Selbstherrschers, Die Instruktion des Grossfürsten Paul von 1788," in Ernst Schulin, ed., *Gedenkschrift Martin Boehring* (Wiesbaden: Studien zur europäischen Geschichte, 1968), pp. 91-106.

The condition of the peasantry required amelioration. All the people were expected to assume carefully prescribed roles; education would enlighten them and show them the benefits to be derived from working faithfully in their prescribed places. In his conclusion (point 33), Paul expressed confidence that "when all the parts of the state have been led in an orderly fashion to the good balance in which they should be, such that the balance cannot be broken or damaged, then one may say that the society has been directed onto its proper path of the well-being of each and of all, which is in accord with the law of God and consequently cannot fail to be blessed in everything by His Heavenly Hand."

It ought to be apparent by this point that the Panins had effectively imparted their vision to the heir. Paul's aspirations were saturated with the thinking of the Panins and the historical lore of Peter I. Peter, like Paul, had thought in terms of *obshchee blago*, the general well-being, and *obshchaia pol'za*, the general advantage. By *obshchaia pol'za*, he meant something familiar to us in Paul's thought, "the capacity of the subjects, depending on their social class, to serve the 'state interest.'" And all were obliged so to serve, the peasants by paying taxes and providing recruits, the nobles by staffing the chanceries and the officers' corps.[46] "If one asks the significance of the great tsar's policy toward the nobility . . . , one must consider two motives as inseparably bound together: the impulse to mobilize all the forces for the state, to leave no force unused, and the need to regulate all social relations and every area of life, to bring them into an order that would transform the incoherent, the arbitrary, and the freely developing into a well functioning mechanism." Peter's purpose in making the nobility into a service class was to enhance his own power and that of the state.[47]

While he waited to govern, Paul had, as he said, nothing to do--nothing except to fantasize, to dream of the day when, if fortune spared him, he would have a sovereign's business of state to occupy him. In the meantime, he drilled his troops and fretted over a fussy schedule, always impatient to begin the era of this constructive statesmanship. In many respects, Martin Malia's observation regarding Herzen and the gentry socialists of

---

46. Nikolai I. Pavlenko, "Petr I: k izucheniiu ego sotsial'no-politicheskikh vzgliadov," in *Rossiia v period reform Petra I: sbornik statei* (Moscow: Nauka, 1973), pp. 40-102, passim, esp. pp. 60-64, 77-78.

47. Reinhard Wittram, *Peter I, Czar und Kaiser: Zur Geschichte Peters des Grossen in seiner Zeit*, 2 vols. (Göttingen: Vandenhoeck & Ruprecht, 1964), 2:144-145.

his generation applies as well to Paul: "Where the entire order of the world, in every detail of its organization, is an affront to the dignity of the [grand prince], the formulation of a specific set of grievances is impossible, and the cry of protest can only find expression in generalities. . . . Under such circumstances . . . to approach politics pragmatically was in effect an abdication of hope, if not downright collaboration with the existing order. Therefore the only thing left to do was to think in terms of general principles; and principles, the longer one lives with them, without any possibility of application, become increasingly pure, ideal, sweeping, and, most crucial of all, uncompromising. The reformer turns intransigent and will settle for nothing less than the complete destruction of the 'old' corrupt world and the creation of a totally 'new' one."[48]

The two chief malefactors in the old, corrupt world were the immoral empress and the pampered nobility. The two chief sufferers were the masses and the heir. Paul's aim would be to undo the work of Catherine, to harness the nobility to state service, and to provide justice and *blazhenstvo* for the people. This might be regarded as a naive program, but it reflected most of what the Panin party had labored to teach him.

---

48. Martin Malia, *Alexander Herzen and the Birth of Russian Socialism* (Cambridge, Mass.: Harvard University Press, 1961), pp. 55, 118-119.

3

THE EMPEROR, 1796–1801

Paul began his reign with mixed emotions. On the one hand, he felt a sense of dread and misgiving. Years before, the French ambassador, the Count de Ségur, had spoken with him about the duties of his inheritance. According to Ségur, Paul was obsessed by the histories of all of his predecessors who had been overturned or assassinated, and he repeatedly expressed the fear of sharing the fate of his father. Ségur responded: "As for the misfortunes you fear in the future, believe me, it is in dreading them that one calls them forth; rise above them and they disappear."[1] It was a remarkably prophetic observation.

On the other hand, he now had what he had been denied for so long: the opportunity to implement the beautiful schemes that he had premeditated. His accession was followed by a flurry of activity such as the Russian government had not witnessed for many years. He was evidently determined to make up for lost time; at age forty-three, he at last had something to do.

---

1. Louis Philippe de Ségur, *Mémoires*, 3 vols. (Paris: Alexis Eymery, 1824-1827), 3:534-535.

One of the more conspicuous elements of the early part of his reign was the wish to reverse as many as possible of the policies of his mother. In some respects, this practice was trivial, as, for example, his inclination to abolish official state decorations instituted by Catherine. In other ways, it was more important: he released the imprisoned journalists Radishchev and Novikov and the Polish revolutionary Kosciuszko and said that he regretted the partitions of Poland. In still other cases, his reversal of policy was of the utmost importance. For example, he recalled an army sent to campaign against the Persians in the Caucasus, and he refused to send the expeditionary corps promised by Catherine to assist the English and the Austrians in the war against revolutionary France.[2]

One of his more notorious early actions designed to rectify the injustices of the preceding reign was the disinterment and reburial of Peter III. Peter had not been buried in the traditionally honored place for deceased Russian sovereigns, the Cathedral of Saints Peter and Paul, but in the comparative obscurity of the Alexander Nevskii Monastery. Paul moved the body and placed it along with that of Catherine in the Cathedral. Moreover, he ordered Peter's murderers to walk behind the coffin in the funeral procession. Apart from this macabre touch, he was astonishingly free of any spirit of revenge against Catherine's former favorites; and given his reputation for impulsive extravagance in the name of justice--and the multiple good examples of it which we have seen and will see yet--it must be admitted that his relative magnanimity to his father's assassins represents a remarkable example of self-control, in fact one so remarkable as to lead to the supposition that it must have been carefully premeditated.

At the time of his coronation in April 1797, he promulgated the new law on succession which he had worked out with Mariia Fedorovna prior to his departure for the Swedish front in 1788. The new law was designed to give Russia more stable government than the nation had had under the law of Peter I of 1722. Peter had provided that the sovereign could choose his own successor, and the competition for preferment and confusion over legitimacy of succession had encouraged palace revo-

---

2. Paul had changed his mind about the desirability of intervening against the French Revolution. He had decided that the powers had done too little too late. Moreover, he told the Austrian ambassador that the condition of the Russian army was not satisfactory and that the empire itself was weakened by the contagion of democratic doctrines. This latter observation was especially improbable. McGrew, "Political Portrait," *Jahrbücher* 18:511.

lutions. Paul hoped to avoid that.   His new law did provide
Russia in the nineteenth century with more orderly succession
than had characterized the Russian throne in the eighteenth
century, but it did not, ironically, spare Paul the fate that he
dreaded.

The law on succession shows that Paul's central ideas
were held with conviction and that they were enduring. It is
striking, as one reviews the statecraft of his short reign, how
faithful he remained to the inspiration which he had set down in
the documents of 1788.

He firmly believed in the absolutism of his own power
and in the necessity to use that power to catalyze the processes
of administration. He was a great advocate of centralization in
the government. One of his more impressive performances was
in the Senate. He found it handling 11,000 cases of law per year
when he came to power; and he arranged for it to handle 44,000
in 1800. One lawsuit, instituted in 1755, had been shunted
back and forth from the Chancery to the College of Justice and
then, in 1777, to the Senate, where it remained without resolution until Paul's time. It was settled during the first year of his
reign. Paul added staff to the Senate and divided its functions
into several departments, and it worked much more efficiently
than it previously had.[3]

In the College of Foreign Affairs, Paul established the
Asiatic Department and inaugurated the study of Asiatic languages. He cut both the staff and the expenses of the college in
St. Petersburg while increasing the staff (and consequently the
expenses) of foreign missions.

He began a close observation of the governors of the
provinces. He punished abuses by the governors and subordinated them strictly to the control of the College of Internal Affairs in St. Petersburg. At the same time, he considerably diminished the number and the prerogatives of the elected provincial officials created by Catherine.

At the end of Catherine's reign, the army was far from
being taut and well disciplined. It was widely known that many

---

3. This assessment relies on Klochkov, *Ocherki,* pp. 180-223. Aleksandr E. Nolde, "Pravitel'stvuiushchii senat v tsarstvovanie Pavla I," in *Istoriia
pravitel'stvuiushchego senata za dvesti let, 1711-1911 gg.,* 2 vols. (St. Petersburg: Senatskaia tipografiia, 1911), 2:695-779, is more impressionistic. Foreign observers were astonished at the volume of business which Paul's administration transacted. On the other hand, these observers deplored and
were shocked by the amount of time that Paul spent in what they considered
trivial ceremony. This situation worsened with the development of the Maltese bauble. McGrew, "Political Portrait," *Jahrbücher* 18:515-516.

persons enjoying position and rank in it served only nominally. Paul abruptly changed that practice. He ordered that persons not actually fulfilling the duties of their office be struck off the rolls. He reduced the size of the army, put it into uniforms like those of the Prussian army, and issued a new military manual like that of Frederick II. After this refurbishing, he held extensive maneuvers in the fall of 1797. He was very pleased and told a convocation of his generals: "I knew, gentlemen, that the formation of the forces according to the new manual was not entirely pleasant; I waited until fall in order that you yourselves might see to what it led. You have now seen the fruits of these labors: the honor and glory of the Russian army." This speech was followed by a generous distribution of honors.[4]

Paul went to some trouble to see that the common soldiers were satisfied. He often asked them if they had any complaints against their officers and took care to see that they were well fed and paid on time. As Sablukov observed, "a second lieutenant (*kornet*) could freely and confidently (*bezboiaznenno*) demand a military trial for his commanding officer, fully counting on an impartial investigation of the case." All contemporary accounts agree that the simple soldiers loved him. On the night of his assassination, one of the chief concerns of the conspirators, who were noblemen and officers, was to do the job before the soldiers discovered their intentions. Sablukov's regiment, the horse guards, refused to take the oath to Alexander until some of them had seen the body of Paul. When one of them, Grigorii Ivanov, had done so, Sablukov asked him if he would then swear loyalty to the new emperor. Ivanov said, "Yes, but he cannot be better than the deceased one."[5]

On the other hand, it has been observed that Paul was more concerned with the trivia of the military calling than with its essentials. "Hence what contemporaries called 'the Gatchina spirit'--a preoccupation with parades and manoeuvres, uniforms and equipment, awards and punishments, in short with the minutiae of army life, and a corresponding neglect of weightier matters likely to prove decisive in war: morale, professional training, technical progress, etc."[6] A contemporary diplomat reported Paul to be as tyrannical a martinet as his assassins

---

4. Klochkov, *Ocherki*, pp. 129-131.

5. Nikolai A. Sablukov, *Zapiski o vremenakh imperatora Pavla I i o konchine etogo gosudaria* (Berlin: Ladyschnikow, n.d.), pp. 65, 85.

6. John Keep, "Paul I and the Militarization of Government," in Ragsdale, *Paul I*, p. 93.

claimed he was: "In general, the slightest mistake committed by an officer on parade, a small irregularity in saluting . . . is punished either by transferring the regiment to the provinces . . . , by cashiering it at once from service, or sometimes by reducing it to the rank of simple foot soldiers. . . . Petersburg has become the domicile of Terror."[7] When these episodes took place, when something gave him offense, he experienced a consistent physical reaction which accompanied his outburst of wrath: he turned pale, his face contorted, his chest swelled, and he threw back his head and breathed with difficulty.[8] Sablukov himself, otherwise so complimentary of Paul, reported that he had always carried money while at drill lest he be sent straight to Siberia from the drill-field without the chance to make appropriate preparations. He had on three occasions loaned money to fellow officers who had failed to take such precautions.[9] But Paul was aware of the damage that he did at such moments, and he was not beyond the reach of reason if someone sought him out for mercy. His son Constantine in particular often did so, as did Mariia Fedorovna and Nelidova.

Christopher Duffy's recent work on the Russian army in the eighteenth century has an interesting assessment of Paul's military reforms. Paul's work, Duffy says, "makes sense only in the context of the run-down, mismanaged army which he had inherited from the last reign." His main aims were:

"(a) to subject the army to the control of the sovereign;

"(b) to eradicate the corruption and tyrannical power of the colonels and senior officers;

"(c) to recall the officers as a whole to their professional obligations, and curb their notorious drinking and gambling;

"(d) to improve the lot of the private soldier, who had been so cruelly abused in the reign of Catherine."

The results, as measured by the Italian campaign of 1799, constitute a brilliant vindication. As one of the survivors of Suvorov's campaign observed, no other army but the Russian was capable of withstanding the armies of revolutionary France.[10]

---

7. McGrew, "Political Portrait," *Jahrbücher* 18:514.

8. Chizh, "Imperator Pavel I," p. 425.

9. Sablukov, *Zapiski*, pp. 43-44.

10. Christopher Duffy, *Russia's Military Way to the West: Origins and Nature of Russian Military Power, 1700-1800* (London: Routledge & Kegan Paul, 1981), pp. 207, 232. It must be admitted that Duffy makes many small mistakes in his account of Paul, and he did not use--though it seems scarcely

Some of Paul's measures were both petty and ridiculous. For example, he outlawed the use of words made notorious by the French Revolution: *otechestvo* (fatherland), *grazhdanin* (citizen), *obshchestvo* (society). He was ready to carry statecraft to almost absurd extremes to make the people conform to his conception of happiness. There were regulations about how houses might and might not be painted, how doors might and might not be decorated. Officers were forbidden by imperial decree to eat lunch with their hats on. Certain kinds of clothing had to be dyed in solid colors. The populace was forbidden to wear colorful neckwear, such as scarves. Small children were forbidden to play unsupervised in the streets.

Paul was not only petty in regulating the state; he was severe in implementing his regulations and notorious for the harshness of his punishments. He publicly humiliated Russia's most illustrious general, Suvorov, because the troops under his command returned from a long and glorious campaign in tatters. At such times, Paul seemed overcome by a sudden access of almost uncontrollable wrath.

On the other hand, he did not entirely lack a sense of humor. One day when Sablukov was standing guard duty near the inner apartments of the tsar, Paul came out of his apartment into the corridor more hastily than usual. Before he managed to get the door closed, a high-heeled slipper flew out the door, barely missing his head. Paul continued on his way, and Nelidova emerged to pick up the shoe. The next day, when Sablukov was again on duty, Paul "came up to me and whispered: Mon cher, we had a little quarrel yesterday.--Yes, sire, I answered."

On a large oak tree which stood opposite the station of the officer of the guard at Gatchina, there were a number of strange growths. One of them resembled Paul to such an extent that Sablukov could not resist making a drawing of it. His fellow officers admired the sketch and asked for copies, which he obligingly supplied. This was obviously observed by someone who reported it to Paul, and one day as Sablukov sat drawing something else, Paul came in unexpectedly and asked him what he was doing. "I am drawing, Sire." "Have you ever drawn my . . . ?" "Many times, Your Majesty." Paul laughed loudly and turned to the mirror, remarking, "What a face for a portrait."

---

credible--Dmitrii A. Miliutin, *Istoriia voiny 1799 g.*, 5 vols. (St. Petersburg: Imperatorskaia Akademiia nauk, 1852-1853). These facts must occasion some reservation about the authority of Duffy's work. Still, his conclusions seem to me quite reasonable.

Then he slapped Sablukov in a friendly fashion on the shoulder and went out, laughing heartily.[11] Unfortunately, such stories of Paul are much rarer than less attractive ones.

He was as suspicious and as given to pervasive surveillance both of Russians and of foreigners as any Russian ruler has been. In this respect, he was the equal of Nicholas I and of Stalin. He forbade Russian students to go abroad to study. He believed that the police must guard the population from malevolent influences in order to achieve the happiness about which his 1788 papers had been so concerned. His ministers received almost daily orders to investigate and read the correspondence of persons near the court.

Paul's penchant for police control was ironically consonant with a similar trend late in Catherine's reign. In matters of censorship in particular, Paul followed Catherine's lead. Catherine's pretensions to enlightenment and especially to the encouragement of education and the development of an exchange of free and refined opinion had led to a remarkable degree of freedom of the press and to an unusual proliferation of journals and reading matter by the latter part of her reign. The high point in legislative encouragement of this trend was reached in the decree of 15 January 1783, which stipulated that a press could be opened in Russian or in a foreign language in any town by simply informing the local police of its establishment. The individual books published by the press then had to be approved by the police as inoffensive to religion. This decree did not alter the situation of those presses that were owned by the state, e.g., the one operated by Nikolai Novikov at Moscow University. Responsibility for censoring Novikov's press rested with the university authorities, and at the time in question, they were liberal and benign.

By the end of her reign, however, Catherine had had a distinct change of heart in the matter of publishing and censorship, one prompted in part by developments in revolutionary Europe, in part by the increasing criticism of her policies by Russian journalists, especially those inspired by the Panin circle. A new decree of 16 September 1796 aimed at putting an end to "inconveniences . . . from the free and unrestricted publication of books." It established censors' offices in St. Petersburg, Moscow, Riga, and Odessa. It closed down all private presses. It required a censor's approval prior to the publication of any book in the empire and for the importation of books from abroad as well. Periodicals were subject to similar restrictions.

---

11. Sablukov, *Zapiski*, pp. 54-55, 62-63.

This was the first officially established system of government censorship in Russian history. Yet, notwithstanding this considerable change of direction in the policy of publishing, the censor's work was carried out more capriciously than systematically or oppressively.

Paul added two further decrees on censorship to those left by Catherine, and these two closed down any pretensions of literary liberalism. The decree of 17 May 1798 established censors' offices in every port for the examination of imported materials. On 18 April 1800, Paul issued a notorious decree simply forbidding imports from abroad of "all kinds of books and music" until further notice. His policy in this area was cruder and more comprehensive than that of Catherine. (It was soon to be reversed by Alexander.)[12]

The management of information had long since become a traditional function of absolutist governments in Europe, and Paul was initially as concerned to acquire information for himself as he was to control the access of others to it. In an episode suggestive of the use to which Nicholas would later put the notorious Third Section, Paul established outside the Winter Palace, soon after his accession, a famous yellow box for receiving petitions and denunciations. For several months he collected the contents and read them daily. This was characteristic of his passion for correcting what Sablukov called "crying injustices" (*vopiuiushchiia nespravedlivosti*). Sablukov and most other contemporary reporters agree that Paul loved the truth and hated deceit and that he reacted to the discovery of lying and cheating with real severity. At length, however, caricatures and criticisms of himself began to appear in the box, and he removed it at once.

When convinced of any dereliction of duty on the part of administrative personnel, Paul was quick to punish and frequently to punish extravagantly. Sablukov gives a personal example. Upon his accession, Paul ordered the redesigning of the army's uniforms to make them more like those of the Prussian army. The dye necessary for the new uniforms, however, was complex and delicate, and not enough of it could be manufactured at once. When this news was reported to Paul by Sablukov's father, the vice-president of the College of Manufacturing, Paul ordered him relieved of his duties and exiled from the capital on the following day. The order reached him when he was quite ill with the flu. Nevertheless, it had to be carried out.

---

12. K. A. Papmehl, *Freedom of Expression in Eighteenth-Century Russia* (The Hague: Nijhoff, 1971), pp. 92-93, 121-122, 137, 139-146.

When Paul subsequently discovered the injustice he had done, he begged with tears in his eyes to be forgiven, restored Sablukov's father to his post, and inquired twice a day about his health.[13]

His social policy, especially where the common people were concerned, contained real elements of paternalist populism. "For the peasants, the reign of Paul signified the approach of a new era: the growth of serfdom was ended, a sudden change took place in the social policy of Russia, the government began to take real measures for the improvement of the mode of life of the peasants, and willy-nilly the wheels of history turned toward the great day of the liberation of the peasants from serfdom."[14] In pursuit of the ideas which he had outlined in the Nakaz of 1788, Paul issued a number of decrees to improve the status of the peasants. Most famous--or notorious--is his prohibition of more than three days of peasants' labor on the demesne land of the landlords in the Ukraine. Ironically, unknown to Paul, the bulk of the Ukrainian peasantry at that time spent only two days a week on such work. Landlords quickly moved to the three-day system. Such was the fate of his benevolence.

On his own estate at Gatchina, he had moderated the obligations of the serfs and aided them during years of bad harvests. Some of the possessional serfs (those attached to factories) were now freed from their private bondage and given the status of state peasants, a considerable improvement in their condition. Paul asked the Senate to take inventory of the landholdings of the state peasants to determine whether their holdings were adequate. He forbade the sale of peasants with land in the Ukraine; he forbade the sale of household serfs; and he forbade the breakup of serf families.

From the beginning, Paul had been regarded fondly by the peasants. The Prussian ambassador reported in 1797 that he was loved by the lower classes. Cobenzl, the Austrian ambassador, reported that during the coronation ceremonies in Moscow, Paul walked into the midst of an angry mob. The people were complaining that officials treated them badly on ceremonial occasions. Paul promptly revised the coronation plans to take their demands into account. Throughout the encounter, he seemed at ease.[15] The legend long persisted that the nobility

---

13. Sablukov, *Zapiski*, pp. 28, 42, 46-52.

14. Klochkov, *Ocherki*, p. 527.

15. McGrew, "Political Portrait," *Jahrbücher* 18:513.

killed Paul solely because of his love for the common people. Allegedly more votary candles burned on the grave of Paul than on that of any other tsar in the days of the empire.

His attitudes toward--and his relations with--the nobility were very different. Considering the nobility to be the mainstay of the throne, Paul regarded it as a class obliged by talent and privilege to serve the state dutifully. He approved the state service which Peter I had required of every Russian nobleman, and he clearly disapproved of the emancipation of the nobility from state service sanctioned in Catherine's Charter of the Russian Nobility (1785). He thought that emancipation had converted the bulk of the class into something like a parasitic order.

Paul did not restore the requirement of universal service for the nobility--perhaps he did not dare. He did determine, however, that those who were listed on the service rolls should serve. Many of them, in fact, were absent from their ostensible posts. On the second day of his reign, he issued a decree ordering all absentee officers on regimental lists to perform their duties or be stricken from the lists. Though he did not formally abrogate the Charter of the Nobility, he ignored several of its guarantees. For example, he subjected the nobility to occasional taxation (by special levies); he sometimes punished noblemen by banishing them to Siberia, by corporal punishments, and by removing their patent of nobility.

Reliable figures on Paul's notorious disposition to punish, and especially to punish the nobility, have recently come to light for the first time. The Soviet historian Natan Iakovlevich Eidel'man has cited the evidence from archival sources. According to Eidel'man, Catherine's police, the *Tainaia ekspeditsiia*, processed 862 cases in 35 years, or an average of about 25 cases per year. In Paul's reign, on the other hand, the *Tainaia ekspeditsiia* processed 721 cases in four and a half years, about seven times more cases annually than in Catherine's reign. What is at least as interesting is the fact that the proceedings against the nobility comprised 44 percent of the whole. In addition, Paul's *General-auditoriat* heard complaints of enlisted men against officers. In the course of his reign, Paul subjected 2,600 officers to disciplinary action, a scale of punishment undreamed of in Catherine's time.[16]

---

16. Natan Iakovlevich Eidel'man, *Gran' vekov: politicheskaia bor'ba v Rossii, konets XVIII-nachalo XIX stoletiia* (Moscow: Mysl', 1982), p. 106. On the scale and severity of Paul's punishments in general and a comparison of them with those of Catherine and Alexander, see ibid., pp. 90-113. I am very

Paul not only made unique demands of the Russian nobility; he also accorded it unique privileges. Only noblemen, he
decreed, should be promoted to officers' ranks in the army. He
established a State Bank for the Nobility, and for that class
alone.

The Bank was an especially revealing aspect of Paul's
approach to the nobility. Its purpose, he said, was to provide
cheap credit which the nobility might use to pay its debts and to
regenerate its financial situation. Paul was afraid that the class
would fritter away its inheritance and find itself in the grasp of
unscrupulous usurers. He wished to maintain the class and its
properties in a sound economic condition. In the opinion of
Roderick McGrew, who has studied the project at some length,
"the Bank plan epitomized Paul's brief reign and dramatized his
tragedy as a ruler. Superficially, the Bank contained praise-
worthy ideas and responded to existing problems; yet it suffered
from a confusion of goals and an inappropriateness of method
which vitiated whatever useful features it might have had.
The . . . Bank was presented as a product of the beneficence of
an all-powerful, all-seeing tsar who stood at the apex of the social hierarchy and whose responsibility was to serve the whole
society. The plan was formulated to help different parts of society recognize their mutual responsibilities while contributing to
the welfare of the whole. No group, including the nobility, could
claim a predominant interest at the expense of the whole; only
the crown had a general social provenance, and the interests of
all groups were always subordinate to the crown, which alone
acted for the whole society."[17] This judgment is entirely consonant with what Paul tells us of his own purposes in the Nakaz of
1788. The project, however, was a failure, and Paul closed the
Bank in 1799. The Russian nobility was never very provident in
economic matters, and it preferred to enjoy its privileges, in the
main, without troubling itself much about service and dedication. As a class, it found Paul's views and his measures extremely distasteful and recalled fondly the more casual attitudes
of Catherine.

In church policy, Paul was both tolerant and exacting.
He appointed Prince A. V. Khovanskii to the Ober-Procuracy of
the Holy Synod. Khovanskii introduced a rigidly bureaucratic
regime of administrative practice. He required lengthy reports

---

grateful to Natan Iakovlevich Eidel'man for the generosity with which he offered to me his manuscript before it was published.

17. Roderick E. McGrew, "The Politics of Absolutism: Paul I and the
Bank of Assistance for the Nobility," in Ragsdale, *Paul I*, p. 119.

on the transaction of church business and sent to Paul weekly summaries of the meetings of the Synod. In 1798, he forbade the provincial clergy to bring its grievances to the capital or to travel to the capital at all without special passports provided by their superiors. Violators of this order were drafted into military service. The church hierarchy chafed under Khovanskii's administration, and in 1799 Paul asked the Synod to select a new procurator. The Synod nominated three persons and especially recommended Count D. I. Khvostov, whom Paul then appointed. Khvostov left the business of church administration largely in the hands of Metropolitan Amvrosii.

Paul was, on the other hand, as supportive of the church as Catherine had been negligent. He more than doubled the state's appropriations to the church (from 462,868 rubles per annum to 982,597). He granted the parish clergy freedom from corporal punishment for crimes tried in civil courts. He took measures to protect the widows and orphans of priests. He increased financial support for ecclesiastical schools. He founded new seminaries at Vifaniia, Kolomenskoe, Tula, Kaluga, Penza, Perm, and Orenburg. And in a controversial innovation that the church historian Kartashev characterizes as theocratic, Paul began the practice of granting secular awards, orders, and ribbons to members of the clergy.[18]

He had an altogether singular approach to foreign religions in Russia. On his estate at Gatchina he had tolerated every confession of faith. When he became sovereign, though he is often regarded as a conservative on the order of Nicholas I, he did something that many more enlightened princes did not dare to do: he decreed general religious toleration. The decree explained that he considered it his "holy duty to secure freedom of confession of faith to everyone."[19] His predilection for the Knights of Malta, partly for religious reasons, is well known. The Jesuits had found a refuge in Russia when an increasingly anticlerical Europe turned against them, and Paul continued to befriend the Order. Noting Paul's favoritism for the Catholic Church, the papacy sent a special nuncio, Lorenzo Litta, to St. Petersburg, to work out a more formal and protected position for Catholics and their affairs in the Russian Empire than they had previously had. The timeliness of this move derived from the great increase in the numbers of Catholics within the empire,

---

18. A. V. Kartashev, *Ocherki po istorii russkoi tserkvi*, 2 vols. (Paris: YMCA Press, 1959), 2:551-557.

19. Klochkov, *Ocherki*, p. 125.

which had resulted from the partition of Poland as well as from Paul's friendly attitude.

Litta demanded an increase in the number of bishops, the freedom of the papacy to select and invest the bishops, and a statute regulating the legal status of clerical orders. Paul was not pleased by these demands, but he consented to negotiate. Before the negotiations were concluded, however, he resolved the issues to his own satisfaction by unilaterally decreeing a solution. He granted much of what the papacy demanded, but one of his decrees stipulated that correspondence between the pope and his bishops must be submitted to Paul. Though he gave up any claim to the selection or investiture of bishops, he forbade the appointment of foreign priests in Russia. The papacy accepted this resolution.

In his administration of internal affairs, Paul strove to achieve happiness in his empire through the introduction of order, authority, legality. He thought that the chief evil of Catherine's reign was its personal quality and the abuses of favoritism. He annotated the memoirs of the Duc de Sully thus: "The first law of the sovereign is the observance of all the laws. Above him there are two masters: God and the law."[20] According to the closest student of Paul's administration, Klochkov, "the foundation of strong power above, the aspiration to centralization and bureaucratization in administration, the effort at an equalitarian policy in social life--here are, in my opinion, the fundamental points of the governing activity of the time of Paul I."[21] A recent student of the administration of Paul emphasized somewhat different things, without disagreeing with Klochkov. According to John Keep, "Paul's policies of 'militarization' implied the conscious adoption of a foreign model. . . . Paul hoped to copy Frederick's achievement in building a *Polizeistaat* or 'regulated State' in the eighteenth-century understanding of this term: that is to say, he sought to centralize real decision-making power in the autocratic Sovereign, whose will was to be law; to demarcate clearly administrative responsibilities among officials within a hierarchical structure dedicated to the pursuit of efficiency, strict discipline and economy in the use of resources; and to harness all his subjects' energies, within the

---

20. Ibid., p. 116.

21. Ibid., p. 574.

limits technically possible at the time, to the achievement of certain state-approved tasks."[22]

Paul's reforming activity was largely confined to the years 1797 and 1798. Russia was at peace during those two years and went to war in 1799. After that date, foreign affairs dominated the government's attention. (Catherine's reign had followed the same pattern, and Alexander's was to do so as well: involvement in foreign war brought reform to a halt.)

In 1798, too, peace in Paul's family setting was destroyed again. By this time, two antagonistic factions were recognized in Paul's entourage. One of them consisted of Mariia Fedorovna, Catherine Nelidova, and Vice-Chancellor A. B. Kurakin. The other was made up of Chancellor A. A. Bezborodko, F. V. Rostopchin, Peter Pahlen, and that curious character, the former Turkish barber now become Paul's chamberlain and confidant, Ivan Kutaisov. Intrigue and counter-intrigue were soon heavy in the atmosphere. This particular intrigue was full of significant data on Paul's behavior, and its outcome was to have serious consequences for the formulation of policy during the remainder of the reign.

Mariia Fedorovna, whose homeland of Württemberg was so palpably threatened by the expansion of the French Revolution, was naturally sympathetic to the growing numbers of French émigrés in St. Petersburg, and it was perhaps inevitable that she should encourage an active Russian role in the coalitions against France. Chancellor Bezborodko, on the other hand, was opposed to the propaganda of the émigrés and to the growing number of émigré army units which were finding a benign asylum in Russia (one of them was commanded by Prince Louis-Joseph de Condé, who had been the host of Paul and Mariia Fedorovna at Chantilly during their European tour). Bezborodko and Fedor V. Rostopchin were to stand for more independence of Russian policy, for a less ideologically oriented foreign policy, for a more rational pursuit of Russian interests, a policy position which has given rise to the rubric "national party." Bezborodko enjoyed in the reign of Paul a unique status: he was immune in some mysterious fashion to the whims of Paul's irascibility, which battered and buffeted all others, a status which he perhaps owed to the alleged fact that he introduced Paul on the day of Catherine's death to the document that would have dispossessed him of the succession.

---

22. Keep, "Paul I and the Militarization of Government," in Ragsdale, *Paul I*, pp. 92-93.

Fortuitous developments in the spring and summer of 1798 provided the party of Bezborodko, Rostopchin, and Kutaisov a capital opportunity. Toward the end of 1797, Mariia Fedorovna's father died suddenly and unexpectedly. In January 1798, she gave birth to the Grand Duke Michael. Mariia Fedorovna had a history of difficult deliveries, and this one was no exception. A doctor had been summoned from Berlin especially for the occasion. Mariia Fedorovna was weakened by the delivery, and the doctor from Berlin gave his opinion that further childbirth would put her life in jeopardy. It was rumored at the time that Kutaisov had bought this opinion--Frederick the Great had said that good court intrigue should always begin with a physician. Mariia Fedorovna understood how gravely this medical advice threatened her position, and she objected vehemently, to which Paul responded that he did not want to be responsible for her death.

In these unhappy circumstances, Mariia Fedorovna was cheered briefly by the news of a visit from her mother, only to be further afflicted by the subsequent news of her mother's untimely death. In the wake of these developments, all of the court physicians agreed that she was not sufficiently robust to accompany Paul on the spring 1798 trip to Moscow, and consequently Paul was left largely in the company of the evil genius of the enemy party, Ivan Kutaisov.[23]

Moscow welcomed Paul with its usual warmth, "even with love." A crowd of 20,000 people turned out to "express devotion to him." He enjoyed it immensely, and when he commented on it, Kutaisov engaged him in the conversation that allegedly ruined the other party at court.

"How gratifying today was to my heart! The people of Moscow love me a great deal more than those of Petersburg; it seems to me that there they fear more than love me."

"That doesn't surprise me," answered Kutaisov.

"Why is that?"

"I don't dare explain."

"Then I order you to explain."

"Promise me, sire, not to tell anyone."

"I promise."

"Sire, the fact is that here they see you as you really are--good, generous, sensitive; whereas in Petersburg, if you show any favor, then they say that either the empress, or Nelidova, or the Kurakins have asked you for it, so that when you do

23. Shumigorskii, *Nelidova*, pp. 113, 120-123.

good, it is really they [that do it]; and when you punish, then it is you who punishes."

"Which means, they say that . . . I let myself be ruled."

"Exactly so, sire."

"Very well, I will show how they rule me!"

Paul then went to a table and began to write, but Kutaisov begged him to restrain himself for a time.

The following day, Paul went to a ball in Moscow. There he noticed the young and beautiful Anna Lopukhina. He sent Kutaisov to negotiate with the family, and a bargain was struck. Lopukhina was soon brought to St. Petersburg, married to Prince Gagarin, and installed in the imperial apartments to become Paul's mistress.

The source for this damning account is the memoirs of Baron Heyking,[24] an adherent of the Mariia Fedorovna/Nelidova party who could not have been present when the crucial conversation took place. It is accepted as essentially authentic, however, by the best authority on Paul's family history, E. S. Shumigorskii,[25] and much of it can be documented from a variety of other sources. A. M. Turgenev's memoirs give some of the details of the negotiations with the Lopukhin family.[26] It was well known that Paul noticed Lopukhina for the first time when he was in Moscow for the coronation in 1797. Rostopchin tells us that Bezborodko at that time flirted with the elder Princess Lopukhina "in spite of himself" and arranged to have her husband appointed a senator in a Moscow administrative department and decorated with the order of St. Andrew.[27]   Grand Prince Alexander Pavlovich's friend Adam Czartoryski has left a similar account of the events in question: "It was necessary to draw Paul away from (*arracher*) his attachment to Mlle. Nelidova and to embroil him (*brouiller*) with his wife. Therefore, it was suggested to the Emperor that he was under their tutelage (*en tutelle*), that these two women reigned in his name, that everyone was convinced of it."   And so, Czartoryski says, the

24. Baron Karl-Heinrich von Heiking, "Imperator Pavel i ego vremia," *Russkaia starina*, 1887, Vol. 56, pp. 784-786.

25. Shumigorskii, *Nelidova*, pp. 120-158.

26. A. M. Turgenev, "Zapiski," *Russkaia starina*, 1885, No. 4, pp. 81-82.

27. F. V. Rostopchin, "1812 god," *Russkaia starina*, 1889, No. 4, p. 651.

Lopukhina affair was arranged, and "the ruin (*naufrage*) of the other party was complete."[28]

On the way back to St. Petersburg, Paul wrote to Mariia Fedorovna in a facetious fashion that Lopukhina had declared her love for him and expressed her jealousy of the presumption of other women in his life. When the entourage arrived in St. Petersburg, Mariia Fedorovna interceded with Lopukhina herself by letter, but the letter was brought by intercept to Paul, and it simply aggravated the split.

Paul wrote to Nelidova an extremely interesting letter. "As you know, I submit very little to the influence of this or that person. No one knows my heart or understands my words better than you, and I thank you for giving me the occasion to talk with you candidly. . . . You can see . . . that I am not afraid to be unworthy of your friendship."[29] This letter suggests that Baron Heyking's account came from Paul himself through Nelidova.

Nelidova was exiled from court to Schloss Lode in the vicinity of Reval, and in a period of six weeks in the fall of 1798, Paul issued eighteen separate instructions having to do with the interception of the correspondence between Nelidova and Mariia Fedorovna. In January 1799, he ordered that the surveillance of the correspondence stop. In January 1800, Nelidova asked permission, on account of a malady of her eyes, to return to Smolny Institute. Paul consented.[30] It was the ruin of the Mariia Fedorovna/Nelidova party that would make possible the Russian flirtation with Bonaparte after the collapse of the Second Coalition.

The remainder of the reign was devoted chiefly to foreign affairs. It had been through imperial expansion especially that Catherine had distinguished herself. Paul proposed to proceed in foreign affairs, as in internal affairs, in a manner entirely different from Catherine's. She was notorious for war; he announced his intention of living at peace with all the world. She was regarded as the author of the demise of Poland; he received in audience the leader of the last Polish revolt, Thaddeus Kosciuszko, and said that he regretted the partitions. He had made it clear long ago, in the Razsuzhdenie of 1774 and the Nakaz of 1788, that he thought Russia powerful enough to sus-

28. Adam Czartoryski, *Mémoires*, 2 vols. (Paris: Plon, 1887), 1:177.

29. Shumigorskii, *Nelidova*, pp. 146-147.

30. Ibid., pp. 152-154.

tain her own security without entangling alliances. He reneged on Catherine's promise to participate in the coalition against the French. In fact, all his early actions signified a real dedication to peace.

Europe, however, was not peaceful. Bonaparte had recently embarked on the ascendant phase of his career. In the spring of 1797, he was in Italy humiliating the Austrians. Both sides in this war hoped to profit by the accession of a new Russian ruler. The French made overtures through the Prussians about a restoration of diplomatic relations, which had been broken upon the execution of Louis XVI in 1793. Meanwhile, the Austrians, more desperately, asked for Paul's mediation of the conflict. Paul was glad to oblige. He designated Prince Repnin to go to Vienna and Berlin and to say there that Paul would mediate under two conditions: first, that the French formally request it; and second, that the Prussians be associated with Russia as mediators. Repnin was prepared to meet in Berlin with the French ambassador, Citizen Caillard, and to discuss terms with him, but he was in no circumstances to lend himself to French plans hostile to Austria. Before Repnin's mission was under way, however, the Austrians were forced by Bonaparte's victories to sign preliminary terms of peace. The treaty of Campoformio, which followed in October 1797, established France in northern Italy and southern Germany and thus realized precisely what Paul had sought to avoid.

In the meantime, French efforts to restore relations with the Russians continued. Paul instructed his ambassador in Berlin not to seek but not to avoid meetings with his French counterpart. Conversations soon began. Kolychev, the Russian ambassador, talked of mediation while Caillard spoke only of friendly relations and commerce. Talleyrand would have nothing to do with Russo-Prussian mediation in Germany. The Directory had decided to avoid Russian meddling there. The French maintained that the Russians had political rights in Germany only in the Bavarian question (Treaty of Teschen, 1779). When Campoformio was signed, Paul ordered the negotiations in Berlin broken off. French émigré regiments were taken into Russian military service, and in November 1797 Paul established Louis XVIII with a handsome subsidy at Mittau in Courland.

In April 1798, Paul sent Prince Repnin to Berlin to work out an alliance to include Russia, Prussia, England, Austria, and perhaps Denmark, Sweden, and various states in Germany. Paul's primary goal was to protect the status quo in Germany from the ambitions of both the Habsburgs and the Hohenzollerns. The alliance was to be conventional but should contain secret articles providing protection against the harmful ideas of the French government.   Prussia, however, would not budge from neutrality, so the whole project was spoiled.

By this time, Bonaparte had sailed to Egypt.   On the way, he took Malta. Paul's response to this affront was war. He was both offended in his moral sentiments by the seizure of Malta and threatened in his national interests by the French campaign in Egypt. The Russians had been inclined to regard preying upon the Ottoman Empire as their special privilege, and they could not live comfortably with a major French military establishment there. Furthermore, Paul had been impressed since childhood with the Knights of Malta. When he acceded to the throne, he found emissaries of the Knights at the Russian court trying to regularize by negotiation the anomalous situation in which the partitions of Poland had left a Catholic order in a Russian Orthodox state. These emissaries found Paul generous with both privileges and subsidies.

The Order had been experiencing hard times.   Its Mediterranean influence was declining, it was plagued by the Barbary pirates, and the French Revolution had dispossessed it of some valuable properties. When Bonaparte captured Malta, his purpose was to establish a French naval outpost in the Mediterranean, to deny Malta to the English navy, and to seize the wealth of the Order both for the declining fortunes of the Directory and to finance his own campaign in Egypt. The conquest was made with such ease that treason was suspected and charged. The Grand Master of the Order, Ferdinand Hompesch, had not defended the island vigorously.

Some of the Knights themselves were scandalized by the conduct of Hompesch. A group of French émigré knights convoked a council of the Order in St. Petersburg. There Hompesch was deposed as grand master, and Paul was elected (9 November 1798). This was an extraordinary proceeding. There was no precedent for the deposition of a grand master. Several of the divisions of the Knights had not been able to send representatives to the council in time for the election. Most importantly, the election made a Russian Orthodox potentate the chief of a Roman Catholic order, for which reason Pius VI, despite his appreciation of Paul's generous intentions with respect to both the Church and the Order, refused to ratify his election. The advantages for the Order were clear: Paul was a passionate partisan of its cause, and a wealthy and powerful one. What was Paul's object?

The closest study of this question has been made by Roderick McGrew. "If the presence of the Russian nobility strengthened Paul's control over the order, the order also gave the tsar an instrument for indoctrinating that nobility. . . . Absolute monarchy as Paul conceived it required a devoted and loyal serving aristocracy. . . . The Knights of Malta could be a vehicle for educating the nobility to values supportive of the tsar's political vision. . . . Russia was to be [their] new homeland, a stable fortress in a world of threatening change. And behind those parapets, the Knights of Malta would provide an organizational center and an ideological form with which to shape the Russian nobility to the contours of Paul's own particular version of absolutism, and thus prepare them for the struggle in which they would have to play a leading role."[31]

So Paul allied with the Porte, Naples, England, and Austria against the French. At this point, Paul began to take a more serious interest in the threat of revolution. His correspondence, his thoughts, the notes of his ministers, all his doings were full of concern about the French Revolution and the best means of dealing with it. If the people around him were not similarly concerned, they were punished or dismissed or both. He gave careful instructions to his army commanders abroad not to allow his troops to become infected with the madness of French freedom.

There now began the glorious campaign of 1799. General Suvorov went to Vienna to take command of the Austro-Russian forces charged with liberating Italy and marching into France itself. Paul's reformed army gave a good account of itself. Militarily all went well for the coalition and badly for the French. The allies beat one French army after another. With the French chased out, Suvorov began to make moves toward the restoration of the previous sovereigns. In particular, he prepared to reestablish the King of Sardinia and the Grand Duke of Tuscany. The protection of such sovereigns from the ravages of the revolution and the restoration of their thrones was what Paul understood the Italian campaign to be about. The Austrians, it turned out, understood matters quite differently. Vienna refused to countenance the restoration in Italy. The Habsburgs also refused now to pursue the previous plan of carrying the campaign into France. Paul became convinced--and rightly--that the Austrians were more interested in annexations for themselves than they were in containing the menace of the

---

31. Roderick E. McGrew, "Paul I and the Knights of Malta," in Ragsdale, *Paul I*, pp. 61-62.

revolution.   The English ambassador in Vienna agreed with Paul's appraisal, warning his government that the whole object of the Austrians was to capture the French conquests in Italy for themselves.   Paul denounced Austrian perfidy, said that he would not sacrifice his soldiers for Austrian aggrandizement, and late in 1799 withdrew his troops from the campaign.

His alliance obligations, however, required that he offer some explanation of this extraordinary conduct to his other ally, England.   Paul wrote to George III to explain.   He had entered the conflict in the first place, Paul said, because of the French threat to the integrity of Germany and because of the solicitations of the Austrian government.   At that time, Paul said, there was no discussion of either acquisitions or indemnifications. Rather, the accord was based on the commitment to free France of revolution, to restore the monarchy there, and to put an end to the bloodshed in Europe.   Paul's only orders to Suvorov were "to restore thrones and altars."   But the conduct of Austria was unworthy of these high purposes.   When Italy was liberated, the Austrians set up governments that were effectively satellites of Vienna.   They taxed the people illegally, refused to restore the King of Sardinia, and forbade the formation of a Piedmontese army.   When Paul raised questions about these policies with Vienna, the response of the Austrian chancellor, Thugut, did not contain a word about the original purposes of the alliance, but centered on the problem of acquisitions and indemnities.   At this point, Paul ordered Suvorov to withdraw from the coalition and return his army to Russia.   "The Emperor Paul coveted nothing from anyone else, except the general well-being; honor is his only guide."   He was led unsuspectingly into the secret designs of others.   "However, withdrawing now His cooperation, the Russian Emperor does not lose sight of the general welfare, and when the time comes, He is ready to take up arms again."[32]

Paul soon broke with England as well, though the reasons why are less obvious.   An Anglo-Russian expedition against the French in the Netherlands, much smaller than in Italy, foundered in November 1799.   Paul was disappointed, but this did not cause the break.   There were in fact no substantive disagreements between Russia and England over European affairs. The best explanation of the break is probably this: England, though she understood that justice in the Austro-Russian dispute was on the side of the Russians, also recognized that in order to continue the battle against France, Austria was, for geographical reasons, more important to the alliance than Russia

32. Miliutin, *Istoriia voiny 1799 g.*, 5:312-320.

was. Thus the English continued their cooperation with the Austrians and tried to persuade the Russians to return to the coalition. This eventually irritated Paul, and he asked for the recall of the English ambassador in St. Petersburg.

Paul's attitude toward his former allies soon changed from irritation to antagonism. The Austrians and the Russians together had captured the Italian town of Ancona from the French in the fall of 1799, yet the Austrians raised only their own flag over the town. Paul demanded that the Austrian officers involved in this insult to the Russian Empire be punished and that amends be made. When amends were offered, he rejected them. Meantime, the Austrian war with the French took a disastrous turn for Austria, and Paul's menacing maneuvers on his own Austrian frontier helped to frighten Vienna into making peace with the French (Lunéville, February 1801).

The English had a similar experience with Paul. Their relations with him continued, for some time after the recall of their ambassador, to be cool but not hostile. In the summer of 1800, English abuses of neutral trade prompted Paul to take an interest in the rights of neutrals. In late summer, he invited the neutrals of northern Europe to revive the League of Armed Neutrality. They all responded positively. This represented a considerable escalation of Anglo-Russian tension, but worse was yet to come. In September, Paul learned that the French garrison on Malta had fallen to the English siege. He demanded the fulfillment of the previous agreement that the island should be garrisoned jointly by Russian, Neapolitan, and English troops. The English, persuaded now of Paul's unfriendly intent, refused, though they had assured him in positive terms during the summer that they intended a joint occupation. Paul was furious, and he now attempted to use the Neutral League as a device of revenge against England. He demanded that all the signatory powers, Sweden, Denmark, and Prussia, close their ports to English trade. They did so. England had just experienced two disastrous grain harvests. At such times, she looked to the Baltic for grain imports. Paul's embargo on trade aggravated the English situation enormously, and the high price of grain, and the rioting and social disturbances which it set off, drove the English to begin negotiations with Bonaparte.

Paul's policy with respect to Austria and England, then, had benefited Bonaparte greatly, and it has been explained by Bonaparte's flattery of Paul. In the summer of 1800, Bonaparte offered, with mock magnanimity, to return all the Russian prisoners taken by France in 1799; simultaneously he offered to give up to Paul the island of Malta, then on the verge of capitulating to the English. Paul is supposed, in madcap fashion, to have been entirely charmed by these two offers. In fact, he was embarrassed by the first, not wanting to accept gratuitous favors from Bonaparte, and entirely undeceived by the second.[33] Instead of hastening to accept Bonaparte's offers, he attempted to organize another Russo-Prussian effort to mediate between the belligerents. His specific object was to prevent either France or Austria or the two in league from arrogating to themselves the disposition of territories in Italy and Germany. Having quarreled with England and Austria and failed to get action from Prussia, Paul then turned to France and explained that he would consider an alliance with France, which was what Bonaparte sought from him, on condition of the restoration of Malta, Sardinia, Bavaria, Naples, and Württemberg. These terms were entirely consonant with what Paul had understood the coalition *against* France to be fighting for in 1799--that is, the integrity of Italy and Germany.

The French delayed a response to Paul's offer, for the terms were not to their taste. Paul stated to his intimates that he would do no further business with France until his terms were accepted. They were eventually accepted, at least ostensibly, whereupon Paul sent an emissary to France to negotiate. His instructions demanded approximately the territorial integrity of Italy and Germany. The French made difficulties, and no agreement was reached.

Throughout, in the area of foreign policy, Paul's diplomatic methods were as volatile and unstable in his political alignments and his choice of allies as he was reputed to be. However, he was as stable and consistent in his attachment to foreign policy objectives as he was willing to change allies in the pursuit of those objectives. His first aim was to sustain good order and good government in Europe by supporting the principle of autocracy, which he considered indispensable to good government and to mastering the threat of the revolution.[34] He

---

33. This interpretation and what follows is quite untraditional. It is based on my article "Was Paul Bonaparte's Fool?: The Evidence of Neglected Archives," in Ragsdale, *Paul I*, pp. 76-90, and on Ragsdale, "Russia, Prussia and Europe in the Policy of Paul I," *Jahrbücher für Geschichte Osteuropas* 31:81-118 (1983). For different views of the matter, see Old Feldbaek, "The Foreign Policy of Tsar Paul I, 1800-1801: an Interpretation," ibid. 30:16-36 (1982), and Paul Schroeder, "The Collapse of the Second Coalition," *Journal of Modern History* 59:244-290 (1987).

34. Paul did not support what Talleyrand called legitimacy. As he told Dumouriez, agent of Louis XVIII in St. Petersburg, "l'authorité réunie dans une seule personne constitue un gouvernement." Dumouriez to Ros-

instructed his emissary, S. A. Kolychev, for example, to encourage Bonaparte to make the crown of France hereditary in his family. (Kolychev did not.) For similar reasons, he supported the church (and the Knights) and the appurtenant virtues of chivalry and justice. He also strove to protect the weak against the abuses of the strong. He did not seek gains for Russia; he did not shop for quid pro quo. He was not concerned to find reciprocal advantages for Russia before involving the country in the support of defenseless governments in Italy or Germany.

Recent research has lent support to the view of Paul's diplomacy as restrained and consistent. Muriel Atkin has examined a little-known aspect of Paul's policy, his diplomacy in the Caucasus and especially his relations with Iran. As has been pointed out already, Paul immediately terminated the expedition which Catherine had sent against Persia in 1796. Simultaneously he announced his intention of following a policy of peace in that part of the world as in Europe. His chief problem was how to protect Russian vassal states in the Caucasus, especially Georgia, without the resort to force and expansion that had characterized Catherine's policy. He did so by forming a league of Muslim princes, whom he treated, in contrast to Catherine, with respect, in order to discourage Turkish and Iranian attacks. He declined to exploit the weakness and turmoil in Iran in the wake of the assassination of Shah Aqa Mohammad Khan Qajar in 1797. He befriended the next shah, Fath 'Ali, who was weak and vulnerable. Paul annexed Georgia, of course, in December 1800, but he did so, in deference to repeated demands of the Georgian monarchy, in order to avoid civil war and anarchy and the almost certain invasion of Georgia by Iran or Turkey or both. He always refused to support the expansionist aspirations of the Georgian state. "Paul was willing to support his protectorate in the claims that his officials said were legitimate, but he was equally determined to restrain Georgia from acting unfairly or antagonistically toward its Muslim neighbors. . . . Reluctance to use force was a reflection of Paul's basic approach to this part of the world, not an expedient necessitated by more pressing demands for Russian troops in other quar-

---

topchin (copy), fall 1800; Ministère des affaires étrangères, Mémoires et documents, France 1891 (Daudet, Moscou), p. 334. "Instruction secrète donnée par l'Empereur Paul Ier au conseiller privé actuel Kalitscheff," *Russkii arkhiv*, 1874, pp. 961-970.

ters. . . . He adhered to his Caucasian policy for the remainder of his reign whether or not he was at war elsewhere."[35]

Paul's policies, both foreign and domestic, eventually provoked a dangerous amount of discontent among the Russian nobility near the court. In foreign affairs, the apparent and sudden switch from the coalition cause to the side of the revolutionary French was not as well explained by Paul as it can be by historians, and it aroused grave misgivings. The conspirators who took Paul's life were conspicuously Anglophile in their sentiments. England was fighting, in this war, after all, for the conservative cause. The English ambassador Whitworth may have been involved in the conspiracy before his expulsion from the country in the spring of 1800.[36] Moreover, the break in trade relations with the English threatened the grain exports and the luxury imports on which the nobility's way of life, to a great degree, depended. The memoirists of his time and the historians of ours have repeatedly commented on the burden of his ambitious autocracy on the serving class, the Russian gentry. The organization of the state into the smoothly functioning harmony that Paul sought was not comfortable for those on whom it was imposed. In particular, he made heavy demands of duty and devotion of the nobility, and that nobility at length would endure it no more.

---

35. Muriel Atkin, "The Pragmatic Diplomacy of Paul I: Russia's Relations with Asia, 1796-1801," *Slavic Review* 38:60-74 (1979); quotes from pp. 63, 62.

36. On this point and other aspects of the conspiracy that took Paul's life, see Chapter 4.

4

THE ASSASSINATION

During the last months of Paul's life, there are considerable signs of a deterioration of his mental balance. We have first
the report of Mariia Fedorovna to Nelidova from Gatchina in the
fall of 1800: "As to the course of our life [here], it is far from
cheerful because our dear master is not at all [cheerful]; but at
least there is no violence. He carries within his soul a fund of
sadness which consumes him, his appetite suffers from it, and
he does not eat as he used to do, and a smile is rare on his lips.
I look at him often, and my heart constricts to see him in this
condition."[1] In spite of all of her travails and difficulties with
Paul, Mariia Fedorovna at this point in her life was still a
friendly observer, and there is no reason to doubt the rectitude
of her judgment in this matter.

Much more dramatic evidence of Paul's mental deterioration, however, is the story of the deeds which form the history
of St. Petersburg politics during the winter of 1800 and the
spring of 1801. Because this evidence bears with special pertinence on the subject of this study and because it is not at all a

---

1. Kaznakov, "Pavlovskaia Gatchina," p. 165.

familiar part of the history of Paul's reign, it requires a closer examination than the account of his policy in the preceding chapter.

There were in the closing months of his reign a whole series of inexplicably puzzling events that impinge in one way or another on the question of his mental condition. For example, he casually commissioned an expedition of Cossacks to drive the English out of India. Without any explanation, he dismissed the chancellor, F. V. Rostopchin, whom all of the foreign diplomats had come to regard as the oracle of Russian policy. He published in the press an invitation to the sovereigns of Europe to resolve the wars of the continent by personal combat. He summarily expelled the Danish ambassador, Nils Rosenkrantz, who was at the very heart of the Armed Neutrality. He made a major issue of extraditing from Sweden a skulking French émigré who had given him offense in some fashion. And finally, he, or someone in Russia, virtually sponsored a plague in Spain. Gogol himself did not invent more madness in St. Petersburg than was paraded there in fact in the spring of 1801.

There is in some of the accounts of Paul and his diplomacy of this period a strange story that appears to confirm his madness beyond a doubt. According to Waliszewski and others, Paul decided to resolve the problem of war and peace by challenging several of the sovereigns of Europe to a series of duels. He allegedly published such a challenge in the *Hamburgische Zeitung* of 16 January 1801, the *Sankt-Peterburgskiia vedomosti* of 19 February 1801, and the *Moskovskiia vedomosti* of 27 February 1801.[2]

In fact, the article did not appear in the *Hamburgische Zeitung* of 16 January nor at any other date thereabouts. Neither did the *Sankt-Peterburgskiia vedomosti* of 19 February or the *Moskovskiia vedomosti* of 27 February print the document in question. Rather, they printed on these dates reports of the story of the challenge that had appeared in the London *Times*. The challenge also failed to appear in the Russian edition of the Russian court gazette, but it did appear in that version of the court gazette most read by foreigners, the German edition, the

---

    2. Kazimierz Waliszewski, *Paul the First of Russia* (Philadelphia: Lippincott, 1913), p. 376.

Sankt-Peterburgische Zeitung, No. 101, 18 December 1800 os.[3]
What is the meaning of this bizarrerie?

Our most authoritative account of the episode is from the well-known German writer who undoubtedly translated and edited the document for publication in the Hamburg paper, August von Kotzebue. He has left the full story in his memoirs. On the morning of 16 December 1800 os, he was summoned to Paul's presence by Count Pahlen, military governor of St. Petersburg. To his astonishment, Paul dictated to him the text of the challenge in French and asked him to translate it into German. Within a matter of hours, Kotzebue presented his translation, and then he and Paul together worked over the text until they had agreed upon it, giving special attention to the last line. When Paul was satisfied, he instructed Kotzebue to have it published in the *Hamburgische Zeitung.* It reads as follows:

"We learn from [St.] Petersburg that the Emperor of Russia, seeing that the powers of Europe cannot agree among themselves, and wanting to put an end to the war that has desolated [the continent] for eleven years, has proposed to invite all the other Sovereigns to meet and to fight a duel, accompanied as equerries, arbiters, and heralds by their most enlightened ministers and most able generals, such as Messieurs Thugut, Pitt, [and] Bernstorff, himself proposing to be accompanied by Generals Pahlen and Kutuzov. We do not know if the story ought to be credited; in any event, it does not appear to be unfounded, as it bears the mark of what he has often been accused of (*toute fois la Chose ne paroit pas destituée de fondement, en portant l'empréinte [sic] de ce dont il a souvent été taxé*)."[4]

Perhaps the acceptance of such a strange story ought to require the testimony of more than one witness. We do not have

---

3. August von Kotzebue, *Das merkwüdigste Jahr meines Lebens,* 2 vols. (Berlin: Sander, 1801), 2:157-166. The Library of Congress Rare Book Room has a substantial file of the *Sankt-Peterburgskiia vedomosti* for this period. The *Moskovskiia vedomosti* and the *Sankt-Peterburgische Zeitung* are available in the Lenin Library on microfilm. The Hamburg paper, whose real title is *Kaiserlich-priviligierte Hamburgische neue Zeitung,* is a very rare and elusive item, but a complete file of it can be found in the Deutsche Presseforschung in the Bremen Universität Library. There is no information in the Hamburg Staatsarchiv on the reasons for the failure of the article to appear there or on any other aspect of this episode, as the fire of 1842 destroyed all the correspondence with St. Petersburg from 1787 to 1817.

4. Kotzebue, *Das merkwürdigste Jahr meines Lebens,* 2:162. Kotzebue also gives his own German translation, p. 163. There are insignificant variations in punctuation and wording between the German text in his memoirs and that which appeared in the *Sankt-Peterburgische Zeitung.*

Paul's account or Pahlen's, and, according to Kotzebue, only the three of them were present. Still, we do have partial confirmation of the story of Kotzebue in a diplomatic report of the Danish ambassador, Nils Rosenkrantz. He does not tell us how he knew what he reported, but what he tells us is compatible with and simultaneous with Kotzebue's version.

There was, Rosenkrantz said, a "*rédaction primitive*," which Paul was not satisfied with. "Not being pleased with the version of his *Secretaire de Cabinet* for German affairs, [Paul] charged Count Pahlen to have one done by the famous Kotzebue." Pahlen brought Kotzebue in a coach to the emperor. Together they made some slight alterations in the text, and Paul was so pleased with the work of Kotzebue, "whom he had sent this spring to Siberia," that he presented him with a "beautiful and rich snuff-box."[5]

This account makes Kotzebue's more credible. But what did Paul have in mind? Rosenkrantz speaks to just this point. "This article is absolutely the consequence of the ill humor of his emissaries and spies, especially in Vienna, where M. D'Entraigues [a French royalist agent in Russian service] records for him the smallest details and the greatest secrets. These people do not hesitate to report to him that they are saying of him that he is a fool."[6] Count Rostopchin had already explained to the Neapolitan diplomats, who were trying to persuade Paul to undertake some démarche in Vienna, that it was extremely hard to speak to him at all of Vienna, because he was so irritated at reports of rumors there that he was crazy. "It seems that the antipathy with which he is animated against the diplomatic

---

5. Rosenkrantz to Bernstorff, 13 January 1801; Copenhagen Rigsarkivet, Dpt. f. u. A. Rusland II, Depecher.

6. D'Antraigues had been in Russian pay for some time. When Austro-Russian relations were broken in the spring of 1800, Rostopchin ordered him to remain in Vienna and to compile a history of the recent relations of the two powers, a volume that was to be published in London but never was. In the spring of 1801, d'Antraigues was reproached by St. Petersburg for including the letters of Marie Caroline of Naples and the Archduke Palatine in his dispatches. Evidently these letters were full of complaints that Paul's desertion of the coalition left Naples at the mercy of French and Austrian imperialism. He was dismissed, 12 March 1801, from Russian service. Léonce Pingaud, *Un agent secret sous la Révolution et l'Empire: le Comte d'Antraigues* (Paris: Plon, 1894), pp. 199-200. Some of his very voluminous correspondence is preserved in the Archives du Ministère des Affaires étrangères at the Quai d'Orsay, but most of that is done in *encre sympathique*. What is legible does not throw any light on the circumstances of his dismissal from Russian service.

corps which resides at his court comes chiefly from the fact that he supposes that the Ministers take a special interest in his person, in his precipitate decisions, and in the interior of his court." He had excluded the diplomats from several recent balls given by distinguished Russian families, and thereby he effectively closed all the doors of Russian society to them. "There are only a few relatives of my wife [a Viazemskaia princess] who dare to receive me; and the Minister of Prussia no longer knows where to find a single house open to him, except that of the Minister of Naples, from which, finally, the Russians themselves have disappeared."[7]

In the strange sense of this explanation, then, Paul's challenge to the sovereigns of Europe may be understood as a joke, as a piece of macabre irony, though one that would have appeared less macabre and more funny had it been understood to be a joke. In the circumstances, it was taken literally, not facetiously, and it made a most unfortunate impression. The English were amused. The French were positively distressed. As for the disloyal opposition at the Russian court, the malcontents among the Russian nobility, how could they, in their fondest dreams, have devised a better excuse than this one for the deed which they were about to do? Or did they devise it? Perhaps we shall see.

In any event, this was the merest beginning of the spectacle. The Danish ambassador, Rosenkrantz, was naturally puzzled to see the name of his own Chancellor Bernstorff alongside those of Pitt and Thugut in the strange challenge in the *Sankt-Peterburgische Zeitung*. Wishing to find out the reason for the appearance of Bernstorff's name, he tried to arrange an interview with Rostopchin. He was unable to do so for several days, apparently, but was scheduled to see him mid-morning on 1 January. He had scarcely gotten out of bed that morning when he was visited by Count Pahlen. Pahlen said that he was distressed by the duty with which he was charged. He explained that when the morning drill was over, the emperor had called him aside and instructed him to order Rosenkrantz to depart for home immediately.

Rosenkrantz nevertheless kept his appointment that morning with Rostopchin, and he now brought to it more questions. First, he wanted to know the reason for his expulsion. Astonishingly, he found the chancellor entirely ignorant of it and therefore disconcerted and embarrassed. Rosenkrantz asked

---

7. Rosenkrantz to Bernstorff, 13 January 1801; Copenhagen Rigsarkivet, Dpt. f. u. A. Rusland II, Depecher.

the reason for including Bernstorff's name in the challenge to a duel. Rostopchin said that he could give no explanation. Rosenkrantz asked if Paul had a personal grievance against him. Rostopchin said "that he had nothing to say to me on this subject." Rosenkrantz asked if he should leave a *chargé d'affaires* at the head of the Danish mission. Rostopchin said that the whole mission must leave. Rosenkrantz asked if this action represented a rupture of good harmony between the two states. Rostopchin said that the Russian minister in Copenhagen, M. Lizakevich, might remain at his post. Rosenkrantz persisted and asked stubbornly several times what had provoked such an order from Paul, and from the stubborn lack of an answer, he got the distinct impression that Rostopchin had been forbidden to discuss the point. Rosenkrantz had to content himself with the request that Lizakevich be given an explanation in Copenhagen. Finally, he said, "Imagine . . . how much they will rejoice on account of this in England. . . ." Rostopchin shrugged his shoulders and said that he understood perfectly well the merit of the remark.[8]

All observers began searching for an explanation of the inexplicable. The Swedish ambassador, Baron Stedingk, reported rumors that a *valet de chambre* had sold Rosenkrantz's cyphers to the Russians, but there was only lively speculation about what caused his ouster.[9] The Danes were left in much confusion. Rostopchin reassured them. He related to Dannewold, a newly arrived Danish diplomat who had come on a special mission, that Paul's sentiments in the matter of expulsion were purely personal, that they had entirely to do with Rosenkrantz and nothing to do with the court of Denmark.[10]

In the meantime, the Russian envoy in Copenhagen, Lizakevich, had received what he said was a stupidly written instruction to withdraw from the capital without an explanation of the reason.[11] He soon returned, however, and assured Bernstorff that there was no cause for concern about relations between the two courts.[12] Rosenkrantz learned in Berlin, on his

---

8. Same to same; ibid.

9. Stedingk to court, 20 and 22 January 1801; Stockholm Riksarkivet, Ur Muscovitica 465.

10. Rostopchin to Dannewold, 24 January 1801 os; Copenhagen Rigsarkivet, Dpt. f. u. A. Rusland II, Depecher.

11. *Arkhiv kniazia Vorontsova*, 20:428.

12. Bernstorff to Bourke, 7 February 1801; Copenhagen Rigsarkivet, Gesandtskabarkiver Sverig I, Ordrer.

way home, that the Russian ambassador to Prussia, Baron Kriudener, had received a confidential letter from Rostopchin in
which the latter expressed his esteem for Rosenkrantz and said
that he regretted the incident.[13]

Several months later, there was a move to engage in a
very guarded explanation with the Danes. On 5 March, Pahlen
paid a visit to Rosenkrantz's successor, M. Dannewold. He said
that Paul wanted Dannewold to remain as Danish minister
plenipotentiary, that it had not been his intention in expelling
Rosenkrantz to damage relations between the two courts. He
explained that "the Emperor believed himself obliged to expel M.
de Rosenkrantz because of the excessively vehement truculence
of his opinions and because of unbecoming ironies that had occurred in his intimate society, and especially in the midst of his
family . . . that His Majesty had decided to expel M. de
Rosenkrantz for fear that his style of perception and the accounts that he gave to the court of Copenhagen would damage
the good harmony that he more and more desired to see established between the two courts."[14]

What Pahlen told Dannewold is eminently plausible, and
it suggests a further explanation for Rosenkrantz's problems.
His connections in Russian society were better than those of his
diplomatic colleagues, it seems, probably because he had married into the distinguished Viazemskii family. In any case, the
quantity and quality of the information which Rosenkrantz reported to his court was, as we have seen (and will see again), really extraordinary. To give but one example, an example especially pertinent to the affair of the challenge and that of his expulsion, he reported that the "*rédaction primitive*" of the sum-
mons to a duel had contained the names of Moreau and Bonaparte. He is our only source for that allegation, and, as he was
not present at the drafting of the document, it is a matter of
pure speculation how he got it. On the other hand, even he was
surprised to see the name of Bernstorff in it. In any event, he
discovered by the end of December what his Swedish colleague
Stedingk had already reported, that the Russians were in possession of his cypher and were perhaps reading what he was
saying about them. Still, he claimed that he had allowed for
"perlustration" and had been accordingly prudent in his corre-

---

13. Rosenkrantz to Bernstorff, 10 February 1801; Copenhagen
Rigsarkivet, Dpt. f. u. A. Rusland II, Depecher.

14. Dannewold to Bernstorff, 10 March 1801; ibid.

spondence.[15]   The historian reading that correspondence must disagree. In view of Rosenkrantz's own report that Paul was increasingly sensitive to opinions about himself in the diplomatic corps, and in view of the numerous examples of perlustration which preceded his own, Rosenkrantz was not nearly so prudent as the situation required.

The next puzzling development was the Indian expedition. On 24 January 1801, Paul sent his famous order to the Cossack General Orlov. "The English are preparing a land and sea attack on us and our allies--the Swedes and the Danes. I am ready for them, but at the same time it is necessary to attack them where it would be most felt and least expected. . . . I order you and your forces, Vasilii Petrovich, to undertake this expedition [to India]. Gather your forces and set out for Orenburg . . . , then straight through Bokhara and Khiva to the Indus River onto the unsuspecting English. . . . All the wealth of India will be ours. . . . I am getting all the maps that we have. God be with you."[16] This somewhat madcap adventure did not reach India. It was recalled by Alexander on the day after Paul died. Orlov received Alexander's order in the village of Mechetnyi near Orenburg.[17]

What is more intriguing, because of the variety of machinations proceeding in the St. Petersburg underground at the time, is the question of a joint Franco-Russian expedition to India. There have been legions of gossamer suggestions of it. So far as I know, there are, in order of their importance, only three pieces of evidence of it worth consideration. There is Bonaparte's claim, in his memoirs, that he and Paul had concerted just such an expedition based on a plan allegedly provided by himself. He gave suspiciously grandiose details.[18] Somewhat more substantive is the plan of a joint expedition carried by General Duroc, Bonaparte's aide-de-camp, to St. Petersburg late in March 1801. Duroc left Paris before the news of Paul's death

---

15. Rosenkrantz to Bernstorff, 13 and 30 December 1800; ibid.

16. *Russkaia starina*, 1873, No. 8, p. 409.

17. Alexander to Orlov, 24 March 1801; *Vneshniaia politika Rossii XIX i nachala XX veka: dokumenty Rossiiskogo ministerstva inostrannykh del*, Series I: *1801-1815*, A. L. Narochnitskii et al., eds., 8 vols (Moscow: Gospolitizdat, 1960-1972), 1:No. 1.

18. *Correspondance de Napoléon I*, J. P. B. Vaillant et al., eds. 32 vols. (Paris: Plon & Dumaine, 1858-1870), 30:323-324.

arrived there.[19] Most importantly, we have indubitable evidence that Bonaparte was thinking about such a plan, as he discussed it with the Danish ambassador, Dreyer. According to Dreyer, Bonaparte said "that the Emperor of Russia could not attack England more effectively and with more advantage than by sending from the Caucasus an army of 100,000 men across Persia in order to fall on the English in the Indies. . . . It is certain that the execution of this project has very seductive charms for the Court of Petersburg, and like a good Dane who prefers to see the Russians turn their gaze onto the Orient rather than the Occident, I strongly urged Bonaparte to advise Paul I [to undertake] the expedition against the English in the Indies."[20] Eight days later, too soon for the content of this conversation to have reached St. Petersburg, Paul did so.

It is not at all unlikely that there were communications between Paris and St. Petersburg on this subject--as on a variety of others--of which we know nothing. We know that Dreyer in Paris had been in touch with Rosenkrantz in St. Petersburg (see below), though at the time of Dreyer's conversation with Bonaparte about India, Rosenkrantz was no longer there. Both Dreyer and Rosenkrantz were encouraging the Russians to attack the English. We do not know the subject of their direct communications. The French foreign office files of the time contain a number of projects of Franco-Russian expeditions to India.[21] The most pretentious examination of the subject, a Russian General Staff study of 1886, alleges an enormous volume of such communications between the two capitals. It offers more information than is found anywhere else, including detailed exchanges between Paul and Bonaparte as they coordinated plans for the venture. But this account nowhere cites evidence of documents. It may be that the dark recesses of the archives contain the information that it presents, but there is no compelling reason to accept it without a full presentation of evidence.[22]

---

19. Curt Bogislaus Ludvig Kristoffer von Stedingk, *Mémoires posthumes*, 3 vols. (Paris: Bertrand, 1844-1847), 2:6-7. *Russkaia starina*, 1876, No. 15, p. 216.

20. Dreyer to Bernstorff, 16 January 1801; Copenhagen Rigsarkivet, Dpt. f. u. A. Frankrig II, Depecher.

21. Ragsdale, *Détente in the Napoleonic Era*, pp. 24-25.

22. Aleksandr A. Batorskii, "Proekt ekspeditsii v Indiiu, predlozhennykh Napoleonom Bonaparte imperatoram Pavlu i Aleksandru v 1800 i 1807-1808 gg.," in *Sbornik geograficheskikh, topograficheskikh i statisticheskikh*

The eminent Soviet historian S. B. Okun' undertook to explain the relationship between the unilateral and the joint expeditions. "While working out the project of a joint invasion of India, it was well understood in Petersburg that if the problem of a joint struggle with England had united Russia and France, then in case of a successful issue from this enterprise, India might become the apple of discord between Paul and Napoleon." Thus there evolved a corollary plan to the joint expedition, one intended to insure to Russia a "dominant position" both in the course of the expedition and in the results of it. "This independent project not only did not exclude, but rather was motivated by, the joint project of an Indian campaign." Okun' says that the historians who ridicule the campaign are wrong, that Paul was very serious about it, and that it caused great alarm in London.[23] Unfortunately, Okun' cites no more evidence than did the Russian General Staff study.

In summary, it is clear that they were thinking about the Indian expedition in both Paris and St. Petersburg and that the Danish ambassadors in both capitals were in contact with each

---

materialov po Azii, 85 vols.   (Moscow: Voennaia tipografiia, 1883-1914), 23:passim, esp. 37-48.

23. S. B. Okun', *Istoriia SSSR: konets XVIII-nachalo XIX veka* (Leningrad: Izdatel'stvo Leningradskogo universiteta, 1974), pp. 86-88. It is true that English diplomatic agents in Naples, Vienna, and Hamburg reported various Russian and French plans on India to London.   Paget (Palermo) to Hawkesbury, 3 March 1801; Sir Arthur Paget, *The Paget Papers: Diplomatic and Other Correspondence*, A. B. Paget, ed.   2 vols. (London: Heinemann, 1896), 1:323.   Minto (Vienna) to Hawkesbury, 15 April 1801; Gilbert Elliott, first earl Minto, *Life and Letters*, E. E. Elliott, ed.   3 vols. (London: Longmans, 1874), 3:214.   Crawford (Hamburg) to Hawkesbury, 4 April 1801: PRO, FO 33, No. 21.   Still, to say that it caused "great alarm" is an exaggeration.   One little-known study of the campaign debunks and ridicules the whole thing.   P. Iudin wrote that he was familiar with the territory over which the expedition allegedly passed, that the area would not sustain the numbers of troops supposed to have been involved, that the timetable alleged in the story of the expedition was not feasible, and that there were no records of the expedition in the Orenburg archives.   P. Iudin, "Na Indiiu," *Russkaia starina*, Dec. 1894, pp. 231-241.   He argues simply that no such expedition ever took place.   He does not explain the documents in which Paul ordered it to go and Alexander ordered it to return.   What may be the earliest and most obscure study of the expedition presents details nearly identical with those of the General Staff study of Batorskii and draws them straight from the Orenburg archives.   A. Filonov, "Orenburgskii pokhod," *Donskie voiskovye vedomosti*, Nos. 1-2 (7 and 14 January os) 1859.   I am indebted to Sergei Ignashev for supplying this source.   Is it possible that Batorskii removed the documents from the Orenburg archive after Filonov saw them and before Iudin worked there?   The study that he published was marked "Secret."

other and were urging Russian action against the English. Rostopchin himself may have been involved in this planning, and it may have played a role in his downfall.

Both the affair of the challenge to the sovereigns of Europe and that of the expulsion of Rosenkrantz show Chancellor F. V. Rostopchin to have been left quite on the sidelines of the policy-making process. On 20 February 1801 os, the *Sankt-Peterburgskiia vedomosti* announced that Rostopchin was being relieved of all of his offices in the government. He was replaced by Count Peter Pahlen at the Colleges of Foreign Affairs and the Post.[24] Rostopchin had already withdrawn from active business in the government several days earlier. For example, Swedish ambassador Stedingk reported on 16 February os that he had not seen Rostopchin for a week.[25] Prussian ambassador Lusi reported the same day that it was impossible to get an appointment with Rostopchin.[26]

The only explanation that we have of Rostopchin's dismissal from office is his own. *Russkii arkhiv* published in 1876 the Russian translation of the French text of a letter of 17 February 1801 os in which Rostopchin explained to an "unknown person" the causes of his fall. The letter was actually written to Victor Pavlovich Kochubei in Dresden, as we know from the fact that Kochubei quoted from Rostopchin's letter in his own letter of 28 March 1801 to S. R. Vorontsov in London. Rostopchin explained that he had decided to ask for his retirement because he could no longer sustain the struggle with the intrigue and slander carried on against him. He cited in particular the return to the capital of his old enemy, Count Nikita Petrovich Panin, the nephew of Paul's old mentor and son of General Peter Panin, whom Rostopchin called "a veritable demon of intrigue and worthy son of Machiavelli." Panin had, according to Rostopchin, formed a great association of intriguers, including the Kurakins, and, "at the head of everything," Pahlen.[27]

---

24. N. K. Schilder, *Imperator Aleksandr I: ego zhizn' i tsarstvovanie*, 4 vols. (St. Petersburg: Suvorin, 1897-1898), 1:254 (note 378), 408.

25. Stedingk to court, 16/27 February 1801; Stockholm Riksarkivet, Ur Muscovitica 465.

26. Lusi to court, 16/27 February 1801; Deutsches Zentralarchiv, Historische Abteilung 2, Merseburg (DDR), Ministerium für auswärtige Angelegenheiten, AA I, Rep. 4, No. 487.

27. *Russkii arkhiv*, 1876, No. 2, p. 422. *Arkhiv kniazia Vorontsova*, 14:146-148.

Rostopchin's explanation is not satisfactory. There are several other possible explanations, and they all depend on the development of one important story in his background. In fact, his fall may have been precipitated in part by the discovery of his own intrigues. Rostopchin had been for some time the object of a French cabal at the Russian court. The French agent in Hamburg and Copenhagen, Citizen Bourgoing, had done his intelligence reconnaissance conscientiously and reported to Paris an imaginative plan for acquiring influence at the Russian court. Count Nikita Petrovich Panin, to whom most of Talleyrand's unction and overtures had been addressed in the summer of 1800, was reported by Bourgoing, correctly, to be Anglophile and Francophobe and hence quite beyond the reach of French influence. Rostopchin, he suggested, was a much more likely prospect. Bourgoing found a French émigré named Bellegarde, a man formerly in Russian service and then on his way back to St. Petersburg, who told interesting stories about the distribution of influence at the Russian court. Bellegarde said that Paul was very sensitive to the persuasion of Count Kutaisov, who was the lover of a French actress, Mme. Chevalier. Bourgoing reported to Talleyrand that he proposed to contact Rostopchin through Bellegarde-Chevalier-Kutaisov.[28]

Naturally, such plans do not leave a clear account of their implementation, but we have a rather surprising record of what followed nevertheless. There are two important points in particular. Rostopchin himself not only associated openly with the Kutaisov-Chevalier party at the Russian court, but admitted his association candidly in his correspondence. Moreover, it was precisely in the aftermath of Bellegarde's mission that Rostopchin produced a well-known policy paper in which he recommended a Russian alliance with France based on a partition of the Ottoman Empire.[29]

Now we may suggest what might have happened to the political stock of Rostopchin. One of the curious items on the agenda of Baltic politics in the winter of 1800-1801 was a minor issue of extradition between the Swedes and the Russians. It involved a mysterious personality of whom nothing is known but

28. Bourgoing to Talleyrand, correspondence of May, June, July 1800; Archives du Ministère des Affaires étrangères, Correspondance politique, Hambourg 115, Nos. 9, 31, 50, 56, 66, 78. See also Ragsdale, *Détente in the Napoleonic Era*, pp. 33-35.

29. Rostopchin to S. R. Vorontsov, 8 April 1801; *Arkhiv kniazia Vorontsova*, 8:276. *Russkii arkhiv*, 1878, No. 1, pp. 103-110. Ragsdale, *Détente in the Napoleonic Era*, pp. 35-40.

his surname--not his other names, not his origins. His surname was Bellegarde. It is not clear whether he was the same Bellegarde as the one through whom Bourgoing and Talleyrand sought to contact Kutaisov, Chevalier, and Rostopchin. Bourgoing was very sensitive to the case, however, as he reported to Talleyrand that among a variety of Swedes who had been purchasing grain in Russia, one of them, "named Bellegarde, has excited the animosity of the Russian government and escaped its severity by taking refuge in Sweden."[30]

About the time that he drafted his policy paper on the French alliance, Rostopchin himself took up the question of Bellegarde with the Swedish government--obviously at Paul's initiative. He explained that Paul had information that a Frenchman named Bellegarde was in Swedish Finland, that he had requested entry into Russia, and that he was a suspicious person. The Russians asked the Swedes to seize his papers and to determine the nature of his business. The Swedish ambassador explained to his court that Bellegarde was formerly in the Russian army, that he had recently written a diatribe against Paul, and that the Russians wanted to investigate him.[31]

The Swedish government detained the man and seized his papers, and he was duly delivered to the Russian authorities at the border. As Ambassador Stedingk reported to court, "I had a conference with Monsieur le Comte de Rostopsin last Saturday in which I communicated to him the orders given by Your Majesty to surrender the said Bellegarde." Rostopchin expressed Paul's gratitude for this assistance.[32] This is the last official communication that is preserved on the subject, but there is one additional comment from the redoubtable Rosenkrantz. "M. de Bellegarde, formerly in the service of Russia, who had withdrawn into Swedish Finland, has been handed over at the Russian frontier. The king requested mercy for him, and the ambassador has been promised that no harm would come to him. But he will undoubtedly be more guarded in manner and not cause the Emperor any more trouble."[33] If this Bel-

---

30. Bourgoing to Talleyrand, 11 frimaire an 9 (2 December 1800); Affaires étrangères, Correspondance politique, Danemarc 176, No. 144.

31. Copy of Rostopchin to Stedingk, 17 October 1800, and Stedingk to court, 19 October 1800; Stockholm Riksarkivet, Ur Muscovitica 464.

32. Copy of Rostopchin to Stedingk, 21 November 1800, and Stedingk to court, 21 November 1800; ibid.

33. Rosenkrantz to Bernstorff, 17 December 1800; Copenhagen Rigsarkivet, Dpt. f. u. A. Rusland II, Depecher.

legarde was Bourgoing's Bellegarde, it is possible that the Russians found the means to make him disclose something damaging to Rostopchin's reputation.

Rostopchin had other connections--assets and liabilities--that might have made him vulnerable. We have seen that the Danish ambassadors both in Paris and in St. Petersburg were urging Franco-Russian cooperation against England. Since September 1800, Rosenkrantz was in regular correspondence with his colleague Dreyer in Paris. The Danish archives evidently do not contain any of this correspondence, as it was unofficial. But Rostopchin was informed of it. As Rosenkrantz reported, "I have already spoken to M. de Rostopchin, who approved my idea of corresponding with my colleague [Dreyer]."34 So the two Danish ambassadors trying to encourage a Franco-Russian alliance were joined somehow by the Russian minister who was in league with the French party at the Russian court. The Danish diplomatic correspondence in these circumstances provided at least a potential clandestine channel of communications between Rostopchin and the French government. If such contacts had been discovered, it would explain much about the fates of Rosenkrantz and Rostopchin.

One of the more arcane interlopers in the Rostopchin circle was a Frenchwoman named Bonneuil. Panin took note of her relationship with Rostopchin as early as July 1800: "Until now the presence of Mme. de Bonneuil has not contributed anything to further our investigation to discover the agents of propaganda. M. le comte de Rostopchin, who has conferred with her alone, seemed enchanted after the first two interviews." But Rostopchin subsequently lost interest in her. It appears from the intercepted letters of Queen Marie Caroline of Naples that she came to play a role about Paul like that which she had formerly played about the chief minister Godoy in Spain, where she was allegedly an agent of the French government.35 Rostopchin's biographer, La Fuye, places Mme. de Bonneuil in the entourage of Bellegarde and Bourgoing and links her with Mme. de Chevalier. Bonneuil "seems to have gained, no one knows how, some influence with the Minister [Rostopchin]." She boasted of a "tender friendship" with him and pretended that

---

34. Same to same, 23 September 1800; ibid.

35. E. D. Verbitskii, *Russko-frantsuzskie otnosheniia v 1800-1803 gg.*, Kandidatskaia dissertatsiia, Kherson Pedagogical Institute, 1950, p. 43. *Materialy dlia zhizneopisaniia grafa N. P. Panina*, Alexander Brückner, ed., 7 vols. (St. Petersburg: Imperatorskaia Akademiia nauk, 1888-1892), 5:574-575.

she had used him in favor of Bonaparte.[36]   According to the historian of the French emigration, Mme. de Bonneuil arrived in Berlin from St. Petersburg in June 1801, alleging that she had known Rostopchin and that she had given him a letter from the entourage of Louis XVIII which contained aspersions on the character of Paul.   Rostopchin had to obtain Louis's cypher to read the letter, and having done so, he was able to read much more, most of which he did not like.   This was the series of events which led to the expulsion of Louis from Mittau.[37]

Not all of these rather wispy allegations are compatible. Bonneuil, if she came from Bonaparte, may have contributed to the undoing of Louis XVIII, or she may have contributed unwittingly to the undoing of Rostopchin.

Of course, Rosenkrantz, too, gave an account of this elusive Frenchwoman, whose political affiliations everyone found so confusing.   "She is understood to have been the mistress of the Prince of the Peace [Godoy]. That she mixes in political intrigues is not open to doubt. But no one knows [on whose side]. Le Comte de Caraman [Louis XVIII's representative in St. Petersburg], whom Count Rostopchin encouraged to talk to her, was never able to understand clearly just what is this woman, who is taken for a royalist *par excellence*. . . . More than one person believes that this woman has contributed to accustom the Emperor to the idea of an understanding with the French Government."[38]   Strange as it may seem, by the time of this dispatch, Rosenkrantz knew that the Russians were reading his correspondence, and the information in the dispatch, had it fallen into the right hands, could have damaged his presumed ally Chancellor Rostopchin.

We have seen by now a number of examples of the vulnerability of allegedly secret diplomatic dispatches from St. Petersburg.   It was one of the traditional risks to which a diplomat's business was exposed in that age--and, of course, not only in St. Petersburg.   It seems, however, that the Russian government mounted in the winter of 1800-1801 a special effort to gather and to read an unusual quantity of diplomatic correspondence.   Baron Kriudener in Berlin was ordered to buy the

---

36. Maurice de la Fuye, *Rostoptchine: européen ou slave?* (Paris: Plon, 1937), pp. 83-84, 89.

37. Ernest Daudet, *Histoire de l'émigration pendant la Révolution française*, 3 vols. (Paris: Hachette, 1904-1907), 3:199-210.

38. Rosenkrantz to Bernstorff, 30 December 1800; Copenhagen Rigsarkivet, Dpt. f. u. A. Rusland II, Depecher.

papers of the French ambassador, Beurnonville.[39]   Rostopchin obtained both the Sardinian and the Saxon cyphers.[40]   The cyphers of the English ambassador, Whitworth, had been cracked in early spring 1800.   In December 1800, the Prussian ambassador discovered that the Russians had his cypher and were reading his reports.[41]   They had bought it from one of the domestics in the ambassador's home.[42]   The Swedish ambassador, Stedingk, developed doubts about the security of his own codes, and he soon confirmed them.[43]

But if breaking the codes provided the Russian government with the means of reading such diplomatic correspondence as came into its possession, how did it gain possession of large quantities of it?   The answer, though it requires a certain Siberian style of cerebration to grasp it, is through the plague in Spain.   What was the plague in Spain?

There was news of an epidemic in Spain in the diplomatic dispatches of the Baltic as early as October 1800.   Bernstorff informed his ambassadors and said that the Danes were taking ordinary precautions.   The disease was said to be prevalent along the western and southern coasts of Spain and to be especially conspicuous in Cádiz.[44]   Somewhat later, the *Sankt-Peterburgskiia vedomosti* reported the news that over 40,000 persons were said to be ill in Barcelona.[45]

The curious thing about this epidemic is that it received so much more attention, it caused so much more stir, in the Baltic, in the remoteness of northern and eastern Europe, than it did in countries contiguous to Spain.   It does not fill the columns of the London *Times* or the Paris *Moniteur*.   It does not figure in the correspondence of the diplomats there.   It receives

---

39. Paul to Rostopchin, 7 August 1800 os; *Russkii arkhiv*, 1912, No. 3, p. 270.

40. Ibid., p. 271.

41. Lusi to court, 12 December 1800; Deutsches Zentralarchiv, Historische Abteilung 2, Merseburg (DDR), Ministerium für auswärtige Angelegenheiten, AA I, Rep. 4, No. 487.

42. Stedingk to court, 22 January 1801; Stockholm Riksarkivet, Ur Muscovitica, 465.

43. Ibid.

44. Bernstorff to Oxenstierna, 6 October 1800; Stockholm Riksarkivet, Ur Danica 357.   Bernstorff to Dreyer, 7 October 1800; Copenhagen Rigsarkivet, Gesandtskabarkiver, Frankrig I, Ordrer.   Bernstorff to Bourke, 8 November 1800; ibid., Sverig I, Ordrer.

45. 30 November 1800 and 18 November 1800 os.

so little attention in western Europe that one wonders if the reports in eastern Europe are mistaken. But a check of the proper sources indicates that they are not. For example, the *Gazeta de Madrid* of 28 October 1800 reported the presence of plague in Cádiz,[46] and the English fleet was forced to avoid Cádiz about the same time in deference to it.[47] So the plague was there, but it caused little commotion in the western European countries that were most exposed to it.

On the Russian frontier, on the other hand, extraordinary precautions were taken. Rosenkrantz reported late in December that the last dispatches from Copenhagen were held up at the frontier by precautions taken against the "*maladie contagieuse*" that had broken out in Spain.[48] Lusi reported that the Russians had for some time been opening all letters from abroad and that they had just quarantined a courier at the border.[49] Rosenkrantz later observed that the Russians were fumigating correspondence at the frontier.[50] Rostopchin explained to Kriudener, 1 February 1801, that the precautions taken in Russia were motivated by the epidemic of yellow fever in Spain. This was to explain the lethargic flow of correspondence between the two capitals.[51] By the middle of January, letters, couriers, and ordinary travelers were being detained on the frontier to prevent the spread of the Spanish contagion. The letters were "*piquées et parfumées.*"[52] Still, no one reported a single case of this mysterious sickness inside the Russian Empire.

---

46. Supplément, p. 1011. I am indebted to Juliette L. Sobon, Hispanic Society of America, for this and the following reference.

47. *Enciclopedia universal ilustrada Europea-Americana*, 70 vols. (Barcelona: Espasa-Calpe, 1930), 10:334: "En 1800 presentóse nuevamente la escuadra inglesa delante de Cádiz, pero en vista de la epidemia que en aquel entonces asolaba a la ciudad, la respetó."

48. Rosenkrantz to Bernstorff, 30 December 1800; Copenhagen Rigsarkivet, Dpt. f. u. A. Rusland II, Depecher.

49. Lusi to court, 30 December 1800; Deutsches Zentralarchiv, Historische Abteilung 2, Merseburg (DDR), Ministerium für auswärtige Angelegenheiten, AA I, Rep. 4, No. 487.

50. Rosenkrantz to Bernstorff, 13 January 1801; Copenhagen Rigsarkivet, Dpt. f. u. A. Rusland II, Depecher.

51. Copy of Rostopchin to Kriudener, 21 January 1801 os; Deutsches Zentralarchiv, Historische Abteilung 2, Merseburg (DDR), Ministerium für auswärtige Angelegenheiten, AA I, Rep. 4, No. 487.

52. Lusi to court, 23 January 1801; ibid.

The English minister in Berlin suggested that the fuss and bother on the Russian frontier were prompted by political considerations rather than by concern for public health. The Earl of Carysfort surmised that the Russians were using the pretext of plague in Spain to close their frontier in an effort to stop the flow of correspondence between St. Petersburg and the rest of Europe.[53]

The Prussians finally protested the inconvenience which the Russian frontier procedures caused in the transaction of diplomatic business. Chancellor Haugwitz pointed out, among other things, that there was no sign of the Spanish disease in Russia. He said that the extraordinary precautions would only give rise to misunderstanding and suspicions. Paul responded that he could not be too careful in such a matter and that the quarantine would continue through the spring.[54]

In Paris, Talleyrand's reaction was similar. He was frustrated by the delay in the arrival of the promised Russian plenipotentiary, a "delay [that] can be imputed only to . . . false alarms that are spread abroad about a sham plague."[55] Haugwitz wrote to Lusi in February 1801 that the disease that had broken out in Spain the previous summer was entirely gone, that not a trace of it was left.[56]

The Russians were evidently not so sure, and some confusion persisted in their precautions throughout the spring. Rostopchin told Lusi on 17 February that the quarantine was lifted.[57] But a Danish mission on its way to St. Petersburg two weeks later reported that it experienced all possible purifications.[58] Late in February, Stedingk received letters that were not

53. Carysfort to Grenville, 24 January 1801; London Public Record Office, FO 64/60.

54 Lusi to court, 3 February 1801; Deutsches Zentralarchiv, Historische Abteilung 2, Merseburg (DDR), Ministerium für auswärtige Angelegenheiten, AA I, Rep. 4, No. 487.

55. Talleyrand to Joseph Bonaparte, 4 February 1801; *Histoire des négociations diplomatiques relatives aux traités de Mortefontaine, de Lunéville, et d'Amiens*, Albert du Casse, ed., 3 vols. (Paris: Dentu, 1855), 2:305.

56. Haugwitz to Lusi, 9 February 1801; Deutsches Zentralarchiv, Historische Abteilung 2, Merseburg (DDR), Ministerium für auswärtige Angelegenheiten, AA I, Rep. 4, No. 487.

57. Lusi to court, 17 February 1801; ibid.

58. Dannewold to Bernstorff, 1 March 1801; Copenhagen Rigsarkivet, Dpt. f. u. A. Rusland II, Depecher.

"*piquées.*"[59] But in March, the quarantine was reported in effect again.   The former Russian ambassador in England, S. R. Vorontsov, observed late in March that letters reaching him described the frontier as cordoned off by troops and officials who opened all correspondence. They dipped the letters in vinegar on the pretext of containing contagion.   "The singular thing is that this supposed malady is communicated only by paper."[60] This situation was genuinely strange, and we are entitled to suspect, along with several of the diplomats, that the motivation behind the measures on the frontier had something to do with political machinations in the Russian capital.

The sum of the weird developments reviewed here was to leave a devastating impression of Paul's mental condition. We have seen the reports in Vienna that he was mad. Even before his alleged deterioration of the last eight or ten months of his life, in March 1800, the Sardinian ambassador, Balbo, informed his court cynically and unequivocally, "The Emperor is mad, nevertheless one can draw great advantage from [the fact] if one seizes favorable moments."[61] At the same time, the English ambassador, Whitworth, reported similarly, "The fact is, and I speak it with regret, that the Emperor is litterally [sic] not in his senses. . . . This truth has been for many years known to those nearest to Him, and I have myself had frequent opportunity of observing it. But since He has come to the Throne, his disorder has gradually increased, and now manifests itself in such a manner as to fill everyone with the most obvious alarm."[62]

Later, such opinions were to multiply. Prince I. M. Dolgorukov, who had participated in the theatrical productions of the young court and who continued after Paul's death to remember his kindness more poignantly than his dreadful qualities, nevertheless wrote that Paul's "judgment was darkened, [his] heart filled with bile and the spirit of wrath." He spoke of

---

59. Stedingk to court, 27 February 1801; Stockholm Riksarkivet, Ur Muscovitica 465.

60. Vorontsov to Novosil'tsev, 29 March 1801; *Arkhiv kniazia Vorontsova*, 11:397-398.

61. Chizh, "Imperator Pavel Pervyi," p. 662.

62. Whitworth to Grenville, mid-March 1800; London Public Record Office, FO 65/46.

Paul's faults as the "weaknesses of a person blinded and almost losing [his] judgment."[63]

More striking is the opinion of Count S. R. Vorontsov, who represented the view common to his former diplomatic post in London. Paul's challenge to the sovereigns of Europe had left an indelible impression in London. In February 1801, Vorontsov wrote to a friend in St. Petersburg a letter altogether daring in its conception. "It is as if we . . . were on a vessel. . . . I am sea-sick and cannot leave my bed. You come and announce to me that the storm is violent and the vessel will perish, for the captain has gone mad, thrashing the crew of more than thirty persons who do not dare to oppose his extravagances. . . . I believe then that the vessel will perish, but you tell me that there is yet hope of being saved, as the second in command is an affable and reasonable young man who has the crew's confidence. I pray you to return to the deck and persuade the young man and the sailors that they must save the ship, a part of which, together with the cargo, belongs to the young man; that they are thirty against one, and that it is ridiculous to fear being killed by this fool of a captain, when in a little while all will be drowned by him."[64]

The delivery from disaster for which Vorontsov appealed was not long in coming. Count Pahlen, who masterminded the plot quietly from the sidelines, put the heir, Alexander Pavlovich, in contact with the man who was the more conspicious organizer of the conspiracy, Count Nikita Petrovich Panin. Alexander gave his consent to the coup, stipulating only, whether naively or not, that his father's life be spared. The conspirators were joined by the Zubov brothers and by General L. L. Bennigsen. There was a distinctly Anglophile and Francophobe disposition among the parties to the plot, and it was in this sense a reaction against the triumph of the Rostopchin-Kutaisov clique in mid-1798. On the night of 23/24 March, their resolve fortified by massive libations of vodka, the conspirators broke into Paul's bedroom in the Michael Palace, flourished a document stipulating abdication before a cowering and distempered emperor, and in the course

63. I. M. Dolgorukov, "Kapishche moego serdtsa," *Russkaia starina,* 1890, Prilozhenie, pp. 253-256.

64. S. R. Vorontsov to Novosil'tsev, 5 February 1801; *Arkhiv kniazia Vorontsova,* 11:397-398.

of a thoroughly confused struggle, struck him unconscious by a blow to the head and strangled the life out of him.[65]

After the assassination, we get clearer indications of what other contemporaries thought of the affair. One of the most important opinions is that of Baron Andrei L'vovich Nikolai, a distinguished littérateur who had served under Nikita Ivanovich Panin as one of Paul's tutors. He was in 1801 president of the Russian Academy of Sciences. Soon after Paul's death, he wrote to Vorontsov in London, describing "the great event of March [24]" as "so fortunate in one respect, so terrible in another. . . . However careful I formerly was to envelop myself in obscurity, however far away I was from any intrigue, ambition or avarice I swear to you that I did not pass a day without expecting some disgrace and that the security which the benevolence of the present government gives me [is like] a new existence and restores [my] youth. In the midst of the perpetual fears in which we lived, still I never forgot either the loyalty that I owed to my Master or the gratitude that I owed to my benefactor. I always recognized in him the strangest combination . . . a most amiable person and a most violent one. [It was] his unhappy fate in the end to have the latter [quality] constantly triumph over the former."[66]

Nikolai did not say that Paul was mad. He said rather that Paul's government had become intolerable. Vorontsov soon responded to Nikolai's letter. "You tell me that the character of the deceased emperor was a mixture of the most amiable with the most violent qualities . . . but I believe that you should have added that the violence was constantly growing and that it had reached the point of alienating his mind (*aliéner son esprit*): because it is plain that in the last 8 to 10 months he was in a visible dementia. The challenge by him to several sovereigns to personal combat, published by his order in the papers, and several other things prove beyond a doubt that his mind was deranged."[67]

In order to appreciate properly these opinions, we must remember that, unlike Paul's assassins, Nikolai regarded Paul

---

65. The latest contribution to the subject of the assassination is James J. Kenney, Jr., "The Politics of Assassination," in Ragsdale, *Paul I*, pp. 125-145. All the pertinent bibliography is cited there. The memoirs of the assassins are published in *Tsareubiistvo 11 marta 1801 g.: zapiski uchastnikov i sovremennikov*, 2nd ed. (St. Petersburg, n.p., 1908).

66. Nikolai to S. R. Vorontsov, 10/22 April 1801; *Arkhiv kniazia Vorontsova*, 22:107-108.

67. S. R. Vorontsov to Nikolai, 6/18 May 1801; ibid., 532.

quite properly as his benefactor and that S. R. Vorontsov was far enough removed from St. Petersburg to be out of harm's way. The sum of this evidence considered together weighs rather heavily against a clean bill of health for Paul's mental condition.

On the other hand, there is a tradition in Napoleonic historiography that we cannot afford to ignore, and it developed on the very morrow of the assassination itself. The heart of the matter appeared in Bonaparte's daily paper, the *Moniteur universel* (27 germinal an 9/17 April 1801): "Paul I died in the night of 24-25 March [sic: the date is 24 hours late]!!! The English squadron passed the [Danish] Sound on the 30th!!! History will teach us the connections between these two events!!!"

Napoleon's official historiographer, Louis Pierre Bignon, has elaborated the idea. Pahlen, the soul of the conspiracy, had, according to Bignon, sold himself to the English. (There is, in fact, some circumstantial evidence of English financial support of the conspiracy,[68] and there was open rejoicing in England at the news of the death of Paul--Paul the Last, they called him.) Then, to secure himself, he engaged in what might be called *désinformation familiale*, i.e., he sowed those seeds of suspicion between Paul on the one hand and the other members of the family, especially Alexander, on the other, that eventually won the qualified approval of the heir that was indispensable to the security of the conspirators.[69] This allegation is rather common both in the memoir literature and in the histories, but it cannot be satisfactorily documented.

The argument of this tradition is amplified somewhat in French histories in a fashion that departs from Russian sources. Bignon and Adolf Thiers suggest that Pahlen appended private notes to diplomatic correspondence on the eve of the assassination in order to inform Russian diplomats and foreign governments that communications from St. Petersburg were not to be taken seriously.

Thus, according to Bignon, Paul's ultimatum to Prussia demanding the occupation of Hanover and the closing of the German ports to English trade contained the note, "The Emperor is not well today."[70]   In Thiers's version, this note is more

---

68. James J. Kenney, Jr., "Lord Whitworth and the Conspiracy Against Tsar Paul I: The New Evidence of the Kent Archive," *Slavic Review* 36:205-219 (1977).

69. Louis Pierre Edouard Bignon, *Histoire de France depuis le 18 brumaire jusqu'à la paix de Tilsitt* (Brussels: Méline, 1836), p. 116.

70. Ibid., p. 117.

provocative still: "His Majesty is indisposed today. This may have consequences." Thiers adds that the dispatch bearing the note was shown to the French ambassador, who reported it to his government at once.[71]

If we consider together the suggestions of the Napoleonic historiography, the conventionally inexplicable nature of the apparently mad events of the last eight to ten months of Paul's reign, and the near total power which Count Pahlen had acquired at the time, we can hardly avoid another line of inquiry. Pahlen was then governor-general of St. Petersburg, with all of the police powers implied by that title, president of the College of Foreign Affairs, president of the College of the Post, and, by any standard but the purely literal, chancellor or premier. Every administrative lever of the control of the traffic of information was in his hands. This fact gave him the possiblity of *désinformation universelle*. He could have used this control in either of two ways. Most obviously, he could have used it to misrepresent Paul to society both large and small, i.e., the society of the family, of the court of St. Petersburg, of the court of St. James. But a mastery of the flow of information such as he may have had would have opened to him a far grander and more devious opportunity yet, the opportunity to influence public opinion in the question of Paul's sanity itself. Pahlen could select from his far-flung sources information suitably skewed to provoke in Paul behavior inappropriate to the un-misrepresented reality; and therefore Pahlen had the capacity, in a sense, to prompt Paul to misrepresent himself and to give evidence against himself in the delicate issue of his own sanity.

We have circumstantial evidence of just this phenomenon in the affairs of Rostopchin's dismissal, Rosenkrantz's dismissal, the Indian expedition, the challenge to the sovereigns of Europe, and the plague in Spain. We do not have enough evidence to make a sound case. But let us consider one pertinent contemporary opinion. V. P. Kochubei was observing these events in the remote safety of Dresden when he received the news of Rostopchin's dismissal. He wrote at once to S. R. Vorontsov in London: "[Pahlen] is the soul of everything. His

---

71. Adolphe Thiers, *Histoire du Consulat et de l'Empire*, 21 vols. (Paris: Paulin, 1845-1874), 2:430. There is no reference to these notes, naturally enough, in the materials published from Russian archives. See *Sbornik IRIO*, 70: 672. More significantly, they did not turn up in the thorough research of Guy Stanton Ford in the Prussian archives: see his *Hanover and Prussia, 1795-1803* (New York: Columbia University Press, 1903), pp. 231-235.

influence is beyond comparison with that of any other person in this reign. He is immune to espionage by his place in the government. Correspondence cannot touch him, and he may confide in whom he likes."[72]

It is time now in this mode of purely conventional history to venture a provisional conclusion in the question of Paul's madness. It is obvious that his capricious policy was a grossly uncomfortable burden on that part of society most exposed to it. It is obvious that he was far from being a well-adjusted personality or an effective ruler. It is not obvious that he was mad. In fact, the issue is deeply ambiguous. The probable truth of the matter is suggested by a source of only marginal reliability, but the reliable and the correct are not absolutely exclusive, and perhaps in a question as tortured and tangled as this one it would be more strange than ironic if they were not sometimes compatible. According to the memoirs of Fedor Golovkin, Platon Zubov and Catherine were once discussing the Grand Duke Paul when Zubov said to her, "He is mad." She responded, "I know it as well as you. Unfortunately, he is not mad enough to [enable us] to protect the state from the evils that he is preparing for it."[73] That, probably, is the heart of the matter. Pahlen addressed himself to the problem of making Paul mad enough to put the state beyond the reach of the evils which he was preparing, because without the help of Pahlen, Paul was merely mad enough to do damage, not mad enough to be easily rendered harmless.

---

72. *Arkhiv kniazia Vorontsova*, 14:147.

73. Fedor Gavrilovich Golovkin, *La cour et le règne de Paul I* (Paris: Plon-Nourrit, 1905), p. 120.

5

Paul as Exemplar of Enlightenment Values

How big a misfit was Paul in his time?

If we analyze the content of Paul's education and state-craft and compare it with the prevailing trends and opinions of the age, we find that it was composed of the characteristic thought and practice of the Enlightenment, though not a precisely balanced selection of them, a subtle point to which we shall return later.

Our one detailed guide to the intellectual influences in Paul's life is Poroshin's diary. We know a great deal about what Paul read, what was read to him, what was discussed, and what he saw in the theater during the year and a half when Poroshin kept notes on his activities. There were three items that stand out above the others in the extent of Paul's exposure to them.

The first is Voltaire's *History of the Russian Empire Under Peter the Great* (1759). Voltaire's *Peter I* is a rather ironic piece of work. His scathing comments on warfare in his *Philosophical Dictionary* (1764) are well known, as are his tauntings of Frederick II for loving war too much. When he turns to Peter I, a monarch of whom Kliuchevskii said that "war was the most important circumstance of his reign," Voltaire conveniently forgot his former outlook, or, rather, he suspended it. Most of the material for his history he got from the Russian court, and he flattered Elizabeth I as fulsomely as he did Catherine later, though with less reason, as the leading patroness of the arts in Europe at the time. In fact, the history is almost entirely an account of the military dimension of Peter's reign. But Peter's military operations, unlike those elsewhere in Europe, were not the frivolous stuff of vanity and hubris: for the battle of Poltava, unlike the other "more than two hundred pitched battles in Europe from the commencement of this century," occasioned the "happiness of the greatest empire under the sun."[1]

The account of Peter's reforms, on the other hand, is conspicuous only by its absence. On one of the most important themes of eighteenth-century historical and political writing, the law, Voltaire merely observed that "it is well known that good laws are scarce, and that the execution of them is still more so." Scarcer yet is his comment on them: Chapter 32, "The Laws," consists of two cursory pages. Paul obviously did not learn his love of peace or any of the details of domestic statecraft from this work.

On the other hand, Voltaire did treat at length the conflict between sovereign and heir in the reign of Peter that again troubled Paul's own time, and his treatment of it was one from which Paul could not have drawn much comfort. Voltaire portrayed Peter's heir, Alexis, as an altogether inadequate student of his father's heroic mold of statecraft. "The reading of ecclesiastical books was his undoing (*ce qui le perdit*)."[2] Peter he entirely excused. Alexis allegedly died, after long bouts of torture, in a fit of apoplexy. "One sees thus at what a high and frightful price Peter the Great purchased the happiness which he procured for his peoples."[3] Given Paul's already acute conflicts with his mother, it would be interesting to know if these observations made him uncomfortable. Of course, Poroshin may have avoided these passages when he read to Paul, as he tended to avoid the subjects of Peter III and Ivan VI in general.

The second conspicuous item in Paul's education was Fénelon's *Télémaque.* Published in 1699 as a thinly veiled attack on the policy of Louis XIV, it was immensely popular and went through sixteen printings in the first year. In Russia, it was published seven times in four translations in the eighteenth

---

1. François-Marie Arouet, Voltaire, *Oeuvres complètes,* 52 vols. (Paris: Garnier frères, 1877-1885), 17:509.

2. Ibid., p. 572.

3. Ibid., p. 592.

century.[4] The story in which the critique is couched is that of Ulysses's son Télémaque, who went traveling in search of his missing father, accompanied by his tutor, Mentor, actually the goddess of wisdom, Minerva, in disguise. As they sailed about the Mediterranean, they had a variety of adventures, which Mentor exploited to teach wisdom, virtue, prudence--in short, politics--to young Télémaque.

A major theme of the book, running through it like a refrain, is the need to subject the passions to the careful control of reason. It cost Télémaque much hard work to meet Mentor's standards of holding aloof from pleasure and the passions. A mysterious voice from a cave in Egypt warned him: "You will be great only to the extent that you are moderate and courageous in conquering your passions." Télémaque learned quickly and mused to himself: "Happy are those who tire of violent pleasures and who know how to content themselves with the sweetness of innocence! Happy are those who amuse themselves in learning and who take pleasure in cultivating their mind." He observed that the "failing of negligent and indolent princes is to give themselves up with a blind confidence to corrupt and crafty favorites." When they encountered King Idomeneus of Salentum, then on the brink of military disaster, Mentor instructed him, "War is the greatest of evils with which the gods afflict mankind." When his visitors had delivered Idomeneus from this crisis, Mentor accompanied him on a walking tour of the kingdom, dispensing the reforms necessary to structure a good government. Though trade was to be "perfectly open and free," all merchants must give an account of their business to the magistrates, and limits were established on the proportion of their capital that merchants may put at risk. Mentor prohibited the sale of all foreign commodities that might encourage luxury and effeminacy. He established a code for dress and for the decoration of houses. Society was divided into seven distinct ranks, determined by considerations of ancient lineage and current merit, and each was to be distinguished by the color and style of its dress. Mentor outlawed two kinds of music, the soft and effeminate kind that encouraged languor and desire, and the bacchanalian kind that prompted tumultuous passions. The superfluity of artisans in the cities was moved onto the idle lands of the countryside. Finally, Mentor required that magistrates be appointed to superintend the conduct of every family and the morals of individuals. Thus an infinite number of disorders and

---

4. Walter Gleason, *Moral Idealists, Bureaucracy, and Catherine the Great* (New Brunswick, N.J.: Rutgers University Press, 1981), p. 97.

crimes were prevented. When Télémaque returned from a military mission to behold this transformation of Salentum, Mentor summed up the duties of the prince: "The unique and essential purpose is never to want authority and grandeur for oneself . . . but one must sacrifice oneself, in the infinite cares of the government, in order to render men good and happy."[5]

The third among the most commonly used books of Paul was Jean Heuzet's *Histoires choisies des auteurs profanes.*[6] Heuzet (1660-1728) was a professor at the Collège de Beauvais who had previously published a similar selection of Latin texts drawn from the Old Testament. In both works, he explained, "My purpose . . . has been to place in the hands of children . . . some small work that might be both easily understood and morally edifying. It is beyond doubt that the Holy Scriptures combine these two advantages." In the new work, the author was confident that "one will see . . . that these pagans, even in the midst of the shadows of idolatry, teach us that the providence of God attends not only all men in general, but each of us in particular, that he knows our most secret thoughts; and that it is he who inspires the good and punishes the bad; that the true worship which we owe him consists in purity of heart; . . . that the happiness of man consists neither in pleasures nor in honors or riches but in virtue; that we must concede to the body only what is necessary to sustain it; that we must suffer injuries, not return evil for evil, do good to everyone, including our enemies; that there is no true friendship but that whose foundation and purpose is virtue: that we must follow virtue and justice in everything; that it is better to lose repose, liberty, life than to fail at one's duty." The examples of the ancients were replete with such lessons. Book I was "Of God"; Book II, "Of Prudence"; Book III, "Of Justice"; Book IV, "Of Fortitude"; Book V, "Of Temperance." The most common sources were Seneca's *Moral Epistles* and Cicero's *On Duties* (*De officiis*). Selected subjects include moral lessons like the following: "Knowledge is the nourishment of the soul"; "Belles-lettres serve as the ornament and the solace of mankind"; "It is not important to have and to read many books, but to have and to read good ones"; "The wise man lacks the will, rather than the power, to

---

5. François de Salignac de la Mothe-Fénelon, *Oeuvres complètes*, 10 vols. (Lille: Lefort, 1848-1852), 6:407, 414, 466, 478-483, 558.

6. Jean Heuzet, *Histoires choisies des auteurs profanes, traduites en françois, avec le Latin à côté; ou l'en a mêlé divers Préceptes de Morale tirés des mêmes Auteurs*, 2 vols. (Lyons: Frères Perisse, 1780). See especially unpaginated Preface.

become rich"; "Justice is the Queen of all the Virtues"; "The mere wish to sin is a sin"; "Who would acquire true glory must bind himself to fulfill all the duties of Justice"; "A teacher must have no vices and suffer none [in others]"; "Friendship is common, but fidelity is rare." This extremely popular book was published over and over again from 1728 to 1858.

A similar kind of material in Paul's reading was Sumarokov's journal, *Trudoliubivaia pchela* (Busy Bee). It contained articles "On the Usefulness of Mythology," "On the two chief virtues necessary to the writer of history, that is, sincerity and piety without superstition." The February 1759 issue taught that "prestige is not as worthy as godliness." The March issue contained the fable of Phaeton from Ovid's *Metamorphoses*, a selection from Erasmus's *Familiar Colloquies*, and Lucian's *Dialogues of the Dead.*[7] Other selections include more of Ovid and part of Locke's *Treatise on Human Understanding.* Sumarokov himself contributed pieces "On the Beauty of Nature," "On Pride," and "On Distinction." "Many consider illustrious birth as a great ornament of genuine distinction: I do not know how it is possible to affirm it: for there is no evidence of it." Rather, he said, distinction arose from merit. In June he gave his opinion "On the reading of novels": "The usefulness of them is small, and the harm great."[8] Later selections included a part of Corneille's *Polyeucte*, Swift's *Tale of a Tub* (translated from German), a eulogy of Peter I by Sumarokov on Peter's nameday, a selection from the history of Livy, and Sumarokov's vision of the "Happy Society," a utopian story of a country ruled by a good governor, with rare qualities of leadership, who rewarded the virtuous and punished the lawless.

In the same genre was Carl Gustav Tessin's *Letters to a Young Prince.* Panin was acquainted with both the author/teacher and the pupil, Prince Gustav of Sweden. The book consists largely of maxims, parables, and fables. Some of them the author allegedly dreamed, but most are drawn from the common fund of fable in which the century abounded. Something of the prince's daily regimen and the pedagogical plan are revealed in Letter XIX: "You converse with learned men upon subjects of speculation; with public ministers on the state of foreign courts, the characters of kings, their employments and

---

7. Lucian (c. A.D. 115-c. 200) studied under the Stoic Demonax. The *Dialogues* deal with the vanity of human pretences. They exhibit a grimly ironic, melancholy resignation.

8. Aleksandr P. Sumarokov, *Trudoliubivaia pchela*, p. 363 (May 1759), and p. 374 (June 1759).

their amusements; with military men on wars, heroic acts, campaigns, and sieges. The administrators of the finances acquaint you with the state of the revenues, the condition and the wants of the kingdom." The lessons here are not pointed lightly. "In the beginning of the world, all animals admired the beauty and the expanded tail of the peacock; but they no sooner heard his voice than they shunned so unpleasant a sound and crowded to the decent nightingale, whose enchanting song was universally applauded. The application is easy. The peacock represents a foolish proud man, and the nightingale is an emblem of the affable and the friendly. Pride is, in my opinion, the most despicable of all vices." "Christian and royal virtues are the foundation upon which a prince is to build his own happiness and that of his people."[9]

Tessin compiled "a list of those worthies who have merited your favor, and deserved particularly well of the commonwealth." Among these were "Celsius, who, with great reputation, hath contributed his part towards investigating the true figure of the earth; Polhem, who hath so often subdued a wild uncultivated nature, and brought her under the yoke and discipline of art; Linnaeus, who has digested, in order, the most minute plants and reptiles, which had almost escaped the sight of man, and ascertained their utility; Ahlstrom, who has, in defiance of an infinite number of calumnies, established manufactures, at the hazard of his fortune, his vigor, his health, and his life; Grill, who has, with great credit, acquired an immense substance, in extending our trade, and furnishing employment for a vast number of his countrymen, and a subsistence for many of the poor."[10]

He presented a list of virtues which the prince ought to emulate: "You will become a sincere Christian; a magnanimous prince; an impartial judge; a calm hero; a humane warrior; and a meek and merciful conqueror. You will be great in adversity; cheerful in distress; moderate in joy; continent in pleasures; regular in amusements; provident without fickleness; resolute without obstinacy; liberal without prodigality. You will be imperious in discouraging vice; your dignity will be supported without pride, your mirth without voluptuousness. You will be the friend, the delight, the ornament, the blessing, the hope and the

---

9. Carl Gustav Tessin, *Letters to a Young Prince* (London: Reeves, 1755), pp. 83, 90, 70. Paul used the German edition.

10. Ibid., pp. 139-143. The worthies listed are Anders Celsius, 1701-1744; Christoph Polhem, 1661-1751; Carl von Linné, 1707-1778; Jonas Alsroemer Ahlstrom, 1685-1761; Claude Grill, 1705-1767.

protector of your subjects." After the fashion of Télémaque, Gustav was assured that "kings and princes were not instituted merely for their own sake, . . . but that it behooves them to be as anxious for the prosperity of their subjects, as for their own."[11]

Paul several times asked for a reading of *Robinson Crusoe*, an adventure story that is amenable to morally didactic uses as well. One chapter is titled, "My Reason Began to Master My Despondency." Robinson's diary became a record of a well regulated household. It is a story of hard work rewarded.

Paul's admiration of Henry IV is well known. Much of it came from two works which were among his favorites, Voltaire's *Henriade* (1723) and Sully's *Mémoires*. Sully's work was saturated in the spirit of Calvinism and all the orderliness, miserliness, and work ethic that accompany it. He was much concerned to put the account books of the French monarchy in order and to regulate what he regarded as the excess of luxuries among the French aristocracy (Book XVI). He believed that "the causes of the ruin or of the weakening of monarchies were enormous subsidies, monopolies, especially on grain, the neglect of commerce and communications, of labor, of the arts and handicrafts, the great number of public offices and their cost, the excessive authority of those in office, the expense, the long delays and the inequity of the [dispensation of] justice; idleness, luxury . . . , debauchery, and corruption of morals, the confusion of ranks, the instability of money, unjust and imprudent wars, the despotism of sovereigns, their blind attachment to certain persons, . . . the greed of ministers and favorites, the degeneration (*avilisement*) of people of quality, the suspicion and neglect of men of letters, the toleration of bad customs, and the infraction of good laws." Finally, he says the most valuable principle in politics is this: "That good customs and good laws give rise to each other."[12]

There are three subjects in both the *Henriade* and Sully's *Mémoires* that must have fixed Paul's attention. The first is regicide (of Henry III in the *Henriade* and of both Henry III and Henry IV in the *Mémoires*).[13] The second is the threat posed to

---

11. Ibid., pp. 297, 278-279.

12. Maximilien de Béthune, duc de Sully, *Mémoires*, 10 vols. (London: n.p., 1778), 5:290-291, 292.

13. It is striking in how many of Paul's childhood readings either a regicide or the death of a prince takes place: in addition to the two mentioned, Voltaire's *Peter I* and his *Mérope, Oedipe,* and *Phèdre; Télémaque,* Book 5 (Idomeneus); Racine's *Phèdre;* and the deaths of Ivan IV's son and Peter I's son in Lacombe's *Histoire.*

thrones by a rebellious nobility. The third is the social and political evil of religious fanaticism. This is perhaps the primary impact of the *Henriade*. Both Voltaire and Sully left graphic and gruesome accounts of the St. Bartholomew's Massacre. This theme is also subject of Voltaire's play *Mahomet*, subtitled *Fanaticism.*[14]

Much of the history that Paul read was quite compatible with the moral outlook of *Télémaque*, the *Histoires choisies*, and the letters of Tessin. Montesquieu's study of the "grandeur et décadence" of the Romans emphasized values familiar to Paul. It was a "well-regulated society" that enabled the Romans to establish their dominion over much of the world. It was the evils of riches and corruption that were responsible for their undoing.[15] More explicitly, in Chapter 9, "Two Causes of the Fall of Rome" were cited: (1) the farther away from home (Italy) the army went, the more it lost the spirit of the citizen and the patriot and became the creature of the local commander; (2) the mixture of races which took place when citizenship was extended to all the inhabitants of the empire spoiled the civic spirit of the population.

Paul studied ancient history in Charles Rollin's famous *Histoire ancienne*. The author, a colleague of Heuzet at Beauvais, specifically designed the history for "young people," but it was popular and widely read among adults as well. Frederick II read it, admired it, and corresponded with the author about it. Trediakovskii translated all twelve volumes into Russian.[16] The French censor who passed the work assured the reading public that it exhibited "the same principles of religion, of probity, and the same happy efforts to improve the minds of youth, which are so notable in all the writings of this author."[17]

Rollin's was a distinctly pious work. He subscribed to Archbishop Usher's idea that the world was created in 4004 B.C. He was concerned not only to relate the fortunes of the ancients, but also to exhibit the reasons for good and bad fortune. Cyrus

---

14. Is it ridiculous to suggest that in pursuing his strange fantasy of the reunion of the two churches Paul was somehow in his imagination following in the footsteps of Henry IV?

15. Charles-Louis de Secondat, baron de Montesquieu, *Considérations sur les causes de la grandeur des Romains et de leur décadence* (Paris: Garnier Frères, 1954).

16. Harold B. Segel, *The Literature of Eighteenth-Century Russia*, 2 vols. (New York: E. P. Dutton, 1967), 1:54.

17. Charles Rollin, *Histoire ancienne*, 12 vols. (Paris: Etienne, 1780), 1:preface, xxxiv-xxxv.

the Great he regarded as the most accomplished prince in profane history. He had "wisdom, moderation, courage, grandeur of soul, nobility of sentiments, marvelous dexterity for leading men and winning hearts," along with great military art and a "vast breadth of spirit sustained by a prudent resolution in designing and executing grand projects." "But what was greater in him, and what was more truly royal, was the intimate conviction which he had that all his cares and all his attention should work to make his people happy . . . by an indefatigable application to attend to their interests."[18]

Xerxes, on the other hand, "by a blindness too ordinary among the great and among princes born in the abundance of all the blessings, with power unlimited, in a glory that cost them nothing, . . . was accustomed to judge his talents and his personal merit by the outward signs of his position and his rank. He mistrusted the wise counsel of [those] who alone had the courage to tell him the truth; and he gave himself up to courtiers who admired his destiny and [were] only concerned to flatter his passions. . . . In a word, in order to judge Xerxes properly, it is only necessary to put him beside a simple bourgeois of Athens, a Miltiades, a Themistocles, an Aristides. On one side is all the good sense, the prudence, the skill in the art of war, the courage, the grandeur of soul: on the other, one sees only vanity, pride, arrogance, a baseness of sentiments that calls forth pity, and occasionally even a brutality and a barbarism that inspire horror."[19]

Of Alexander the Great: "Of all the vices, there is none so base, nor so unworthy, I will not say of a prince, but of an honest man, as drunkenness: . . . What shameful pleasure to spend days and nights drinking, to continue debauches for weeks at a time . . . without speaking of the infamies that accompany these debauches."[20]

What Rollin especially admired was the character of the Athenians, and he found Plutarch's delineation of them exemplary. He appreciated, too, the virtues of the Spartans, and his reaction to the two peoples was much like that which has become a cliché in our own textbooks.[21]

---

18. Ibid., 2:305, 309.

19. Ibid., 3:342-344.

20. Ibid., 6:702.

21. Ibid., 4:581-592.

Paul read Russian history in Jacques Lacombe's *Abrégé chronologique de l'histoire du Nord*.[22] The history of Russia here is just over two hundred pages in length. Happily for Paul and his tutors, it ends at the death of Elizabeth, sparing everyone the agony of Peter III. It is curious history. It gives a straight Norman theory of the origins of Russia, presumably relying here on the Primary Chronicle, proceeding year by year. Much of the early history is done in cursory fashion. Alexander Nevskii is missing. The chapters on the fifteenth and sixteenth centuries are full of mistakes. There is no substantial account of Peter's reforms. It is rather primitive history, not a distinguished piece of work.

Paul also saw Molière's *Tartuffe* and *Le bourgeois gentilhomme*. He read a good deal of Lesage's *Gil Blas* (1715-1735). Poroshin read to him unspecified parts of Diderot's *Encyclopédie* (1751-1772). He probably read Fontenelle's *Entretiens sur la pluralité des mondes* (1686). He saw some of the work of the now forgotten French playwright Destouches. "Of a strongly religious character, Destouches aimed at making comedy moral and edifying and thereby worthy of esteem."[23] He read Racine's *Phèdre*, of which Racine said that he was not sure it was the best of his plays, but that he had written "none where virtue has been more emphasized."[24] There are two titles that remain mysterious. One of them is an anonymous work called *Histoire des rois philosophes Marcu-Aurèle, Julien, Stanislas et Frederic*. The other, *O zhitiiakh slavnykh gosudarei i velikikh polkovodtsev* (On the Lives of Famous Sovereigns and Great Captains), may be Plutarch. It would have been strange in that age, given the nature of Paul's education, if he had not been exposed to Plutarch.

Our information about Paul's reading and his reaction to it is not so full after the departure of Poroshin. We have his student notebooks, it is true, some of them. We have some indication of the contents of his enormous personal library of 40,000 volumes. The library was burned in 1837, with the exception of a few volumes which eventually found their way to the

22. Jacques Lacombe, *Abrégé chronologique de l'histoire du Nord ou des états de Dannemarc, de Russie, de Suède, de Pologne, de Courland*, 2 vols. (Paris: Hérissant, 1762).

23. Sir Paul Harvey and J. E. Hesseltine, eds., *Oxford Companion to French Literature* (Oxford: Oxford University Press, 1959), p. 200.

24. Jean Racine, *Complete Plays* (New York: Random House, 1967), 1:235.

Helsinki University Library.[25] Klochkov's work in the archives at Pavlovsk before the revolution indicated that Paul read quite widely. Chizh agreed with Klochkov, and the people at the French court who met Paul on tour there were obviously astonished at the breadth and depth of his education. This evidence compels us to think that Paul continued long after the departure of Poroshin to use his time as Poroshin would have had him do, in the fashion of Télémaque under the direction of Mentor.

We know that he read the Scottish historian Robertson's *History of Charles V* (1769). His library contained the complete works of Racine and Corneille, Bossuet's *Histoire universelle* (1781), Voltaire's complete works, Claude De Ferrière's *Histoire de droit romain* (1718), a great number of works on Frederick II, Necker's budget of 1781, Catherine's 1767 *Instruction* to the Legislative Assembly, Golikov's *Acts of Peter I* (1788 ff.), Mably's *Observations sur l'histoire de France* (1765) and *Droit public de l'Europe* (1748), some of the work of the Physiocrats, Bielfeld's *Institutions politiques* (1760), and the works of Blackstone and Hume. We do not know which works of Hume he had, but virtually the whole corpus had been translated into French and published in Amsterdam by 1767. Another work in Paul's library was a *Collection des moralistes anciens*,[26] which included fifteen volumes of Epictetus, Confucius, Seneca, Cicero, Plutarch, and others.

One of the more impressive things about this list is its variety. Though it is clear that Paul was nourished with a rather definite moralizing point of view by Panin and Poroshin, he was also treated to a wide selection of viewpoints. Hume's work is obviously more skeptical than that of Heuzet and Rollin. Mably stood for the abolition of private property, public credit, commerce, the sciences, letters, libraries, museums, and most of the marks of civilization. Paul bore the stamp of some of the influences to which he was subjected, and he rejected others.

The content of Paul's childhood readings suggests one of the two fundamental ways in which he mirrored the outlook of his times. His education reeked of the influence of Stoic moralism. It is explicit and prominent in Télémaque, where Fénelon mined the renaissance of Roman Stoicism for the values which Mentor taught. It is more obvious yet in the *Histoires choisies*, where about half the references are to Seneca's *Moral Epistles*,

---

25. Correspondence with the librarians there indicates that there is little of value for the biographer in what remains.

26. Klochkov, *Ocherki*, pp. 110, 587-588.

and Cicero's *De legibus* (On Laws) and *De republica* (On the Republic).

Of course, Cicero was not, like Seneca, explicitly a Stoic but an eclectic. He was, however, strongly influenced by the Stoics, and his pronouncements on law and morals in particular are heavily indebted to them. In *De legibus* and *De republica*, he repeatedly referred to and exemplified the Stoic philosophers Panaetius, Posidonius, and, less frequently, Chrysippus. The extent of the Stoic influence in the Enlightenment is detailed in Peter Gay's study. "In the Enlightenment, Stoicism had become a part . . . of a comprehensive view of the world." Montesquieu studied Cicero carefully, especially the *De officiis* (On Duties), and recognized in him the influence of Panaetius. Montesquieu especially admired the Stoic attitude toward duty. Hume and Voltaire admitted owing much of their philosophic impulse to Cicero, Seneca, and Plutarch, whose *Lives* exhibits militantly Stoic criteria. Montesquieu was aware of the affinity of Stoic ethics and Christian ethics. The Belgian Christian Stoic Justus Lipsius (*De constantia; Politicorum libri sex*) was much prized by Gibbon, Montesquieu, Voltaire, Diderot, Thomasius, and Wolff. Charron's *Traité de la sagesse* (1601) was widely read in the eighteenth century. It relied much on Montaigne--the transmitter of Stoic influence to modern Europe--as well as Lipsius, Cicero, and Seneca.[27]

Frederick II sketched the ideal sovereign and suggested that he was "the archtype of the Stoics, the idea of the sage that they had portrayed, that never existed but was approached most closely perhaps by Marcus Aurelius . . . and whose object was the happiness of the people."[28] There were five Russian editions of Marcus Aurelius's *Meditations* between 1740 and 1798.[29] The reading list for the new Moscow orphanage established by Catherine's educational adviser, Ivan Betskoi, included Cicero, Seneca, Plutarch, and Marcus Aurelius.[30]

---

27. Peter Gay, *The Enlightenment: An Interpretation*, 2 vols. (New York: Alfred A. Knopf, 1966-1969), 1:1, 50, 64, 95, 98ff., 106, 109, 162, 165, 296, 300-304.

28. Frederick II, *Oeuvres posthumes*, 15 vols. (Berlin: Voss & Decker, 1788), "Essai sur les formes de gouvernement," 6:87-88.

29. Gleason, *Moral Idealists*, p. 97.

30. J. L. Black, *Citizens for the Fatherland: Education, Educators, and Pedagogical Ideals in Eighteenth-Century Russia* (Boulder, Colo.: East European Quarterly, 1979), p. 81.

Of course, the Stoicism of the eighteenth century was a Roman Stoicism,[31] farther from the Cynics than the Stoicism of Greece and less world-denying. It was bound up inextricably with notions of managing a vast empire, and it was intimately connected with the traditions of the Roman law. This form of Stoicism was evident in Europe in the work of Montaigne, prominent in the neo-classical drama of France in the seventeenth century, and pervasive in the outlook of Fénelon toward the end of the seventeenth century and the beginning of the eighteenth. By the time of Paul's reign, however, it had serious competitors on the European scene in the sphere of moral theory.

There were two rivals in particular. First, there was that body of tradition that has been called so well *L'esprit du mal*.[32] This tradition incorporates much of the salacious literature of the time, both serious and pornographic. It includes the picaresque work of the Abbé Prévost (*Manon Lescaut*), much of Defoe (*Moll Flanders* in particular), Lesage's *Gil Blas*, Laclos's *Les Liaisons dangereuses*, and especially, of course, the various works of the Marquis de Sade. To group all of this work together under the rubric "l'esprit du mal" requires a loose interpretation of the title, for some of the authors explicitly protest (Laclos) and others evidently intend (Lesage) that their work show the seamy side of life for the sake of teaching the innocent to avoid it. De Sade portrayed the most extreme and forceful view of this tradition: "I am convinced that crime serves nature's intentions as well as wisdom and virtue; let us sally forth into this perverse world."[33] Paul was not in touch with this body of work and was explicitly hostile to the outlook, with the single exception of *Gil Blas*, which is the tamest part of it and is easily capable of edifying interpretation.

The other viewpoint rivaling that of the Stoics was more modern and progressive. It was sensationalist, hedonist, and utilitarian. This corpus of work was represented by Helvétius, La Mettrie, d'Holbach in France, and, more preeminently, by

---

31. Ransel, *The Panin Party*, p. 212, calls it neo-Stoicism, and the term is appropriate, for reasons suggested above, but it is by no means a commonly used term. Note, for example, its general absence from histories of ideas and encyclopedias of philosophy.

32. Marcel Ruff, *L'esprit du mal et l'esthétique baudelairienne* (Geneva: Slatkine, 1972), pp. 12-62.

33. Donatien Alphonse François de Sade, *Histoire de Juliette, ou les Prospérités du Vice*, as quoted in Lester G. Crocker, *An Age of Crisis* (Baltimore: The Johns Hopkins University Press, 1959), p. 10.

Smith and Hume in Scotland. It is a revision of Stoic notions of the relationship between the passions and reason. It envisioned a reciprocal relationship of the two such that passion comes to play a positive and essential role in this new ethical theory. It argued the notion of the actuating forces of pleasure and pain, and before the century was over, it spoke of the greatest happiness of the greatest number. This theory is more sophisticated and realistic than the older Stoic one, and it probably is the origin of the modern form of learning theory. This set of ideas, too, was foreign to Paul. It is true that he discussed the work of Helvétius with Poroshin, almost certainly *De l'esprit* (1758), but if he learned much of it, it is not evidenced in his own freely expressed ethical ideas. Radishchev reflected Paul's somewhat outdated view of these matters: "I recalled all the times when my soul, stirred by my senses, chased after their gratification, falsely considering the hired partner of amorous satisfaction an object of true love."[34]

In western Europe by the end of the age, this new theory of hedonic ethical utilitarianism had won many influential adherents. But there seem to have been two distinct groups that were left untouched by it, pedagogues in general and Russians in particular. As we are not concerned here with pedagogues in general, let us look at the Russians.[35]

One of the most widely used textbooks of the time in Russia was N. Kurganov's *Pis'movnik*. It contained several substantial selections from Epictetus and Seneca. Several educational journals, for example, *Utrennii svet* and *Rastushchii vinograd*, carried translations of Seneca and Diogenes Laertius (biographer of the Greek philosophers).[36] The prominence of Stoic material in Sumarokov's *Trudoliubivaia pchela* has already been mentioned. "A survey of the many books on moral training circulating in Russian society in the second half of the eighteenth century leads us to the conclusion that the demand for

---

34. Alexander Radishchev, *Journey from St. Petersburg to Moscow*, Leo Wiener, tr. R. P. Thaler, ed. (Cambridge,Mass.: Harvard University Press, 1966), p. 126.

35. There are two exceptions to the Russian rule: S. E. Desnitsky and I. A. Tret'iakov, professors at Moscow University in Catherine's reign, had studied at Glasgow under Adam Smith. See A. H. Brown, "S. E. Desnitsky, Adam Smith, and the *Nakaz* of Catherine II," *Oxford Slavonic Papers* 7:42-59 (1974).

36. Marc Raeff, *The Origins of the Russian Intelligentsia* (New York: Harcourt, 1961), p. 233.

moral education was rather strong at the time."[37]   In that age, "political moralizing was a characteristic, in varying degrees, of all forms of Russian literature."[38] Catherine instructed the tutor of Constantine and Alexander that virtue and morality must be the main burden of their training.[39]

The anonymous *Nauka shchastlivym byt'* (The Science of Being Happy), translated from German and published by the Academy of Sciences Press in 1759, is full of similar wisdom. "The brave and magnanimous man masters his passions, struggles against sin, and always wishes for virtue." "Try to make sincerity the ballast and virtue the cargo of the ship of your soul." "If you wish to live happily, then let your thinking be prompted by reason, put away harsh opinion, and live according to nature." "Spiritual peace and bodily health are the essence of perfect happiness in the life of man." "Genuine happiness does not consist in great strength, power, or riches, but only in the mastery of the passions and in just and reasonable conduct." There were many similar manuals and similar observations. There were the *Moral Fables and Expositions of Baron Goldberg*, translated and published by Denis Fonvizin in 1756, Epictetus's *Encheiridion* and *Apothogems* in 1767, a translation of Maupertuis's *Essai de philosophie morale* in 1751, showing the debt of Christian morality to Stoicism, something called *The Book of the Flowers of Virtue and the Thorns of Prophecy* (1785), translated from Greek and containing articles on love, joy, mercy, reason, truth, fidelity, constancy, conciliation, and moderation. There is a book by M. Bertrand, "a member of many European Academies," titled *The General Foundations of Moral Teaching* (1796).

At the same time, that slightly more charming medium of moral teaching, fabulism, flourished in a nearly genuine native form. Collections were gathered and published by Sumarokov, Novikov, Khemnitser, and, finally, Krylov; and Trediakovskii translated Aesop.[40] Walter Gleason writes about what he calls "the moral fraternity of the early 1760s" among a group of young Russian journalists: Ippolit Bogdanovich, Denis Fonvizin,

---

37. M. M. Demkov, *Istoriia russkoi pedagogiki*, 2 vols. (St. Petersburg: Stasiulevich, 1886-1897), 2:580.

38. Black, *Citizens for the Fatherland*, p. 62.

39. Catherine II, "Instruktsiia kniaziu N. I. Saltykovu," *Sochineniia Imperatritsy Ekateriny II*, 3 vols.   (St. Petersburg: Smirdin, 1849-1850), 1:199-248.

40 Segel, *Russian Literature*, 1:239.

Nikolai Novikov. They were all dedicated to religious principles. Their ideals were rational, virtuous conduct; the passions under the control of reason; the "twinned ideals of rationality and virtue." The journals amid which they moved were Russian variants of the "moral weeklies" of western Europe: *Useful Entertainment* (*Poleznoe uveselenie*), *Good Intentions* (*Dobroe namerenie*), *Leisure Time Utilized for the Good* (*Prazdnoe vremia v pol'zu upotreblennoi*), *Innocent Exercise* (*Nevinnoe uprazhnenie*). They were passionately devoted to peace.[41]

Our best guide to Paul's mature thinking about politics and the duties of both sovereign and people to the state as well as the educational background which produced this thinking is Paul's 1788 memo. That memo exemplifies as closely and literally as one short paper can an amalgam of three constellations of ideas that were at the heart of the outlook of the era. They are natural law statecraft, Enlightened Despotism, and the *Polizeistaat.*

The idea of natural law, closely connected with many of the ethical ideas of the era, also derived from the influence of the Stoics. In the seventeenth century, the basic lines of the natural law model of statecraft had been laid out in the resonant works of Hugo Grotius and Samuel von Pufendorf. The natural law, the natural order, was established by God, or providence, in the Christian, Stoic, or deist fashion, but a providential plan of some kind there was, a plan allowing the harmonious functioning of the universe if only man could goad his weak reason to apprehend it. The eighteenth-century manifestations of the idea of natural law are in their most formal aspects represented in Blackstone, Vattel, Wolff, and Burlamaqui. Thus Blackstone: "When the Supreme Being formed the universe, and created matter out of nothing, he impressed certain principles upon that matter, from which it can never depart, . . . when he put that matter into motion, he established certain laws of motion, to which all moveable bodies must conform." There follows the great eighteenth-century metaphor of mechanical natural law: "And, to descend from the greatest operations to the smallest, when a workman forms a clock, or other piece of mechanism, he establishes, at his own pleasure, certain arbitrary laws for its direction. . . . If we farther advance, from mere inactive matter to vegetable and animal life, we shall find them still governed by laws, more numerous indeed, but equally fixed and invariable . . . performed in a wondrous involuntary manner, and

---

41. Gleason, *Moral Idealists*, pp. 53-128.

guided by unerring rules laid down by the great Creator . . . this will of [the] Maker is called the law of nature."[42]

This conception of natural law, when applied to the notion of statecraft, leads to a rather striking ambiguity well summarized by Basil Willey: "Two chief views about the moral order of the universe are to be found in the eighteenth century (often held simultaneously by the same thinkers); one, that the world is a system which automatically works together for good, . . . the other, that in order to secure good results we must make good efforts."[43]

Of the two choices, the very notion of statecraft or of political theory presupposes the latter choice. So, as a consequence of the saturation of notions of natural law statecraft in the eighteenth century, the duty of the statesman/sovereign was to use his reason and his almost celestially impartial station above the welter of conflicts of interest to apprehend the natural law and to use executive force to require everyone in his society to accept the role and the duty allotted him by providence for the end of the happy, progressive, blissful functioning of the whole. And here is Paul.

In the words of Christian Wolff (1679-1754), "men come together to form a Society, with no other View but to be in a Condition with joint Powers to Promote a common Good . . . human Happiness consists in one interrupted Progress towards greater degrees of Perfection."[44] "The purpose of the society . . . is to give mutual assistance in perfecting itself and its condition, consequently the promotion of the common good by its combined power. . . . The perfection of a nation depends upon its fitness for accomplishing the purpose of the state, and that is a perfect form of government in a nation."[45] In the words of Emmerich de Vattel (1714-1767), "the *Aim* or the *End* of Civil Society is to procure for the Citizens all the things which they need for necessities . . . and in general for their happiness. . . .

---

42. Sir William Blackstone, *Commentaries on the Laws of England*, 2 vols. (New York: Dean, 1844), 1:25-26.

43. Basil Willey, *The Eighteenth-Century Background; Studies on the Idea of Nature in the Thought of the Period* (New York: Columbia University Press, 1940), p. 95.

44. Christian Wolff, *The Real Happiness of the People Under a Philosophical King* (London: Cooper, 1750), p. 3.

45. Christian Wolff, *Jus gentium methodo scientifica pertractatum* (Oxford: Clarendon, 1934), 2:11, 20. See also Werner Frauendienst, *Christian Wolff als Staatsdenker* (Berlin: Matthiesen Verlag, 1927), especially pp. 67, 95.

Happiness is the target (*centre*) toward which all the duties of a man, and of a People, aim . . . : It is the great goal of Natural Law."[46]

Wolff was quite influential in Russia in academic circles in the early 1760s. Several of the professors at Moscow University had been his students or were his disciples, and the student journals of the time show the influence of his teachings through that of local professors.[47] Lomonosov himself, the most famous native Russian academic personality of the eighteenth century, had been a student of Wolff at Marburg in the 1730s.[48]

Natural law statecraft took two forms in the late eighteenth century. One of them was Enlightened Despotism. The term is well known in our day, and it was very little known in its own. "It would not be an exaggeration to say that much of the history of the phrase since its inception has revolved around the attempt to find out whether it means anything and, if so, exactly what."[49] The term was first used by the Physiocrats in the 1760s, though they used it very little. More often they used the term "legal despotism." No one else at the time picked up the use of either phrase, and both soon disappeared, until German scholars around the middle of the nineteenth century adopted an approximation of the idea in the term "Aufgeklärter Absolutismus."[50]

A modern study of the idea describes the program of Enlightened Despotism as follows:[51]

"1. A greater sense of responsibility in the handling of public monies.

"2. A greater emphasis on the establishment of a permanent state civil service, which implied appointment on merit. . . .

"3. The attempt to create one or another form of known, uniform, and written fundamental law."

-----

46. Emmerich de Vattel, *Le droit de gens; ou principes de la loi naturelle, appliquées à la conduite & aux affaires des Nations & des Souverains* (Washington: Carnegie Institution, 1916), pp. 23, 110.

47. Walter Gleason, "Political Ideals and Loyalties of Some Russian Writers of the Early 1760s," *Slavic Review* 34:560-575 (1975).

48. Segel, *Russian Literature*, 1:178.

49. John C. Gagliardo, *Enlightened Despotism* (New York: Crowell, 1967), p. v.

50. Fritz Hartung, *Enlightened Despotism* (London: Routledge and Paul, 1957), p. 6.

51. Gagliardo, *Enlightened Despotism*, p. 96.

Most students of the period and of the monarchs who reigned during it could agree easily enough with this characterization, and certainly Paul fits it, though not necessarily adequately or without controversy.

Still, the precise significance of Enlightened Despotism is as slippery and ambiguous as its history is wispy. Presumably, it was designed to embody a strict legality incumbent upon all classes of society and the monarch as well with a monarchy sufficiently exalted to rise impartially above all special interests in the body politic. There was a distinct tendency at the time for the nobility to think that only its participation in the government through the forms of constitutional monarchy could guarantee the strict legality of the monarch. And a contrary tendency insisted that no constitutional monarchy guaranteed by a single class could administer the state impartially.[52] Precisely this problem bedeviled the political projects of Paul and the Panins, the Panins seeking constitutional controls over the monarch through a state council formed of the nobility. Paul as monarch solved the problem unambiguously in his own favor, and in so doing, he was entirely in accord with the Physiocrats, to whom we are allegedly indebted for evolving this theory of despotism.

According to Quesnay, *"the sovereign is unique and superior to all the individuals of society and to all the unjust enterprises of the particular interest*; because the aim of governance and obedience is the security of all and separation of powers (*contreforces*) in a government is a sinister idea which only leads to discord among the great and to oppression of the small. The division of society into different orders of citizens, of whom some exercise sovereign authority over others, destroys the general interest of the nation and introduces the dissension of particular interests among the different classes of citizens."[53]

The most authoritative Physiocratic work on statecraft was Pierre Le Mercier de la Rivière's *L'Ordre naturel et essentiel des sociétés politiques* (1764). The book was written in close consultation with Quesnay, and it was, in Adam Smith's opinion, the best statement of the doctrine. The author maintains vehemently that "the legislative power is indivisible . . . it can be exercised neither by the nation *en corps* nor by persons chosen by the nation . . . it is inseparable from the executive

---

52. This point is elaborated, in somewhat opague and turgid prose, in Leonard Krieger, *An Essay on the Theory of Enlightened Despotism* (Chicago: University of Chicago Press, 1975).

53. François Quesnay, *Oeuvres économiques et philosophiques*, August Oncken, ed. (Paris: Jules Peelman & Cie, 1888), pp. 329-331.

power . . . it is exercised by a *Chef unique*, who is only the instrument of nature (*organe de l'évidence*), [and who] does nothing more than reveal by clear signs and arm with coercive force the laws of an order of which God is the Institutor."[54]

Wherever enlightened despots are mentioned, Frederick II is always included among them. Frederick's attitudes toward the division of royal prerogative are no more indefinite than are those of the Physiocrats. He wrote in his political testament (the first one, 1758) that a prince of Prussia could never share power, not even partially, with ministers. A minister's views were, Frederick maintained, always conditioned by his interests. After a considerable disquisition on the subject, he summed up: "By these already overextended details, you will see how important it is that a king of Prussia govern by himself. As little as it would have been possible for Newton to design (*arranger*) his system of gravity if he had worked in concert with Leibniz and Descartes, so little can a system of politics be formed and sustained if it is not done by a single head."[55]

In his exalted notions of his own perogative, Paul was in good company.

A far more satisfactory model of Paul's style of statecraft than that of enlightened despotism--because it is better grounded in the thinking and writing of the time, though it is less heard of in our time--is the idea of the *Polizeistaat*.

According to the closest student of Paul's administration, Klochkov, "the foundation of strong power above, the aspiration to centralization and bureaucratization in administration, the effort at an equalitarian policy in social life--here are, in my opinion, the fundamental points of the governing activity of the time of Paul I."[56] A recent study of the administration of Paul emphasizes similar things. According to John Keep, "Paul's policies of 'militarization' implied the conscious adoption of a foreign model. . . . Paul hoped to copy Frederick's achievement in building a *Polizeistaat* or 'regulated State' in the eighteenth-century understanding of this term: that is to say, he sought to centralize real decision-making power in the autocratic Sovereign, whose will was to be law; to demarcate clearly administrative responsibilities among officials within a hierarchical

54. Pierre Le Mercier de la Rivière, *L'Ordre naturel et essentiel des sociétés politiques* (Paris: Geuttiner, 1910; 1st ed., 1764), p. 50.

55. Frederick II, *Die politische Testamente*, Gustav Berthold Volz, ed. (Berlin: Reimar Hobbing, 1920), pp. 37, 39, 77.

56. Klochkov, *Ocherki*, p. 574.

structure dedicated to the pursuit of efficiency, strict discipline and economy in the use of resources; and to harness all his subjects' energies, within the limits technically possible at the time, to the achievement of certain state-approved tasks."[57]   In the most general terms, that task was, in the phrases of both Paul and legions of political theorists of the age, some of whom have been cited here, the happiness or general well-being of the nation.   It is strange that historians have treated monarchical policy of the era so extensively in terms of the idea of enlightened despotism, as there is nearly no contemporary use of it, and so little in terms of the *Polizeistaat*, which usage is quite well documented.

The term police state in its eighteenth-century context denoted a well-policed state in the most benign sense.   It derives from the old Greek work *politeia*, meaning government and policy, and it came into modern European usage through Latin borrowing of the Greek.   The Germans called it *Polizeistaat* and the French, *état policé*.

It is perhaps best grounded theoretically in the German tradition of cameralism.   According to Johann Heinrich Gottlob von Justi's *Staatwirtschaft* (1755), "all the methods whereby the riches of the state may be increased, in so far as the authority of the government is concerned, belong . . . under the charge of the police . . . the monarchical form of government is far preferable to all others, in consideration of the rapidity with which it can grasp the means of happiness of a state."[58]   The business of using the apparatus of the state as an instrument of maximizing the power of the nation and, consequently, the prosperity of the people was the essence of the cameralists' conception of *Policeywissenschaft*.

As the system applies to the government of Peter the Great, his leading biographer has explained, "The regulated state is the rational state. . . .   In a word: the police is the 'soul of the bourgeoisie' and of all well ordered conditions (*Verhältnisse*)."[59] A student of the Prussian application of the idea says that "the only proper translation of Polizeistaat is 'welfare state.'. . .   By the eighteenth century the word *Polizei* had become synonymous with *Wohlfahrt* or *Gemeine Nutz*.   It implied legislative and ad-

---

57. John Keep, "Paul I and the Militarization of Government," in Ragsdale, *Paul I*, pp. 92-93.

58. Cf. Paul in Chapter 3 above. The quote is from Albion W. Small, *The Cameralists* (Chicago: University of Chicago Press, 1909), pp. 320, 325.

59. Wittram, *Peter I*, 1:126, 157.

ministrative regulation in the private and public life of the civil community in order to establish good order and security and to advance the common good."[60]

The theoretical traditions of the police state were not so strong and explicit in France, but that is essentially what Fénelon described in Book X of *Télémaque*. The work of Colbert fits the idea far better than does the reign of Louis XIV as a whole, which perhaps explains the eclipse of Colbert's work before the reign had run its ruinous course. In any case, Louis's police took themselves and their charge seriously and conceived of their duties much as they were described by the cameralists.[61] One of these policemen, Nicholas de La Mare, wrote a classic treatise on the subject for Louis XV, *Traité de la police*. His motive, he said, was to describe "that good order on which the happiness of states depends" and to contribute thereby to the "public well-being." He treated decent morals; the honor of families; good faith in commerce; control of blasphemy, irreligion, and heresy; public health; sumptuary legislation; gambling; prostitution; astrology; sorcery; and virtually everything imaginable, including "mauvaises filles de joie" and conventional relations between the sexes.[62]

The Abbé St. Pierre is credited with coining the French variation, *bienfaisance*, of the English word commonweal, the German *Wohlfarht*, the Russian *blazhenstvo* (or *blago*), a term very conspicuous in the police state on the continent. That busy man was a constant maker of projects--for perpetual peace, a graduated land tax, diminishing the number of lawsuits, improving schools, reforming spelling, extirpating the Barbary pirates, making dukes and peers socially useful, improving the system of government, raising the emoluments of authors, making roads passable in winter, dealing with beggars, constructing a portable armchair.[63] The good Abbé was at home in the eighteenth century, and he would have been welcome in Paul's Michael Palace.

---

60. Reinhold August Dorwart, *The Prussian Welfare State before 1740* (Cambridge, Mass.: Harvard University Press, 1971), pp. 3, 18.

61. See in particular Jacques Saint-Germain, *La Reynie et la police au grand siècle* (Paris: Hachette, 1962), especially pp. 26-27.

62. Nicholas de la Mare, *Traité de la police*, 2nd ed.   4 vols. (Amsterdam: "aux depens de la Compagnie," 1729-1738), 1:Preface, not paginated.

63. Paul Hazard, *European Thought in the Eighteenth Century from Montesquieu to Lessing* (Cleveland: World Publishing, 1963), pp. 232-233.

The impulse behind the police state has been summed up by Marc Raeff. "The eudaemonism of seventeenth-century cameralism and police contained *in nuce* this notion of general welfare and happiness, only at that time both welfare and happiness were considered to be the means for the attainment of the primary aim of any polity: the maximizing of potential energies to further the power, independence, and influence of the state. What may be called the 'enlightenment amendment' to this conception was the transformation of felicity from a mere instrument of a transcendental political goal into an end to be achieved for its own sake."[64]

One of the primary functions of the police state was to teach civic virtue and civic duty to the citizens. The Physiocrats, especially Le Mercier de la Rivière, emphasized the *autorité tutelaire* a good deal. In the conception of La Mare, "what the tutor is to the pupil, the magistrate is to the citizen."[65] Bogoslovskii has described the universal tutelage of the policy of Peter I and showed how most of his legislation was accompanied by an explanation proving the utility of it.[66]

One of the most important things taught by the police state was, after the fashion which Paul described in his 1788 memorandum, the special duties of the different social classes. As a bishop of France had once put it, the people served the state with their labor, the nobility with its blood, and the clergy with its prayers.[67] Peter explained the concept of duty to his nobility forcefully and institutionalized it in the Table of Ranks. It was a basic idea in Wolff and Vattel. In Frederick's Prussia, the nobility governed the rural areas of the state, supervised the payment of taxes, served in the army, staffed the civil service. The middle class, largely exempt from military service, paid the taxes from which the nobility was largely exempt. The nobles were not entitled to encroach on the industry and commerce of the bourgeois, and most handicraft activity was forbidden outside town limits. The peasants staffed the army and paid heavy

---

64. Marc Raeff, "The Well-Ordered Police State and the Development of Modernity in Seventeenth- and Eighteenth-Century Europe: An Attempt at a Comparative Approach," *American Historical Review* 80:1239 (1975).

65. La Mare, *Traité de la police*, 1:47.

66. M. M. Bogoslovskii, *Oblastnaia reforma Petra Velikago: provintsiia, 1719-1727* (Moscow: OIDR, 1902), pp. 1-14.

67. John Lough, *An Introduction to Seventeenth-Century France* (New York: McKay, 1954), p. 100.

taxes. Frederick protected them from enclosures and from un-usual abuse.[68]

All the scholars who have seriously studied Peter I's pol-icy agree that it drew heavily on western European ideas, pri-marily those of Grotius and Pufendorf, to a lesser extent on those of Hobbes. Peter's frequently used terms *obshchaia pol'za* and *obshchee blago*, common advantage and common good, re-spectively, correspond to the German *Gemeine Nutz* and *Wohlfahrt* and to similar terms current in France and England. The major apologia for Peter's monarchical style, Prokopovich's *Pravda monarshei voli*, exemplifies this debt. The *politsiia do-braia*, benign police, busied themselves with examining the quality of manufactured goods, with the arts, with machines for the fleet and the army, architecture, the cleaning of canals and rivers, the founding of factories, agriculture and gardens, styles of dress and grooming, prostitution, orphans. Paul drew heavily on this tradition.[69]

The whole conception was alive and well generally in the late eighteenth century. Frederick, in his second political tes-tament, observed: "In a well governed state, rules and principles are needed for everything; they are executed by those charged with the powers of the police. This includes the security of trav-elers, the care of the great roads, the bridges, . . . of the post. . . . In addition, the police must take care that there are fair prices for workers, merchants, and others, that no one plays prohibited games, that the Jews do not take excessive usury, that there are no quarrels in the cabarets."[70]

About the same time, Maria Theresa inquired of the Paris police through her ambassador how they maintained such an admirable system. They replied in a memorandum, full of pride,

---

68. Gerhard Ritter, *Frederick the Great: A Historical Profile*, Peter Paret, tr. (Berkeley: University of California Press, 1968), pp. 159-163.

69. See especially Bogoslovskii, *Oblastnaia reforma*, pp. 1-14; Wit-tram, *Peter I*, passim; A. Lappo-Danilevskij, "L'idée du l'état et son évolution en Russie depuis les troubles du XVII siècle jusqu'aux réformes du XVIII," in Paul Vinogradoff, ed., *Essays in Legal History* (London: Oxford University Press, 1913), pp. 356-383; Nikolai M. Druzhinin, "Prosveshchennyi absoliu-tizm v Rossii," in N. M. Duzhinin, ed., *Absoliutizm v Rossii (XVII-XVIII vv.)* (Moscow: Nauka, 1964), pp. 428-459; Nikolai I. Pavlenko, "Idei absoliutizma v zakonodatel'stve XVIII v.," in ibid., pp. 389-427; Nikolai I. Pavlenko, "Petr I: k izucheniiu sotsial'no-politicheskikh vzgliadov," in *Rossiia v period reform Pe-tra I*, pp. 40-102. For a general treatment of the police state, see Kurt Wolzendorff, *Der Polizeigedanke des modernen Staats* (Breslau: Marcus, 1918).

70. Frederick II, *Die politische Testamente*, pp. 182-183.

that runs to 131 printed pages. It indicates that what they presumed to do in Paris in 1770 was much like their plan of a hundred years earlier. They took care of religion, discipline, health, food supplies, communication, security, arts and sciences, commerce, manufacturing, servants, the poor. If all goes well in Paris every day, they claimed, "it is owing to the Prefecture of the Police."[71]

This is what the police state aspired to do and to be. The Austrians wanted to imitate the French, and the police statutes of 1726 in Prussia and of 1721 and 1782 in Russia indicated that in this respect, the Russians did not intend to lag behind. Of course, both the refinement and comprehension of the concept and the aspirations to complete benign control totally outdistanced the technical capacity of the communications of the time to allow the realization of the aims of the police state.

Paul's conception of his role as autocrat of the *Polizeistaat* reflects the common thought of the age. It was what many of the advanced writers of Germany and France were saying. It was, in the main, what he was taught by the Panins. Paul's own writing on the subject reflects, to paraphrase Pope, what oft was thought as well as better expressed. His policies illustrate the literal nature of his convictions. He differs in one important way from the other ambitious progressive autocrats of his day: he did not allow for the derogation of ordinary humans from the high-flown principles of the age. And even in this, he had peers--such as Joseph II of Austria--who were not mad.

---

71. Jean-Baptiste-Charles Le Maire, "La Police de Paris en 1770," *Mémoires de la Société de l'histoire de Paris et de l'Ile-de-France*, 51 vols. (Paris: Champion, 1875-1930), 5:1 and passim.

6

THE DIAGNOSIS AND TREATMENT OF MADNESS IN PAUL'S TIME

The preceding chapter shows that Paul's ideas and values were in no way unusual in the age in which he lived, and thus there are no grounds on this basis for believing that he was mad. In this chapter, I am concerned to examine the question of his madness from another point of view, that of the more specialized criteria of the medical science of psychiatry of his time. How did the medical men of the late eighteenth century define madness, and how did they treat it once it was identified?

One of the most prominent diagnostic manuals of the time was the *Nosologie méthodique* of François Boissier de Sauvages de la Croix. According to reputable eighteenth-century medical history, "Nosology owes its greatest debt to . . . Sauvages."[1] Sauvages cites much learned literature, especially from the classical authors, and exhibits a real passion to give a comprehensive survey of his subject. He supplies a

_____

1. Lester S. King, *The Medical World of the Eighteenth Century* (Chicago: University of Chicago Press, 1958), p. 205.

great plethora of subdivisions of all the categories of mental illness. The terminology that he uses is typical of the age, though the definitions of the terms differ significantly from author to author.

Judging by his summary classification of mental disease, the category most likely to be of interest in Paul's case is Sauvages's "huitième classe: des Folies," especially "Ordre III: Délires." *Folies* are described as "an illness of the spirit, an error of the imagination, of the desires, and of the judgment: an aberration, a caprice, or a delirium." *Délires* are "errors of judgment caused by damage in the brain."[2]   There are three kinds that might prove of interest in Paul's case.

Démence is "a gentle, continual delirium, without fury, without temerity, with an illness of long duration." "This illness is an inaptitude to reason and judge well." Persons so afflicted do not perceive objects in their environment correctly. They are morose, inattentive, indifferent, apparently stupid, childish, and frivolous, and given to playing with toys.[3]   It seems evident that Paul did not have so serious a derangement as this one.

Mélancholie is "a gentle and particular delirium, with fretfulness, and an illness of duration. . . .   Melancholics are constantly attached to a single thought, are in delirium about themselves [sic], and about their condition, such that they reason properly about all other things." Many of them are sad and depressed, but others are quite happy.   Melancholics make sense on many subjects, unlike maniacs, who rave about everything whatever. "Melancholics do not reason badly; but they often draw correct conclusions from a false principle to which they adhere. The novel *Don Quixote* . . . furnishes a remarkable example of melancholia. The origin of this disease comes from the fixed and constant attention which is paid to [a single] idea, while neglecting others; wherefore it happens that the free actions [sic: *actions libres*] do not correspond to the circumstances, as in the case of a sane person; but to an object the idea of which captures the imagination entirely." The melancholic is extremely introspective, constantly monitoring his own inner condition.   Melancholics are often characterized by excessive religiosity. They are hermits, ascetics, celibates.

Sauvages lists a bewildering and inadvertently amusing variety of melancholic afflictions, *mélancholie ordinaire, mélan-*

---

2. François Boissier de Sauvages, *Nosologie méthodique*, 3 vols. (Paris: Hérissant, 1770-1771), 3:587-588.

3. Ibid., pp. 588, 723-727.

cholie amoureuse (Quixote), *mélancholie d'imagination, mélancholie extravagante,* as well as *vagabonde, dansante, hyppanthropique* (grandeur), *de Scythes* (transvestism), *angloise* (boredom!), and others.[4]

It is difficult to know how to apply Sauvages's criteria of melancholia in view of the enormous variety of manifestations of the problem, which allows for a great many personality types. If we return to the definition given of the syndrome as a whole and concentrate on what would appear to be the most general and pervasive characteristic of it, introspection and inactivity, then it is clear that Paul does not belong to this category. He was not a withdrawn person. In spite of his difficulties in getting along with people, in establishing normal, trusting relations with them, he was never reclusive.

This leaves us with *manie,* "a universal delirium with fury, intrepidity, and a durable illness." "It is a kind of chronic illness without fever, which makes the patients talk nonsensically about all subjects, because of a flaw in their imagination. . . . Mania differs from melancholia in the universality of the delirium." Maniacs become upset about everything whatever. They often refuse all food and drink and yet do not lose their strength. They rarely sleep, they endure extraordinary heat and cold indifferently, and they may go nude in winter.[5]

The mismatch of this definition and Paul's behavior is clear and total. In fact, by reference to the criteria and terminology of Sauvages, we are compelled to conclude that Paul was not mad. Before insisting too much on the point, however, we ought to examine other medical opinion of the time.

One of the standard and very influential medical textbooks of the period was William Cullen's *First Lines of the Practice of Physic* (1784). Cullen was a prominent professor at the University of Edinburgh and, moreover, David Hume's physician.[6] He objected to the quest for ever subtler refinements and subdivisions of diagnostic categories, finding such complex classifications in the work of his predecessors to be lacking in clarity. Consequently, he concentrated his attention on three forms of mental illness--delirium, mania, and melancholia--and these three he explored more thoroughly than many of his peers did.[7]

---

4. Ibid., pp. 588, 727-737.

5. Ibid., pp. 588, 745-750.

6. William Cullen, *First Lines of the Practice of Physic,* 4 vols. (Edinburgh: Elliott, 1784).

7. Ibid., 4:141-143.

Delirium was "a false or mistaken judgment of those relations of things, which, as occurring most frequently in life, are
those about which the generality of men form the same judgment." There were three very particular symptoms of delirium.
First, "false perception of external objects, without any evident
fault in the organs of sense, and which seems therefore to depend upon an internal cause; that is, upon the imagination
arising from a condition in the brain presenting objects which
are not actually present." Second, "a very unusual association
of ideas. As, with respect to most of the affairs of common life,
the ideas laid up in the memory are, in most men, associated in
the same manner; so a very unusual association, in any individual, must prevent his forming the ordinary judgment of those
relations which are the most common foundation of association
in the memory." Third, "an emotion or passion, sometimes of
the angry, sometimes of the timid kind; and from whatever
cause in the perception or judgment, it is not proportional to
such cause, either in the manner formerly customary to the person himself, or in the manner usual with the generality of other
men."[8]

Does this describe Paul? In some respects, it does not.
For example, Paul was not given to false perceptions of objects.
In addition, as the preceding chapter was concerned to show, he
was not characterized by an unusual association of ideas, but
rather by a very ordinary association of the ideas common to his
time and station. In some respects, on the other hand, the
problem is a subtler one, particularly in reference to angry passions disproportionate to their apparent cause. But on this
point especially, Paul must not be judged like the "generality of
other men," for he did not belong to such a social category. He
was an emperor, and he must be judged by standards characteristic of his peers, who constitute the appropriate control
group. If we recall the experience of Gustav III and Gustav IV
Adolf of Sweden or of Joseph II of Austria, we can at least see
examples of other irascible monarchs of the age who sometimes
lost their patience and whose headstrong behavior became a
burden to their subjects.[9] By Cullen's criteria, the case for
Paul's delirium is extremely doubtful.

Cullen describes mania as a "false perception or imagination of things present that are not; but this is not a constant,

8. Ibid., pp. 116-119.

9. For some especially pertinent examples, see Paul Bernard, *The
Limits of Enlightenment: Joseph II and the Law* (Urbana: University of Illinois
Press, 1979).

or even a frequent attendant of the disease. The false judgment is of relations long before laid up in the memory. It very often turns upon one single object: but more commonly the mind rambles from one subject to another, with an equally false judgment concerning the most part of them; . . . what for the most part more especially distinguishes the disease, is a hurry of mind, in pursuing any thing like a train of thought, and in running from one thought to another. Maniacal persons are in general very irascible." Their false judgments lead them to actions of "impetuosity & violence; when this is interrupted or restrained, they break out into violent anger and furious violence against every person near them." Finally, Cullen adds, very significantly, "the disease must be attended very constantly with that incoherent and absurd speech we call raving."[10]

Unfortunately, Cullen's definition of mania does not distinguish it clearly from his definition of delirium. In both cases, he speaks of a false perception of objects (or "things present that are not"). In both cases, he refers to a confused association of ideas "laid up in the memory," using virtually the same words and phrases in the two cases. In the one case as in the other, there is volatile and impetuous anger. The two definitions overlap so much as to warrant the conclusion that a personality that does not qualify for one diagnosis does not qualify for the other, and this is not very helpful. Of the few particulars in the complex of manic symptoms that are not shared by delirious persons, one of them, a "hurry of mind," was distinctly characteristic of Paul in childhood, but it did not incapacitate him as an adult such that he ran incoherently from "one thought to another." Moreover, it is quite clear that Paul did not engage in "incoherent and absurd speech" called raving. All things considered, Cullen's definition of mania is not very satisfactory, and it does not closely describe Paul.

The definition of melancholia is clearer. "The disease which I name Melancholia is very often a partial insanity only. But as in many instances, though the false imagination or judgment seems to be with respect to one subject only; yet it seldom happens that this does not produce much inconsistency in the other intellectual operations." It is "always attended with some seemingly groundless, but very anxious, fear." Melancholics give especially close attention "to one particular object,

---

10. Cullen, *First Lines of the Practice of Physic*, 4:144-146.

or train of thinking. They are even ready to be engaged in a constant application to one subject."[11]

This is a relatively trouble-free definition, and it has the merit of agreeing with part of Sauvages's description of melancholia. The difficulty of applying it to Paul, however, is considerable. How might we choose a particular "one subject only" which reflected his false imagination or judgment? He was much concerned with Stoic virtue, with the threat of the French Revolution, with issues of international and social peace, as well as with the ideals of genuine service on the part of the Russian nobility. He exhibited much anxiety, if not actual fear, in respect to some of these things, but it would be difficult, given his political position, to make the case that these anxieties were abnormal. Rather, they would seem to have been a natural part of his job description.

One of the diagnostic classifications of the time is from a somewhat surprising source. In 1798, Immanuel Kant published an account of the problem in one of his lesser known works, *Anthropology from a Pragmatic Point of View*. Kant distinguished four kinds of mental illness.[12]

Amentia was "the inability to bring ideas into mere coherence necessary for the possibility of experience." Paul did not have unusual problems of coherence. *Dementia* was "that disturbance of the mind, wherein everything which the insane person relates, is in accord with the possibility of an experience, and indeed with the formal laws of thought; but, because of false inventive imagination, self-concocted ideas are treated as if they were perceptions. Those who believe they are everywhere surrounded by enemies, and those who regard all glances, words, and otherwise indifferent actions of others as directed against them personally and as traps set for them belong to this category."

Paul evidently does not belong here. What he was most suspicious of was derogation from the standards of virtue, especially on the part of the Russian nobility. It was not primarily designs against himself that he remarked, but rather negligence, corruption, and lack of dedication in state service. He obviously did not take too many precautions to secure his own safety but, on the contrary, too few.

---

11. Ibid., pp. 174-178.

12. Immanuel Kant, *Anthropology from a Pragmatic Point of View*, Victor Lyle Dowdell, tr. Hans H. Rudnick, ed. (Carbondale: Southern Illinois University Press, 1978), pp. 108-117.

Kant's third category is too vaguely defined to be of much use. *Insania*, he said, "is disordered faculty of judgment in which the mind is deceived by analogies, which are being confused with concepts of similar things, so that the imagination offers dissimilar objects as similar and universal ones in a process resembling that of the understanding. Mental patients of this type are usually very cheerful; they write insipid verse and take pleasure in the richness of what, in their opinion, is such an extensive realm of analogous concepts."

Vesania, on the other hand, is sufficiently defined, but it is clearly not applicable to our subject. It is "the sickness of a disordered reason. The patient disregards all the facts of experience and aspires to the principles which can be entirely exempted from the test of experience. Such a patient fancies that he comprehends the incomprehensible, and that such things as the invention of a method for squaring the circle, perpetual motion, the unveiling of the transcendental forces of Nature, and the comprehension of the mystery of the Trinity are all within his power."

Finally, Kant has a concluding comment which is genuinely useful, and in this he substantially agrees with Cullen: the "only general characteristic of insanity is the loss of a sense for ideas that are common to all (*sensus communis*), and its replacement with a sense for ideas peculiar to ourselves (*sensus privatus*); for example, . . . a man . . . hears a voice which no one else hears." This is the clearest thought which Kant has to offer. We have seen in the preceding chapter that Paul's ideas were, if not common to all, demonstrably characteristic of his age; and with the exception of one very dubious story of a hallucinatory conversation with Peter I, there was no evidence in him of what Kant calls the *sensus privatus*.

Our last and perhaps most important authority is Philippe Pinel. Pinel was active during Paul's lifetime; he had enormous experience in dealing with mental illness; and he was the only physician cited here who specialized in such illness. He became the administrator of the French mental hospital (or detention center) for men, the Bicêtre, in 1793, and of the women's hospital, the Salpêtrière, in 1795. He had a brilliant reputation. He was soon to become the most influential reformer-modernizer of mental hospitals in his time.[13]

Among the symptoms of melancholia, according to Pinel, were a leaden face, a thin body, an irascible character, a suspi-

---

13. Philippe Pinel, *Nosographie philosophique*,   3rd ed.   3 vols. (Paris: Brosson, 1807).

cious defiance, a slow pulse, and sleep agitated by terrors. The melancholic was constantly tormented by singular ideas or possessed by an extreme and dominant passion. Melancholics "have a marked inclination for inactivity and the sedentary life. But the affections of the soul are capable of the greatest violence; love is transported to delirium, piety to fanaticism, anger to a frenetic fury, the desire for vengeance to the most barbarous cruelty. They join an ardent and profound pursuit of an idolized object with the most inconstant volatility in reference to what is alien to them; a somber taciturnity alternates with lively gaiety of an almost convulsive kind. It consists in a lesion of the intellectual and affective functions; which is to say that the melancholic is as if possessed by an exclusive idea or a particular series of ideas with a dominant passion."[14] The behaviors here described, both the fugue and the frenzy, are more extreme than we have observed in Paul's case.

Mania was characterized in Pinel's experience by tension in the stomach, distaste for food, stubborn constipation, agitation, panic, insomnia, fixed staring at the sky, speaking in a very low voice, profound meditation during walks, occasional immoderate laughing, somber taciturnity, unprovoked crying, and extreme anguish. Manics frequently had delusions of grandeur and imagined themselves monarchs and conquerors. Mania occurred either with or without delirium. In the latter case, it might manifest no derangement of understanding, perception, judgment, imagination, or memory, only a perversion of the affective functions, such as blind impulses to acts of violence. In delirious cases, there were serious, even extravagant, malfunctions of judgment. A patient might say: "I am God, I am father of the universe, all of you are my children; give me eau-de-Cologne, let's make a deal, everything will be all right." Patients of this type imagine themselves monarchs or generals and harbor plans of making machines of perpetual motion.[15] This personality type also appears too extreme for the historical personality of Paul.

Finally, there was *démence*, characterized by a "turbulent and irrepressible volatility, a rapid and instantaneous succession of ideas that seem to be born and to multiply in the consciousness without any [external] impression on the senses; a constant and ridiculous flux and reflux of chimerical ideas that collide, alternate with and annihilate each other . . . , the same

---

14. Ibid., 3:91-92.

15. Ibid., pp. 98-112.

tumultuous course of emotions and of moral affections, of sentiments of joy, of sadness, of anger, which are born haphazardly and disappear in the same way . . . without having any resemblance to the forms of external objects. . . ."[16] This condition, too, is much more extravagant than the behavior that we have been reviewing in Paul.

By the psychiatric criteria of his age, then, Paul does not appear to have been mad. Still, his behavior was volatile, impulsive, and sometimes violent, and he was clearly a burden to a certain sector of the service class about him. Perhaps, unacquainted with the specialized medical literature of the age, which would be natural enough, the conspirators jumped to conclusions through overexposure to his behavior and mistakenly judged him mad. In order to test this idea, it is necessary to look at the way in which psychiatric cases were handled in the late eighteenth century and then to see if Paul's case was handled in the same way.

In early modern Europe, attitudes embodying respect for the "wisdom of the fool" were not uncommon--viz. *The Praise of Folly, Don Quixote,* the idea of the *Narrenschiff,* the *Fête des fous*[17]--but the Russian variation on this theme was perhaps unique. Madness or feeble-mindedness was traditionally regarded by the Russians after the fashion of St. Paul in the first letter to the Corinthians; that is, it was considered an especially inspired, childish form of wisdom, "foolishness in Christ" ("ibo mudrost' mira cego est' bezumie pred Bogom"; "My bezumny Khrista radi"). This phenomenon was known as "iurodstvo" and the person exemplifying it as a "iurodivyi." It is seen in the characters of Nikolka in Pushkin's play and of Ivanych in Mussorgsky's opera *Boris Godunov.* Prince Myshkin is a more modern evocation of it in Dostoevsky's *The Idiot.* Russians characteristically looked upon such persons with respect if not with reverence. The last Russian sovereign who was so honored was Fedor I (Fedor Ivanovich, 1584-1598), known as Fedor "the Bell-Ringer" because he wandered about Moscow ringing church bells rather than attending to affairs of state.

If Paul had been clearly mad or feeble-minded, he might well have been regarded by the Russian masses with special sympathy or favor on that account; and though there is some sign that he was so regarded, the reasons have to do with what

---

16. Ibid., pp. 122-125.

17. See Walter Kaiser, "Wisdom of the Fool," *Dictionary of the History of Ideas,* Philip P. Wiener, ed. 5 vols. (New York: Charles Scribner's Sons, 1973), 4:515-520.

was identifiably populist and anti-aristocratic in his policy. But there is no likelihood that the reaction of Paul's courtiers reflected notions of *iurodstvo*, as it was simply not a viable concept among the cosmopolites of St. Petersburg late in the eighteenth century. Rather, attitudes toward madness at the Russian court reflected the standards of modern educated Europeans who were schooled in the Enlightenment.

There was a very substantial interest in abnormal psychology in Europe in the late eighteenth century, and consequently there is an abundance of literature on it. It seems fair to say, by way of summary, that there were four kinds of characteristic treatment of madness in that age. The first was confinement. John Haslam, apothecary of Bethlehem Hospital (Bedlam) and author of one of the standard psychiatric works of the era, explained the uses of confinement in typical fashion. "From long established practice, there has been an usual association between BEING MAD, and confinement in a MADHOUSE. That insanity is a disease, which for its cure, and also for the prevention of mischief, ordinarily requires seclusion, must be admitted."[18] Confinement was virtually a first principle of the handling and treatment of the insane, and it was universally recommended by physicians treating the problem.

A second approach was restraint. Presumably designed in part to prevent the insane from hurting themselves or others, in part to make it easier to manage them, restraint was also considered therapeutic. Inmates of madhouses were commonly chained, and they were frequently restrained by the use of what at that time was called the "strait waistcoat," what we know today as the straitjacket.

A third approach was the ministration of medicine such as opium, iron, bitters, or elixir of vitriol, or forms of treatment presumed to be medical, including warm baths, bleeding, purging, induced vomiting, prescribed diets, and immersion in cold water, especially by surprise.[19]

---

18. John Haslam, *Considerations on the Moral Management of Insane Persons* (London: Hunter, 1817), p. 13.

19. See Michel Foucault, *Madness and Civilization: A History of Insanity in the Age of Reason*, Richard Howard, tr. (New York: Pantheon, 1965), pp. 159ff. Haslam, *Considerations on the Moral Management of Insane Persons*, pp. 2-3, 122ff., 136ff. Michael Deporte, *Nightmares and Hobby Horses: Swift, Sterne and Augustan Ideas of Madness* (San Marino: Huntington Library, 1974), p. 5. Samuel Tuke, *Description of the Retreat: an Institution near York for Insane Persons of the Society of Friends*, Richard Hunter and Ida Macalpine, eds. Reprint of 1st 1813 ed. (London: Dawsons, 1964), ch. 4, passim.

The fourth approach, something new and progressive, the trend of the future, was simply kindness, a more benign regimen than had been characteristic in the past or was characteristic in most madhouses of that time. The two champions of this movement were Samuel Tuke in England and Philippe Pinel in France. Pinel's work is better known, probably because he wrote more, and more theoretically. They were chiefly concerned to stop the savage torments that passed for treatment in many of these institutions and to limit the measures of restraint as much as was consonant with the keeping of good order.[20] Still, it must be pointed out that their sturdy attack on medical barbarism, and on restraint in particular, did not extend to the practice of confinement, which they continued to think essential to problems of "moral management" of the mentally ill.

This was the characteristic outlook on mental illness in the St. Petersburg of Paul's time. During the second half of the eighteenth century, the process of Westernization which Peter I either inaugurated or dramatically catalyzed entailed incorporating the western European view of health and medicine, including mental health. There were ten times more physicians in Russia in 1802 than in 1700 (though nearly half were in military service).[21] Medical and psychiatric textbooks available in Russia were either imports or Russian translations of western European textbooks.[22] Scientific medicine in Russia had long been dependent on the presence of relatively large numbers of physicians imported from western Europe. Peter I changed only the scale of this practice. Throughout the eighteenth century, foreigners dominated Russian medicine, and to employ a native Russian, with a Russian education, as court physician in this age was

---

20. Tuke, *Description of the Retreat.* Philippe Pinel, *Traité médico-philosophique sur l'aliénation mentale*, 2nd ed. (Paris: Brosson, 1809).

21. Heinz E. Müller-Dietz, *Ärtze in Russland des achtzehnten Jahrhunderts* (Esslinger: Neckar, 1973), p. 16.

22. François Amédée Doppet, *Vrach filosof* (Moscow: Universitetskaia tipografiia, 1792). Matvei Khristianovich Peken, *Nachal'nyia osnovaniia deiatel'nyia vrachebnyia nauki* (St. Petersburg: Sukhoputnyi kadetskii korpus, 1790). Georg Friedrich Meyer, *Opyt o lunatikakh, sochinennoi publichnago ucheniia filosofii, i Korolevskoi Akademii nauk v Berline chlenom Georg Friedrich Meyer* (Moscow: Universitetskaia tipografiia, 1764). Johann Daniel Metzger, *Nachal'nyia osnovaniia vseobshchikh chastei vrachebnyia nauki* (St. Petersburg: Gosudarstvennyi meditsinskii kolledzh, 1799). August Gottlieb Richter, *Nachal'nyia osnovaniia rukovoditel'nyia vrachebnyia nauki*, 3 vols. (St. Petersburg: Sukhoputnyi kadetskii korpus, 1791-1795). Simon André Tissot, *Vrach svetskikh liudei* (Moscow: Tip. kompanii tipograficheskoi, 1792).

simply inconceivable.   Even the institutions which would eventually become native and self-sustaining were under foreign
tutelage in the eighteenth century.   Moscow University was
opened in 1755 and acquired a medical school in 1764.   In St.
Petersburg, the Medical and Surgical Academy was opened in
1798.   In the meantime, development in psychiatric facilities
followed the lead of the more general medical institutions.   In
1762, a madhouse was established in St. Petersburg and another in Novgorod.   In the 1770s, asylums for the mentally retarded began to be established, and by the century's end, there
were such institutions in thirteen Russian provinces.[23]   Still,
during Paul's reign, the medical and psychiatric establishments
of St. Petersburg were very much a foreigner's domain, and the
thinking about madness was consonant with that of western
Europe.[24]

(Paul himself had one interesting experience associated
with Russian madhouses and madmen.   One such institution
housed a curious fellow named Kondratii Selivanov, who be-
longed to that strange Russian tradition of "samozvanstvo,"
which is to say that he claimed to be or was regarded as the true
tsar, in this case Tsar Peter III, Paul's father.   In addition, he
was the founder, in the early 1770s, of a group of religious sec-
tarians knows as the *skoptsy*, or castrati.   Paul somehow heard
of him and summoned him for an interview.   Paul is supposed to
have asked him, "Are you my father?" and Selivanov is said to
have replied, "Unfortunately, I am not your father, but if you will
follow my example, I will recognize you as my son."   Evidently,
Selivanov's example did not appeal to Paul, and the tsar ordered
him to be returned to the madhouse.   Alexander I repeated this
royal interview with Selivanov in 1805.)[25]

The question whether Russian practice reflected the new
trends supported by Pinel and Tuke aside, it seems safe to conclude that of the four major psychiatric approaches characteristic of medical practice in western Europe, three--confinement,
restraint, and medicine--were characteristic of the Russian cap-

---

23. See Brokgaus-Efron *Entsiklopedicheskii slovar'*, 21:281, and Ia.
A. Chistovich, *Istoriia pervykh meditsinskikh shkol v Rossii* (St. Petersburg:
Trei, 1883), pp. 569-570.

24. On the question how nearly Russian medical and psychiatric
practice followed in this period in the wake of western Europe, see Kenneth S.
Dix, *Madness in Russia, 1775-1864: Official Attitudes and Institutions for its
Care* (Los Angeles: Ph. D. dissertation, University of California, Los Angeles,
1977), esp. pp. 38-44, 63-103.

25. N. V. Reutskii, *Liudi Bozh'i i skoptsy* (Moscow: Grakov, 1872).

ital as well. Nowhere in western Europe or in Russia at that time was murder prescribed for madness. That is to say, the suggestion that Paul was mad suffers a great deal from the fact that he was not handled by the standards applied to mad persons in that age.

Now, there would seem to be one conceivable objection to this line of argument, and it is that the manuals of medical and psychiatric practice prescribed for, and the madhouses were established for, persons ordinarily of sub-royal stations in society. Paul, so the argument would go, was not an ordinary person: he was too majestic and powerful to be a candidate, therefore, for the ordinary rules of confinement and restraint. This may well be a pertinent objection, and there is a convenient way of discovering whether it is. We must simply compare the fate of other mad sovereigns of Paul's time.

What we need to know about these people is, first, were they subjected to the usual regimen of confinement, restraint, and medication? Second, what arrangements were made to replace them with other persons having the authority to govern once it was recognized that they lacked the capacity to do so? Third, how many of them were murdered?

The case that we know the most about is that of George III of Great Britain (1760-1820). George was a more prominent monarch than some of the kinglets and princelets in lesser countries, and as his illness became well known, it considerably increased the interest of the educated English public in psychiatric questions. But it seems clear that there already existed in Britain before George's illness more interest in mental disease than elsewhere in the world, or at least elsewhere in Europe. The psychiatric literature of the age is overwhelmingly English, and this is probably explained by the fact that both English and other writers clearly believed that the incidence of mental illness--or, to be more precise, of melancholy--was greater in Britain than elsewhere. In *that* age, the "English malady," or *maladie anglaise*, was usually understood to be "spleen" or "hyp," hypochondriasis. The problem was commonly attributed to the frightful climate of the British Isles, although occasionally it was attributed to the English diet.[26] In any event, George's case was conspicuous and politically important, and it attracted a great deal of medical--and other--attention.

---

26. See, for example, in addition to the works cited above, John Haslam, *Observations on Insanity* (London: Rivington, 1798), p. vii; Thomas Arnold, *Observations on the Nature, Kinds, Causes and Prevention of Insanity*, 2 vols. (London: Phillips, 1806), 1:15.

The first of George's several episodes of derangement was in 1788.[27] He developed severe stomach pains, had chronic insomnia, talked rapidly and incessantly for long periods (up to 19 hours), perspired profusely, and was frequently delirious and occasionally dangerously violent. A variety of physicians were called, and they were plainly puzzled. It is clear, however, that he was subjected to restraint relatively early. He was swaddled in a constricting fashion. He did not like it, and it seemed to aggravate his agitation. Nevertheless, he was soon put into a strait waistcoat. In the meantime, he was given various opiates to calm him, but to no avail.

The patient was at this time under the care of seven consulting physicians. In November 1788, they decided that his condition warranted confinement. By this time, the cabinet was involved in most of the consultations on the king's health, and Pitt in particular assisted in the difficult decision to transfer him from Windsor to Kew--difficult because George did not want to go and consented only with the utmost reluctance.

It was at Kew that the subsequently famous Dr. Francis Willis was called for the first time. Dr. Willis was a clergyman and a physician, and he had served for a long time as director of a madhouse in Lincolnshire. He brought his sons, also physicians, to assist. Though he did not possess the social prominence of some of the colleagues whom he joined at Kew, and he was not a member of the Royal College of Physicians, as some of them were, he soon established his ascendance over them, and he was the physician who was to be credited with the curing of the king. There are two features of special interest in his work.

The first is that his coming quickly rendered the crisis as political as it was medical. It was in great part owing to his optimistic prognosis and his very sanguine medical bulletins that the government came to prefer him to his predecessors. The Opposition had obvious interests in disturbing the stability of the government as composed, as did the Prince of Wales. There was much disagreement and jealousy among the attending physicians, and the medical bulletins were actually negotiated among them. Dr. Richard Warren served the Opposition as Dr. Willis served the government. In the meantime, a Regency Bill was written and debated, and had the illness lasted a bit longer, it would probably have been voted.

---

27. The following account is based on Ida Macalpine and Richard Hunter, *George III and the Mad-Business* (New York: Pantheon, 1969), pp. 1-164.

More important for our interest, more pertinent with respect to the case of Paul, Dr. Willis brought to the problem a medical approach that was traditional, old-school, no-nonsense, severe, and authoritarian. Restraint had been used early, and confinement had been accomplished before he arrived on the scene. He approved of both, and with a vengeance. Under his regimen, the king was not generally allowed to see the queen, and he was attended at all times. Dr. Willis put George in the strait waistcoat frequently, though not constantly, sometimes leaving him in it through the night. In addition, George was sometimes put into a restraining chair, and he was sometimes tied to the bed. When he became abusive and obscene, he was gagged.

As for medical treatment, Dr. Willis prescribed cupping and blistering on the king's legs, the theory of the time holding that noxious humors would thus be drawn out of the patient's body. Leeches were applied to his temples with the same intention. He was also given calumel pills, quinine, digitalis, castor oil, purges, and--especially frequently--tartar emetic.

By the end of February 1789, the king was declared cured. The illness returned in February 1801, but this time it was less violent and of shorter duration. On this occasion, he was treated by the sons of Dr. Francis Willis, Drs. Thomas, John, and Robert Darling Willis. Their treatment was a repetition of the regimen of their father. There was another recurrence in 1804 and another in 1810. The last episode proved to be permanent, and on 31 January 1811, the Regency Bill was passed, effectively ending the reign of George III. George spent the remainder of his life under the close medical regimen of the Willises, though it was subjected to much criticism by physicians recommending a more liberal dispensation. He died in 1820.

The admirable research of Macalpine and Hunter has led them to the conclusion that George suffered a rare hereditable disease of the nervous system called porphyria,[28] and they have examined both his case history and the family history in some detail in support of their argument. Their conclusions are by no means generally accepted, but the uncertainty of their particular

---

28. Ibid., pp. 172-175. See also the thoughtful comments of John Brooke, *King George III* (New York: McGraw-Hill, 1972), pp. 339-341. As Brooke correctly points out, the value of the work of Macalpine and Hunter "is independent of the diagnosis of prophyria. Even if it could be proved that this diagnosis is wrong, this would not diminish the value of the book as the only scholarly account of the King's illness." Ibid., p. 399, n. 1 for ch. 8.

diagnosis does not cause difficulties for the problem posed here. It is not our business to decide here what kind of illness George III had. Rather, it is to illustrate how the society of the time responded to the problem of a monarch generally admitted to be mad. We may draw two useful conclusions from his case. George was unambiguously out of his mind, far more deranged than Paul was; and second, monarch though he was, he was not treated as an exception to the rules. Rather, his treatment was a pure and rigid classic of the rules of the age: confinement, restraint, and medical ministration.

The medical aspects of the case of Maria I of Portugal (1777-1792) were remarkably similar to those of the case of George III. She succeeded to the Portuguese throne at a difficult moment and handled herself for a time with admirable aplomb. The reign of her father, Joseph I, had been dominated by his reforming minister, the Marquess de Pombal, who left a legacy of progressive politics and social discontent. Pombal had operated an oppressive, if enlightened, despotism. He had, in a fashion typical of that model of statecraft, alienated the church and the nobility. The Inquisition had been made subject to review at court, the Jesuits had been expelled, education had been advanced, and a thoroughgoing absolutism had been asserted. The nobility grew restless, and there was in 1758 a conspiracy against the king's life. It was broken up by Pombal, and several of the conspirators were executed.

Maria dismissed Pombal, who was tried and condemned. She intervened to pardon him, however, and he was exiled to his estate with a pension. She amnestied his political prisoners and recalled all exiles except the Jesuits. She relinquished the form and some of the substance of absolutism, and her rule soon calmed the more alarming manifestations of discontent among the nobility. She had long, however, evinced a tendency toward religious mania, and when Pedro IV, her husband, consort, and uncle, died in 1786, and the heir Prince Joseph died in 1788, Maria retreated into uncontrollable grief and melancholy. Early in 1792, her ministers recognized her as mad.

She was afflicted by stomach pains, depression, fever, insomnia, and "nervous affections." An assembly of physicians was convened and asked whether there were prospects of improvement and whether she should be allowed to continue in charge of the government. They said no to both questions, so the ministers turned on 10 February 1792 to her second son with the urgent request that he "assume the direction of public affairs." He did so as King Joao VI.

In the meantime, on 4 February, the Portuguese minister in London, Cipriano Ribeiro Freire, was instructed to press the famous Dr. Francis Willis, well known in Lisbon for his cure of George III, to come to Portugal at once in order to treat Maria. The Portuguese government assured Dr. Willis that it would spare no expense to secure his services, and it did not.

Dr. Willis demurred. He was 73 years old, and he was not eager to go to Lisbon (he died in December 1807, nearly 90 years old). Nevertheless, he eventually agreed to go for a hand-some fee. He was paid 10,000 pounds sterling for this long-distance house call, plus all his maintenance and expenses while there, plus the expenses of the trip, and 1,000 pounds a month for the duration of his stay. He departed Falmouth 8 March 1792, arrived in Lisbon 15 March, and saw Maria the next day. His first impression was, as previously in the case of George III, optimistic. I can discover no record of the details of the treatment, but it seems reasonable to assume that it dupli-cated the one that had brought him such fame in the case of George III. Maria showed some early signs of improvement, but they did not long continue. She soon took a turn for the worse, and Dr. Willis wanted to transfer her to England, presumably to his clinic there. Maria was much against it, and the government did not consent to her going. Dr. Willis left Portugal in August 1793 without realizing any improvement in the patient's condi-tion. Maria left Portugal for Brazil with her family in the face of the French attack in November 1807, and she died in Rio in 1816.[29]

The reign of Christian VII of Denmark (1766-1808) is perhaps best remembered for the improbable adventures of Friedrich Struensée. Struensée was a German physician who insinuated himself indispensably into the gap between king and country created by Christian's utter indifference to politics. Christian was as cold to the queen as he was to government, and Struensée stepped into this gap, too. Caroline Mathilda, a daughter of George III, was pathetically lonely, and she sought solace in the medical and other ministrations of Struensée. There followed a passionate love affair, which she had the im-prudence virtually to advertise. She bore him two children, as all the world realized. And so Struensée for a time reigned supreme in the councils of state and in the heart of the queen. Christian, in his curious way, was once heard to remark that the king of Prussia, of whose military talent he was known to be

29. Caetano Beiro, *D. Maria I, 1777-1792*, 4th ed. (Lisbon: Empresas nacional de publicidade, 1944), pp. 399-420.

jealous, had seduced Caroline Mathilda. What king of Prussia? he was asked by his astonished auditors. Struensée, he answered, unconcerned.

Struensée governed much in the fashion of Pombal and other enlightened ministers of the day. He did the accepted progressive things, and he did them boldly and impatiently. In particular, he abolished censorship of the press, and he had the impudence to make German the official language of government in Denmark. His policy, his arrogance, and his violation of the king's marriage naturally provoked indignation. In January 1772, a group of conspirators led by the conservative Ove Hoegh-Guldberg broke into the king's bedroom and persuaded him to sign orders for the arrest of Struensée and Caroline Mathilda. Struensée was tried, condemned, and savagely executed. The marriage of Christian was annulled, and Caroline Mathilda was exiled to Hanover, where three years later she died. Guldberg took over the government, and foreign affairs were given into the capable hands of Count A. P. Bernstorff.

Government in Denmark, however, continued in an unsettled condition. On the one hand, Denmark was a rigidly absolutist country. The basic law of the land was the Lex Regia Perpetua, or Kongelov, of 1665. This document embodied the most unstinting form of absolutist theory. It declared that the Estates had surrendered their authority entirely into the hands of the king, for whom it stipulated just two obligations: he must maintain the Christian faith of the kingdom according to the Augsburg Confession, and he must observe the Kongelov. It was contrary to the law of the land to diminish the power of the king so long as life remained in him.

On the other hand, Christian VII was clearly incapable of governing. No competent ruler would have tolerated the scandal of Struensée and Caroline Mathilda. One of the courtiers often found Christian in the morning sitting in the corner of his room with a pained expression on his face. From time to time he would beat his head against a wall, sometimes until blood flowed. He occasionally attacked his entourage violently. He laughed inappropriately and wildly. His speech was full of word salad and echolalia. He had delusions of grandeur and of persecution. The most competent study of his mental condition concludes that he was schizophrenic.[30]

---

30. Viggo Christiansen, *Christian den VII's Sindssygdom* (Odense: Odense Universitetsforlag, 1978). Christiansen, a psychologist, used the memoirs of Christian's tutor Reverdil, the transcript of Struensée's trial, and other materials, and he was advised in his historical research by the distin-

In 1784, this intolerable situation was resolved when Crown Prince Frederick, taking his cue from the previous practice of Struensée, without warning placed before the king in council a document establishing a regency. Christian unhesitatingly signed it and ceased effectively to rule. In the meantime, however, he continued, according to the Kongelov of 1665, nominally to reign in Denmark until his death in 1808. He was never confined, constrained, or subjected to a medical regimen.

There were other monarchs of the time, impulsive and obstinate, who were sometimes regarded--though it is not clear how seriously--as mad, and it is instructive to compare their experience with Paul's. Two such monarchs were Gustav III and Gustav IV Adolf of Sweden.

Gustav III was tutored as a child by Carl Gustav Tessin, who compiled for his pupil a kind of moral catechism in the form of fables titled *Letters to a Young Prince*. Paul's own tutor, Nikita Ivanovich Panin, made the acquaintance of Tessin while serving as a Russian diplomat in Stockholm. Panin paid careful attention to the educational conceptions of Tessin, and he subsequently used the German translation of Tessin's *Letters* in the education of Paul. The contents of the book are saturated with ideas of Stoic morality and especially devotion to duty.

Gustav was much influenced, in the course of his education, by the political ideas of the Physiocrats, and especially by the work of Mercier de la Rivière, *L'Ordre naturel et essentiel des sociétés politiques* (1767). A stronger statement of the position of absolute monarchy is hard to imagine. At the time, of course, Sweden was passing through that phase of her history known as the Age of Freedom, and the power of the monarchy had been supplanted since the revolution of 1720 by the power of the estates in the Riksdag. Gustav determined to put an end to the ascendancy of the estates, which he did in his own revolution of 1772, a year after coming to the throne. He asserted that henceforth promotion in the state service would be based not on

guished Danish historian Peter Edward Holm. The reliability of his diagnosis was ratified by the Odense University psychiatrist Niels Juel-Nielsen in 1978. See also: Ole Feldbaek, *Danmarks Historie: Tiden 1730-1814* (Copenhagen: Gyldendal, 1982), pp. 75-79; Elie Salomon François Reverdil, *Struensée et la cour de Copenhague, 1760-1772* (Paris: Meyrueis, 1858); J. F. Reddaway, "Struensée and the Fall of Bernstorff," *English Historical Review* 27:274-286 (1912); J. F. Reddaway, "Don Sebastiano de Llano and the Danish Revolution," ibid. 41:78-90 (1926); Stewart Oakley, *The Story of Denmark* (New York: Faber and Faber, 1972). I am much indebted to Professor Ole Feldbaek of the University of Copenhagen for identifying the pertinent materials on the case of Christian VII and for discussing the problem with me.

favoritism, but on experience and ability as well as on birth. In his conception, the aristocracy was entitled to special privilege in Swedish society in exchange for putting its special talents dutifully in the service of the nation. He claimed to restore the ancient Swedish constitutional principle, "The king shall rule the kingdom, he and none other." But in fact, his power continued to be constrained by constitutional limitations in important ways. The highest officials in the kingdom enjoyed tenure of office. The king could not interfere in judicial processes, and he might not declare war without the consent of the Riksdag. The Riksdag had a veto over legislation, and it alone had the power to tax.

Gustav's Russian war of 1788, which he entered without the consent of the Riksdag by guile and deceit, provoked much opposition, and he decided to proceed with another coup d'état. In February 1789, he promulgated the Act of Union and Security, which abolished most of the impediments to absolutism in Sweden, including the Riksdag's authority to declare war. Gustav now enjoyed all the powers of unrestricted absolutism except the power to tax. In the midst of this internal turmoil, he managed to bring the Russian war to a tolerable conclusion. But he had provoked a dangerous level of discontent among the aristocracy. Moreover, as the French Revolution developed, Gustav began to get ideas of leading a general European crusade to restore the power of the Bourbons in France.

By this time, the nobility was conspiring seriously against him. On 16 March 1792, Gustav was shot at the opera by Jacob Johan Anckarström, a former Captain of the Life Guards, and he died thirteen days later. Anckarström, unlike Paul's assassins, was arrested, tried, and punished. He freely confessed his guilt but stubbornly refused to name his accomplices, although he was broken on the wheel and had his right hand amputated. Eventually he was decapitated. Some of his suspected accomplices were exiled.[31]

Like Paul, Gustav IV Adolf was born to parents who were never very harmonious and only after twelve years of marriage. It was often rumored that he was illegitimate, and his father's mother believed it and told him so.

In 1804, he went to visit his in-laws in Baden. While he was there, the affair of the Duc d'Enghien occurred. Napoleon, faced with a royalist conspiracy fomented by the British, violated the territory of Baden to take captive the unfortunate duke who

---

31. R. Nisbet Bain, *Gustavus III and his Contemporaries*, 2 vols. (New York: Bergman, 1970).

happened to be the most proximate of the Bourbon princes, and although it soon became clear that he was entirely innocent, Napoleon executed him anyway. Gustav Adolf was deeply offended, never forgot it, and from this time regarded himself as the archenemy of Napoleon. The treaty of Tilsit simply catalyzed this feeling. By the spring of 1808, only Sweden, of all the continental powers, held out against the Continental System. At that point came the war with Russia to decide the fate of Finland and to force Sweden into the continental blockade. Of course, Gustav Adolf's disposition to fight the French was favored by the unusual Swedish dependence on commerce with England. So in this case material interests and moral inclination coincided. Nevertheless, in the winter of 1808-1809, the pressures mounting on Sweden and on Gustav Adolf were enormous, and he evidently lacked sufficient self-control to deal with his problems. In any event, he began to engage in the punishment of army officers in a fashion that was capricious and cruel. Soon they began to conspire against him.

On 13 March 1809, he was taken prisoner by a group led by Jacob Cederström and Georg Adlersparre. He resisted and was lightly wounded in the struggle. His captors made it clear to him that if he called troops or made any difficulties, they intended to kill him, and to clarify the king's mind, they explained these matters to him with a knife at his throat. Under these circumstances he was persuaded to sign an act of abdication (29 March 1809). He was detained for nine months more, after which he was given a pension and released on the understanding that he would go abroad and never return to Sweden. He soon began to appear at various royal courts--London, St. Petersburg--where he was received in a respectful and pleasant fashion. When he demanded support for his restoration to the throne of Sweden, however, he was disappointed. He appeared before the Congress of Vienna in 1815 to make such a plea. He died in poverty and obscurity in Bohemia in 1837.

The experience of Spain in the eighteenth century largely replicates the pattern that we observe in the other monarchies of Europe. Spain provides the examples of two monarchs who were probably mad, Felipe V (1700-1746) and Fernando VI (1746-1759). Felipe is said to have been virtually the slave of his wives, María Luisa of Savoy (d. 1714) and Elizabeth Farnese, and there are suggestions of erotomania in his attachment to them. Most historians and memoirists describe him as a profound melancholic and hypochondriac. In 1724, evidently world-weary, he abdicated in favor of his son Luís I, whose death two years later, however, forced Felipe to resume the throne. On the field of battle, his unusual courage earned him the title *el animoso*--the brave--but in the chanceries of state he was utterly useless. Like Christian VII of Denmark, he was a prince who, in the words of a contemporary, "neither reigns nor ever will reign." He fairly paraded eccentricities. He confused day and night. He cut neither his hair nor his toenails; consequently he could neither wear a wig nor walk. In the words of Ballesteros y Beretta, he was "un monarca melancólico y abúlico," i.e., melancholic and characterized by abulia, or mute and insensate fugue, a semi-schizoid condition.

Fernando VI (1746-1759) is said to have inherited the hypochondria of his father. When his wife died in 1758, he withdrew into melancholy seclusion also suggesting a schizoid condition. He did not dress, shave, cut his hair, or take solid food. He imagined that his body was being destroyed from within. He abhorred the company of those who had previously enjoyed his confidence. No one at the Spanish court, however, seems to have considered the question of medical care for either of these unfortunates.[32]

Carlos III (1759-1788) was strikingly different. He is one of the more celebrated enlightened despots of the age. He differed conspicuously from his predecessors in that he enjoyed robust mental health and gave systematic attention to affairs of state. It may be that he was not so gifted as the better known triad of his eastern European counterparts, Joseph, Catherine, and Frederick--he clearly lacked the inspired press agentry of Catherine--but he was distinguished for a conscientious devotion to duty, and perhaps none of his peers enjoys a better reputation today. He had two virtues indispensable to governing by the rules of enlightenment in a nation so backward as Spain: he was pious, and he was prudent. He was thus able to pursue progressive measures in the economy and to exile the Jesuits, and still he did not usually require the cynicism of a Frederick II to make his policy work in conservative and clerical Spain. In this respect, the Spanish experience of enlightened despotism differs in part from that of the bulk of Europe.

Yet even here, there were characteristic aristocratic reactions. Carlos's secretary of state for war and finance was a Si-

---

32. Antonio Ballesteros y Beretta, *Historia de España y su influencia en la historia universal*, 9 vols. (Barcelona: Salvat editores, 1918-1941), 5:66, 83, 150. Modesto Lafuente y Zamalloa, *Historia general de España*, 25 vols. (Barcelona: Montaner y Simón, 1887-1891), 13:341; 14:2, 43. Luciano de Taxonera, *Felipe V, fundador de una dinastía y dos veces rey de España* (Barcelona: Editorial Juventud, 1942), p. 261.

cilian nobleman known in Spain as the Marqués de Esquilache. Esquilache imported American bullion to finance Spain's wars, and it encouraged inflation. He introduced a characteristic eighteenth-century police regime in Madrid: there were regular garbage collections at appointed hours; the Madrileños were forced to abandon their habit of throwing refuse through windows and doors into the streets; knives, firearms, and gambling were prohibited; and a system of street lights was established throughout the city. Taxes were of course increased to pay for these measures. In the meantime, there had been three years of bad harvests from 1763 to 1765, and bread prices had spiraled upward. Finally, Esquilache forbade the wearing of traditional Spanish cloaks and broad-brimmed hats on the grounds that they facilitated the hiding of criminal elements, and at this provocation, the populace rose in the "motín de Esquilache," the Esquilache revolt of March 1766.

Carlos was frightened and withdrew from the city. He sacrificed Esquilache to the demands of the mob, and when calm was restored, he summoned the Count of Aranda to conduct an investigation, which concluded that the Jesuits were behind the trouble. It was the prelude to their expulsion. Rodríguez Casado maintains that the Esquilache revolt was a popular uprising organized and managed by the Spanish nobility. In this sense, it was the Spanish exception that adheres to the European rule.[33]

There were at the same time diminutive variations on the universally European theme of the conflict of nobility and monarchy in both England and France. In England, a truculent House of Commons postponed electoral reform, conceived by William Pitt with the consent of George III, from 1785 until 1832, when another prime minister with more robust royal backing forced the legislation through a reluctant House of Lords. In France, Louis XV and Chancellor Maupeou won a brave battle with the French nobility in 1771 when Maupeou banished the parlement of Paris from the city, but it was all undone when Louis XVI, preferring "above all to be loved," relented and allowed the parlement to return in 1774. Most Frenchmen rejoiced mistakenly at the triumph of law over tyranny. Voltaire, more farseeing, regretted the defeat of the "thèse royale." Louis then tried in vain to amend the loss and recoup the fortunes of

---

33. Richard Herr, *The Eighteenth Century Revolution in Spain* (Princeton, N.J.: Princeton University Press, 1958), pp. 20-21, 231-235. Vicente Rodríguez Casado, *La política y los políticos en el reinado de Carlos III* (Madrid: Ediciones Rialp, 1962), pp. 130-144.

his failing government through the appointment of a series of reforming comptrollers of finances--Turgot in 1774, Necker in 1777, Calonne in 1783, Loménie de Brienne in 1787, Necker again in 1788--but he lacked the resolution to sustain the daring measures which they and the situation required.

The age of enlightenment was also the age of the "nobles' revolt." The European nobility was rebounding from its losses of the seventeenth-century age of absolutism, freeing itself from the constraints imposed on it by Louis XIV and his peers, hotly pursuing the medieval license of its Polish and (sometime) Swedish brothers. In the circumstances, a critical conflict with the reforming monarchies of the age was inevitable. The nobility's quarrel was not with royal madness: it was with the semi-egalitarian social policy espoused by the bulk of the practitioners of progressive despotism. At the end of the era, from 1787 to 1789, it was the French nobles' revolt which led to the downfall of the monarchy before it led to the ruin of the nobility itself.

In summary, madness was not treated by homicide in late eighteenth-century Europe, but tyrannizing over the nobility often was.

7

THE TWENTIETH-CENTURY PSYCHIATRIC PERSPECTIVE

The standard guide to classifying mental disturbances in the United States today is the American Psychiatric Association's *Diagnostic and Statistical Manual of Mental Disorders*. It is coordinated with but not identical to the World Health Organization's *International Classification of Diseases*. From 1968 to 1980, the state of the diagnostic art was governed by the second edition of the *Diagnostic and Statistical Manual*, commonly called *DSM-II*. A third edition, *DSM III*, appeared in the spring of 1980. *DSM-III* is naturally regarded by the psychiatric profession as an improvement over the second edition, but parts of it are controversial. It is a considerably larger and more complex manual than its predecessor. I have used both manuals in this chapter, first, because *DSM-II* is simpler. For the layman, especially, it provides a more comprehensible guide through the territory. Second, whenever a new diagnostic manual is introduced, some years are required for the textbooks and the research literature to adjust to and reflect the conventions of the new terminology. In this instance, only the very recent textbooks have made use of the terminology of *DSM-III*, and though most of the concepts of interest in the case of Paul have not changed in the new manual, in some instances *DSM-III* classifications pertinent to him incorporate advances in research or sharper and more concrete definitions rather than merely a new style of terminology.

The mental disorders to which Sauvages, Cullen, Kant, and Pinel devoted the bulk of their attention are known today as psychoses. The psychoses are the most thoroughly deranged category of mental disorders. "Patients are described as psychotic when their mental functioning is sufficiently impaired to interfere grossly with their capacity to meet the ordinary demands of life. The impairment may result from a serious distortion in their capacity to recognize reality. Hallucinations and delusions, for example, may distort their perceptions. Alterations of mood may be so profound that the patient's capacity to respond appropriately is grossly impaired. Deficits in perception, language and memory may be so severe that the patient's capacity for mental grasp of his situation is effectively lost."[1]

There are three kinds of psychosis in modern clinical terminology: schizophrenia, affective disorders, and paranoid states. Our eighteenth-century medical men have described two of them, schizophrenia and paranoia, though under different names, but we have seen that there was much confusion in the diagnostic terminology of that period, and we shall soon see that it was extremely primitive and unclear by comparison with current terminology. Therefore, it makes sense to examine the question with the advantages of a more modern science, while keeping constantly in mind the relationship between eigh-

---

1. *DSM-II*, p. 23. There is one unavoidably pertinent issue in contemporary psychiatry that must be addressed at the outset of this chapter, the issue stated by Thomas S. Szasz in the title of his book *The Myth of Mental Illness: Foundations of a Theory of Personal Conduct* (New York: Hoeber-Harper, 1961). The book is misnamed, and it has been misunderstood. It is misnamed because it is not in fact about mental illness in general; it is about conversion hysteria in particular, and especially in the allegedly flawed thinking of Charcot, Breuer, and Freud. Conversion hysteria is the most vulnerable diagnosis in the whole conception of mental illness because of the fine and often arbitrary line between malingering and illness in pursuit of the profit of "secondary gain" (see below). Because the distinction between malingering and illness is a judgment call, Szasz's not implausible argument that what we know as conversion hysteria is not illness will simply not transfer applicably to a phenomenon like schizophrenia, rooted as it is in heredity and biochemistry. The book has been misunderstood, at least in part, it seems to me, because Szasz was most concerned to do what the subtitle promised, to elaborate a theory of personal conduct, and the argument about conversion hysteria was simply the peg on which he chose to hang his theory. If Paul turns out to be a candidate for the diagnosis of conversion hysteria, we will return to the questions raised by Szasz.

teenth-century behavior and observation on the one hand and twentieth-century terminology on the other.

What *DSM* designates as affective disorders are commonly called manic-depressive illness, a pronounced alteration of highs and lows of mood. They have to do chiefly with emotional skew, as opposed to disorders of cognitive and intellectual processes, which are characteristic of schizophrenia and paranoia.

Affective disorders "are characterized by a single disorder of mood, either extreme depression or elation, that dominates the mental life of the patient and is responsible for whatever loss of contact he has with his environment. The onset of the mood does not seem to be related directly to a precipitating life experience."[2] The affective disorders are easily recognizable: symptoms are simple, and behavior, while extreme, is conventional.

This definition does not describe a prince who, though often discouraged (and rarely elated), persisted in committing to paper the principled programs which he would one day implement in triumph, whose vindication of himself he thus anticipated. He was not described by his contemporaries as habitually depressed.

The most grossly dysfunctional form of mental illness is schizophrenia. According to *DSM-II*, "this large category includes a group of disorders manifested by characteristic disturbances of thinking, mood and behavior. Disturbances in thinking are marked by alterations of concept formation which may lead to misinterpretations of reality and sometimes to delusions and hallucinations, which frequently appear psychologically self-protective. Corollary mood changes include ambivalent, constricted, and inappropriate emotional responsiveness and loss of empathy with others. Behavior may be withdrawn, regressive, and bizarre. The schizophrenias, in which the mental status is attributable primarily to a *thought* disorder, are to be distinguished from the *Major affective illnesses* . . . which are dominated by a *mood* disorder."[3]

The simple type of schizophrenia exhibits a slow but thorough withdrawal into self. The hebephrenic type is marked by bizarre emotionality and infantile behavior. The catatonic type alternates between almost manic elation and mute stupor. The paranoid type is associated with delusions of persecution or

---

2. *DSM-II*, pp. 35-36.

3. Ibid., p. 33.

grandiosity. They all share the basic characteristics described above.[4]

Schizophrenia is strongly correlated with genetic and biochemical factors, and it has existed at all times and places.[5] It was described by the eighteenth-century physicians cited in the preceding chapter as follows:

Cullen: delirium, "false perception of external objects"; mania, "must be attended very constantly with that incoherent and absurd speech we call raving."

Sauvages: *manie*, "the patients talk nonsensically about all subjects, because of a flaw in their imagination . . . differs from melancholia in the universality of the delirium."

Contemporary literature is more comprehensive, more specific, and, especially, more exclusive.[6] In schizophrenia, the content of thought is disordered. Delusions are common, and one of the most common is the idea that one's thoughts and feelings are governed not by oneself, but by an external force. The form of thought is also disturbed, commonly reflecting a "loosening of associations, in which ideas shift from one subject to another completely unrelated or only obliquely related subject, without the speaker showing any awareness that the topics are unconnected." Perceptions are skewed. The usual disturbance of perception is hallucination, especially the hearing of voices. "The disturbance often involves blunting, flattening, or inappropriateness of affect," general emotional immobility, or lassitude. "The sense of self that gives the normal person a feeling of individuality, uniqueness, and self-direction is frequently disturbed . . . [it is] frequently manifested by extreme perplexity about one's own identity and the meaning of existence." The patient loses initiative and may be unable to do his work. "Frequently there is a tendency to withdraw from in-

---

4. Ibid., pp. 33-34.

5. See especially Heinz E. Lehmann, "Schizophrenia: History," in Harold I. Kaplan, Alfred M. Freedman, and Benjamin J. Sadock, eds., *Comprehensive Textbook of Psychiatry*, 3rd ed. 3 vols. (Baltimore: Williams & Wilkins, 1980), 2:1105-1113; Haroutun M. Babigian, "Schizophrenia: Epidemiology," ibid., pp. 1113-1120; Herbert Weiner, "Schizophrenia: Etiology," ibid., pp. 1121-1148; and Lawrence C. Kolb and H. Keith H. Brodie, *Modern Clinical Psychiatry*, 10th ed. (Philadelphia: W. B. Saunders, 1982), pp. 347-348.

6. *DSM-III*, pp. 182-184. James C. Coleman, James N. Butcher, and Robert C. Carson, *Abnormal Psychology and Modern Life*, 6th ed. (Glenview, Ill.: Scott, Foresman, 1980), pp. 400ff. Babigian, "Schizophrenia: Epidemiology," in Kaplan et al., *Comprehensive Textbook of Psychiatry*, 3rd ed., 2:1114.

volvement with the external world and to become preoccupied with egocentric and illogical ideas and fantasies in which objective facts are obscured, distorted, or excluded." A patient may take refuge in a catatonic stupor or bodily rigidity. All authorities emphasize similar phenomena: there is very general agreement about the symptomatology of schizophrenia.[7]

In Paul's case there is no evidence of perceptual problems, of disorganization of thought, or of emotional panic. He nurtured some dreams, and he suffered disappointments in them. There is doubtless a degree of withdrawal from reality in the pious principles and high-flown moralism of his writing and his militant convictions. But it is not of the proportions described by a definition of schizophrenia.

A look at the particular and concrete manifestations of the behavior of schizophrenics will illustrate the point. Hallucinations figure prominently among the symptoms. Paul did not have hallucinations, with the possible exception of one highly doubtful one. Hallucinations, however, do not occur in isolation. If they begin, they recur and become habitual.[8] Advanced schizophrenia is also characterized by autistic behavior, echolalia, echopraxia (imitative movement), bizarre facial expressions, the ability to maintain a bodily position for a long time, disequilibrium of the central nervous system, cold, bluish hands and feet, blotchy skin, widely dilated pupils, hoarding of various items by stuffing them into bodily apertures, swallowing dangerous objects, and/or painting and otherwise decorating the body wildly.[9]

Schizophrenic verbal expression is as strikingly different from Paul's admittedly infelicitous expression as the examples of behavior above are different from his behavior. The following examples of schizophrenic expression demonstrate the difference:

"Anyone can study all science in a compositive way. It takes a compositive mind to be able to understand. Can tell compositive minds by stromonized conception. The mind at

---

7. Andrew McGhie and James Chapman, "Disorders of Attention and Perception in Early Schizophrenia," *British Journal of Medical Psychology* 34:103-116 (1961).

8. Silvano Arieti, *The Interpretation of Schizophrenia*, 2nd ed. (New York: Basic Books, 1974), p. 267.

9. Ibid., pp. 415-433. Kolb and Brodie, *Modern Clinical Psychiatry*, pp. 358-372.

birth takes on a birthification, becomes environmental by the radiation to it."[10]

"I'm too utterly weary from battling with my financial-religious and general-religious problems to be able to survive any shock of learning that unhintably hard-won progress supposed to have been earned in the fraternal-religious problem is illusory. For that would wreck me--in my critically exhausted condition--with horror lest humanity--contrarily from being faith-imbured joy-multipliers or Revelations All Embracing God or Unfathomably Progressive Universe--are duped victims of God's opposite faith deluding us--with illusions of immortality, as Heavenly Father and of progress--into accommodation as evil-absorbers of His unconvertible and endless agonies and struggle."[11]

An inmate of a mental hospital wrote to a doctor: "Dear Dr. _____ 'My Plan,' or as mother used to call you, 'The Little Plant,' or else one little Plant for I was the other Plant, called 'Tant.' Will you please see that I am taken out of this hospital . . . so I can prove to the court who I am and thereby help establish my identity to the world. Possibly you do not remember or care to remember that you married me May 21, 1882, while you were in England and that I made you by that marriage the Prince of Wales, as I was born Albert Edward, Prince of Wales, I am feminine absolutely, not a double person or a hermaphrodite, so please know I am England's feminine king--the king who is a king. . . . Sincerely, 'Tant'."[12]

We have seen that Paul did not write well, but he did not write like these people.[13]

Paranoia is a more plausible suggestion and a subtler problem. The incidence and epidemiology of paranoid problems are unknown, as afflicted persons tend to be secretive about themselves in general and about their disorder in particular. Moreover, such behavior is not entirely maladaptive in Western society and especially in the busy, striving, ambitious sectors of it. It is believed that the vast majority of paranoid persons con-

---

10. Ibid., p. 395.

11. Ibid.

12. Ibid., p. 397.

13. For other examples, see Arieti, *Interpretation of Schizophrenia*, p. 407.

tinue to function tolerably well in society and thus rarely come to the attention of physicians or mental institutions.[14]

The history of the problem is, on the other hand, not nearly so obscure as is the question of its distribution. Paranoia is not a modern phenomenon, and it was well known to physicians for generations before Paul's time. It has historically been known as partial insanity, monomania, *manie sans délire*, or *folie raisonnante*.[15] We have examples of it in the work of John Bowname, *Spiritual Physicke to Cure the Diseases of the Soule* (London, 1600); William Perkins, *A Discourse of the Damned Art of Witchcraft* (Cambridge, 1608); Meric Casaubon, *A Treatise Concerning Enthusiasm* (London, 1655); Richard Baxter, *The Signs and Causes of Melancholy* (London, 1716); Thomas Beddoes, *Hygeia: Or Essays Moral and Medical* (Bristol, 1803); James Cowles Prichard, *A Treatise on Insanity and Other Disorders Affecting the Mind* (London, 1835); Jean Etienne Dominique Esquirol, *Des maladies mentales* (Paris, 1838); as well as those from the eighteenth-century medical men cited in the previous chapter.

The descriptions of paranoia, under the variety of names used, from all these times and places, are entirely consonant with the descriptions of it both in the work of the eighteenth-century physicians and in *DSM-III*. As Casaubon wrote in 1655, "there is a sober kind of distraction or melancholy: not such only wherein the brain is generally affected to all objects equally; never outrageous, nor out of reason, as it were, to outward appearance; but also where the distemper is confined to some one object or other, the brain being otherwise very sound and sober upon all other subjects and occasions . . . there is not any Physician, either ancient or late, that treateth of Melancholy, but doth acknowledge it, and hath several examples."[16]

In May 1800, James Hadfield discharged a pistol at George III at Drury Lane Theatre. He was tried on 26 June 1800, and his lawyer, Thomas Erskine, won an acquittal by

---

14. See especially J. Ingram Walker and H. Keith H. Brodie, "Paranoid Disorders," in Kaplan et al., *Comprehensive Textbook of Psychiatry*, 3rd ed., 2:1289-1290.

15. Richard A. Hunter and Ida Macalpine, eds., *Three Hundred Years of Psychiatry* (London: Oxford, 1963), p. 144.

16. Quoted in ibid., pp. 143-147.

pleading that his client was not guilty by reason of insanity. The description of Hadfield is a classic example of paranoia.[17]

All four of our eighteenth-century physicians described this condition, though they gave it different names:

Sauvages: "Melancholics are constantly attached to one single thought, are in delirium about themselves, such that they reason properly about all other things." Notable is the "fixed and constant attention which is paid to [a single] idea, while neglecting others."

Cullen described melancholia as "false imagination or judgment . . . with respect to one subject only; yet it seldom happens that this does not produce much inconsistency in the other intellectual operations." Melancholics, in his observation, give especially close attention "to one particular object, or train of thinking. They are even ready to be engaged in a constant application to one subject."

According to Kant, "those who believe they are everywhere surrounded by enemies, and those who regard all glances, words, and otherwise indifferent actions of others as directed against them personally and as traps set for them belong to this category," i.e., *dementia*. In *vesania*, "a patient fancies that he comprehends the incomprehensible, and that such things as the invention of a method for squaring the circle, perpetual motion, the unveiling of the transcendental forces of Nature, and the comprehension of the mystery of the Trinity are all within his power."

In the view of Pinel, "the melancholic is as if possessed by an exclusive idea or a particular series of ideas with a dominant passion" whereas in *manie*, there are delirium, delusions of grandeur, extravagant errors of judgment, the patients imagine themselves generals and conquerors and have plans for making such things as machines of perpetual motion.

Modern diagnostic literature gives us a much fuller and clearer account of this problem. The paranoid states are "psychotic disorders in which a delusion, generally persecutory or grandiose, is the essential abnormality. Disturbances in mood, behavior and thinking (including hallucinations) are derived from this delusion. This distinguishes paranoid states from the affective psychoses and schizophrenias, in which mood and thought disorders, respectively, are the central abnormalities." Paranoia is an "extremely rare condition . . . characterized by gradual development of an intricate, complex, and elaborate

---

17. Ibid., pp. 567-572. The other works cited above are from ibid., pp. 55-56, 66-67, 240-243, 578-583, 731-736, 836-843.

paranoid system based on and often proceeding logically from misinterpretation of an actual event. Frequently the patient considers himself endowed with unique and superior ability. In spite of a chronic course the condition does not seem to interfere with the rest of the patient's thinking and personality."[18]

The various paranoid conditions are not nearly so comprehensively debilitating as schizophrenia. The paranoid dynamic operates on that limited part of the personality spectrum which is pathologically hurt somehow. When a paranoid person is approached on some subject independent of his delusional system, he may appear normal and rational.[19] In addition, the paranoid dynamic may not always be incapacitating. The person who labors under persecutory delusions, for example, may work harder on that account to reach his goals and may succeed objectively in doing something that his particular cognitive habits perceive as defeating his enemies. It is in this sense that paranoid behavior, especially in an achievement-oriented environment, may even be in part socially adaptive and effective. "Paranoia is rare in clinic and mental hospital populations, but . . . many exploited inventors; persecuted teachers; business executives . . . ; fanatical reformers; morbidly jealous spouses; and self-styled prophets fall in this category. Unless they become a serious nuisance, these individuals are usually able to maintain themselves in the community and do not recognize their paranoid condition nor seek to alleviate it."[20]

Paranoid behavior is rooted in severe feelings of inferiority or insignificance.[21] As described by Sullivan, paranoid attitudes form in two stages. First: "I am inferior. Therefore people will dislike me and I cannot be secure with them." Second: "It is not that *I* have something wrong with me, but that *he* does something to me. One is the victim, not of one's own defects, but of a devilish environment. One is not to blame; the envi-

---

18. *DSM-II*, pp. 37-38.

19. Coleman et al., *Abnormal Psychology*, p. 431. Kolb and Brodie, *Modern Clinical Psychiatry*, p.444.

20. Coleman et al., *Abnormal Psychology*, p. 429. Though the variety of paranoid diagnoses makes up about 10 percent of hospital admissions, there are no reliable figures on the incidence of the disorder in the population at large (it is believed to be high). See Norman A. Cameron, "Psychotic Disorders, II: Paranoid Reactions," in Alfred M. Freedman and Harold I. Kaplan, eds., *Comprehensive Textbook of Psychiatry*, 1st ed. (Baltimore: Williams & Wilkins, 1967), p. 666.

21. Coleman et al., *Abnormal Psychology*, pp. 433-435.

ronment is to blame. Thus we can say that the essence of the paranoid dynamism is the transference of blame."[22]

This device of the transference of blame is better known as the defense mechanism of projection. Ideas perceived as threatening to oneself are defended against by imagining that they are entertained by others. "Projective thinking is the characteristic most frequently regarded as the *sine qua non* of the paranoid mode. . . . Projection is the natural process by which one's impulses, fantasies or other tensions that are unacceptable or intolerable in one's self are attributed to others."[23]

The paranoid feels that he lives in a hostile world. The very suspicious, easily wounded and angered paranoid tends to perceive a "paranoid pseudo-community," which is the organization of his enemies. This community does not include everybody, but rather those persons associated with the area of mental stress.[24] There is general agreement that the behavior of the paranoid tends to provoke the realization of his suspicions. The community which was initially "pseudo," because it existed only in his imagination, becomes real. The people suspected by the paranoid take his suspicions into account, and, for example, avoid meeting each other where they can be observed by him lest this behavior confirm his suspicions; which it would--but so does the avoidance behavior.[25]

Many paranoid subjects show sexual maladjustment or weakly developed sexuality, and a high percentage of them do not marry.[26]

The paranoid is characterized by hyperalertness and by constant mobilization of his personality. He is sensitive to slights, and he perceives himself as the center of attention.[27]

---

22. Harry Stack Sullivan, "The Paranoid Dynamism," in *Clinical Studies in Psychiatry* (New York: W. W. Norton, 1965), pp. 145-146.

23. David W. Swanson, Philip J. Bohnert, and Jackson A. Smith, *The Paranoid* (Boston: Little, Brown, 1970), pp. 8-9.

24. Norman Cameron, "The Paranoid Pseudo-Community," *American Journal of Sociology* 49:32-38 (1943); and "The Paranoid Pseudo-Community Revisited," ibid. 65:52-58 (1959).

25. Edwin M. Lemert, "Paranoia and the Dynamics of Exclusion," *Sociometry* 25:2-20 (1962).

26. Kolb and Brodie, *Modern Clinical Psychiatry*, pp. 450-451. Harold Rosen and H. E. Kiene, "Paranoid and Paranoiac Reaction Types," *Diseases of the Nervous System* 7:330-337 (1946).

27. Coleman et al., *Abnormal Psychology*, pp. 430-432. Kolb and Brodie, *Modern Clinical Psychiatry*, pp. 445-450.

The more typical approach to his problem is that of the persecutory reaction. Also common is the grandiose (or exalted) reaction. In this case, he regards himself as unique or very superior. He may think that he has been designated somehow as the instrument of a messianic enterprise, or the mastermind of a wonderful invention, or the prophet of a new religion or ideology.[28]

How well does this description fit Paul's personality? Did he have a well-developed system of delusions? He certainly had a well-developed outlook and set of attitudes. The most conspicuous features of his thought as set down by himself were that Catherine had denied him his rightful place on the throne and that the Russian nobles consented to his sacrifice in exchange for their privileges and the continuance of their corrupt existence. Is this a delusion? It is an idea open to challenge. It may lack nuances; it may be exaggerated; it may even be wrong. But we cannot rationally argue that the idea entirely lacked foundation. Hence it is not a delusion. Paul's conception was not one that bore no relation to reality: it was derived directly from the facts, even if it was a case of mistaken judgment.

Paul was perceived by various people whom he met to be normal and even charming. This was the case at his first wedding, his first major exposure to the public. He was similarly received on his travels in Europe, making a good impression there. Such occasions, however, do not constitute satisfactory evidence against paranoid dynamisms, since these would not be in evidence when he was not in touch with his own personal areas of pathological stress.

Did he have feelings of inferiority or inadequacy that were unwarranted? Obtaining good evidence on this question is a tricky business. Paul did not confess whether he had such feelings or not. But his behavior suggests that he probably did. Consider again the observation of Rostopchin: "he is obsessed with the idea that people do not respect him and that they scorn him. Proceeding from that assumption . . . having four marine battalions of 1600 men and three squadrons of horse, he imagines . . . to imitate the deceased king of Prussia . . . now he orders that Count Zinoviev be told that he must show more respect to persons enjoying Paul's favor . . . Countess Shuvalova . . . was . . . told that she must hurry for Paul because she had always carried out all that Prince Potemkin had told her to do." Paul remarked in 1784 that he was thirty years old and had nothing to do, a predicament incommensurate with his dig-

---

28. Ibid.

nity and worth. He had endured enough to give him feelings of inferiority. His father had neglected him and failed to name him as heir. His mother had taken his throne, and her favorites occupied his place in the councils of state.

Did he think that he had unique and superior ability? The gist of his writing about Catherine and the mess that she had made of government as well as his remarks about the corruption, laziness, and shirking of the nobility evince an attitude of superiority. His writing was full of self-righteousness: "If I were in need of a party, then I would be able to hold my tongue about the disorders, in order to humor certain persons; but being what I am, I can have neither party nor interest except that of the State, and it is painful, with my character, to see that things are going awry and above all that negligence and personal views are the cause of it;--I prefer to be hated for doing good than loved for doing evil."

Did Paul feel that he lived in a world which was hostile to him? He evidently felt that a large part of it was hostile. He was quite suspicious of Catherine's intentions. However, suspicion is normal if it is warranted by the facts. To a great extent in this case it was warranted. Paul had a distinct sense of being abused before he came to the throne, and he often reacted strongly to disappointments, as for example in foreign affairs; but there was a sound basis for his grievances against the Austrians, the English, and the French. He did not behave in a conspicuously irrational fashion as if the world were against him.

On the other hand, his decided interest in the military might be interpreted, among other ways, as evidence of an exceptional need to secure himself. In addition, his concern with the happiness and well-being of society might be seen as betraying a need to create a harmonious and peaceful world, less hostile and more secure than the one that he perceived.

We do not have as much information about Paul's sexuality as about Catherine's, but it seems safe to say that his appetite did not match hers. It is clear that he showed some fanciful interest in love affairs during the time of Poroshin's duty as teacher (when Paul was ten to eleven). Paul was happy with his first marriage, though Nataliia evidently was not. Had suspicion on his part been a factor in her unhappiness, he would probably have been better apprised of her relations with Razumovskii. His second marriage was happy for a long time. Neither marriage, then, was sufficiently stormy to suggest the presence of paranoid factors. The remainder of Paul's sexual behavior is open to the label of weakly developed sexuality, but there is nothing conclusive in this evidence. In his case, not to marry was out of the question. It was his duty to marry and to provide an heir. In fact he provided four of them--four sons--and the next two tsars. In addition, he had a number of mistresses, though no grand passion among them.

Was he a hyperalert personality, mobilized to discern slights to himself? Rostopchin, a friendly observer, said frankly that he was and gave examples. As a child, he accused the servants of stealing. He admitted his excessive suspicion to Razumovskii. But Razumovskii himself turned out not to deserve Paul's trust. Paul was suspicious of N. I. Saltykov when Catherine sent him to replace Panin at the young court. Maybe Saltykov was a spy. In a sense, Paul merited spying upon: he carried on a treasonous correspondence with Frederick II. He was also a threat to Catherine by virtue of his very existence, as she was to him.

Did he see himself as the center of attention? To some extent, he did. He did not want the audience in the theater to applaud before he did. His sense of being slighted, his references to being neglected, appear to be in the nature of attention-seeking. When he was grand prince, he seems to have wanted to be the center of more attention than he received. Of course, when he became tsar, he was naturally the center of attention. He must have been aware of this part of his destiny from early childhood, which would have influenced his attitude on the subject. The sense of being the center of attention is not pertinent as evidence of paranoid processes in the case of someone born to be an emperor.

Did he have persecution reaction? Yes, but not in a delusive sense, as explained. On the other hand, he clearly had pretensions of grandiosity. He recalled as a child being told that "the peoples are jealous of you; they often think of you and repeat: 'you are joy, you are love, the hope of all joys.'" The thought and its import are not perfectly clear, but they suggest grandiosity. His fascination with the Knights of Malta and his ambition to use them to restore thrones and to reestablish respect for religion was not modest even for an emperor. He gave himself airs as peace-maker and offered after his accession to the throne to mediate a general peace settlement in Europe. He then crusaded in Italy for a just international settlement. Later, when his other efforts had come to nothing, he attempted to persuade the Prussians to assist him in imposing a peace of their conception upon the powers of Europe. The political testament which he wrote before going off to the wars in 1788 is suffused with the notion that the best means of achieving the blessedness, well-being, and security of the nation was simply to deliver unlimited power to himself. The grandiosity of these attitudes and schemes must be weighed, however, against his position as the ruler of a vast and powerful nation.

One of the more interesting tests of Paul's symptomatology is that of the concept of the paranoid community or pseudo-community. From an early date, he rallied his forces, the Panin party, against Catherine and her lovers. Around 1790, he divided his household between those for and against Nelidova. About the same time, the world was either for or against the French Revolution. Around 1795, the reconciliation of Mariia Fedorovna and Nelidova prompted a temporary alienation between himself and Nelidova. He turned his attentions briefly to another woman at court until a really serious danger, the threat that Catherine would dispossess him of the throne, reconciled him with both Mariia Fedorovna and Nelidova. When this threat passed, at Catherine's death, he was won away from Mariia Fedorovna, Nelidova, and their associates, the Kurakins, by Rostopchin and Kutaisov. This review of his relations with various parties suggests that the principle actuating his behavior was the sense of threat which he felt. If the sense of threat was delusive, then the behavior was paranoid.

The threat from Catherine was not a delusion. The threats from the other parties seem to have been largely delusive. Mariia Fedorovna and Nelidova did not wish him ill. Paul was manipulable by persons near him who suggested that others, their enemies, were trying to use him and manipulate him as they themselves were. Mariia Fedorovna did try to manipulate and manage Paul, to subject him in some ways to her influence: to favor the French émigrés, for example, to combat the French republic, and to restrain the more destructive outbursts of Paul's anger. Nelidova spoke frankly to him and attempted to restrain his volatility. Hence the two of them were excellent prey for Kutaisov's suggestions that Paul was their creature. It was quite blind of him not to recognize the significance of this suggestion.

The question of paranoid process in Paul is, then, complex and ambiguous. He did not have a conspicuous system of delusions. He probably had some sense of inferiority or inadequacy. At the same time, he had a clear sense of unique and superior ability--at least he had a special sense of moral superiority and moral destiny. His feelings that he lived in a hostile world were at least partly justified. When Catherine seized the throne in 1762, she faced the threat of three pretenders. A few years later, two of them had been killed, and only Paul remained. And yet Paul's suspicions of his environment were not sufficient to save his own life later. Or were they sufficient to provoke his death? He saw himself, by and large, as the center of attention, which at times he was. His thinking was grandiose but perhaps not excessively so, given his position. One of the more positive readings on this scale of symptoms is of the paranoid pseudo-community. (One other crucial criterion, the use of projection, will be examined later in connection with another pathological category.)

What degree of these symptoms justifies the name paranoid? Let us look at some modern examples. "There's God who is Number 1, and Jesus Christ who is Number 2, and me, I am Number 3."[29] A middle-aged man drove to a local airport and told army officers that enemy planes were flying overhead, that he therefore must get a message to the president about espionage activities immediately.[30] A paranoid patient reported that he had "founded a religion 'more up to date' than Christianity and one that would supplant the latter and dominate the world. . . . There will come in the western continent a greater man than this world has seen since this civilization began. It will not be through the ignorance of the people that this man will be carried into the White House. 'In some respects this man will be the intellectual and philosophical leader. He will be to the world what Mohammed was to Arabia, Columbus to the New World, Moses to the Jews, Plato to the Greeks.' This, the patient said, referred to him."[31] Cullen and Pinel and their contemporaries reported similar examples of grandiosity in the eighteenth century.

Paul did not exhibit this order of derangement. He did, on the other hand, exhibit elements of paranoid behavior. He was perhaps characterized by what might be called a paranoid style, or what Sullivan calls "a paranoid slant on life."[32] Some of this paranoid slant he learned naturally and normally. Some of it he brought to situations in which it was not adaptive and appropriate. We will return later to the question whether he exhibited paranoid behavior in a mode less deranged than the psychotic.

29. Coleman et al., *Abnormal Psychology*, p. 431.

30. Swanson et al., *The Paranoid*, p. 70.

31. Kolb and Brodie, *Modern Clinical Psychiatry*, p. 452.

32. Sullivan, *Clinical Studies in Psychiatry*, p. 145.

The concept of neurosis helps to elucidate Paul's behavior.[33] Neurosis is a less severe mental disturbance than psychosis. "Anxiety is the chief characteristic of the neuroses. It may be felt and expressed directly, or it may be controlled unconsciously and automatically by conversion, displacement, and various other psychological mechanisms. Generally, these mechanisms produce symptoms experienced as subjective distress from which the patient desires relief. The neuroses, as contrasted to the psychoses, manifest neither gross distortion or misinterpretation of external reality, nor gross personality disorganization. . . . Traditionally, neurotic patients, however severely handicapped by their symptoms, are not classified as psychotic because they are aware that their mental functioning is disturbed."[34]

Though there may be no sharp line between psychoses and neuroses, and one often merges with the other in scarcely perceptible stages, there are key indexes that distinguish between them. First, neurotics, unlike psychotics, understand that something is abnormal about them. Second, neurotics do not experience the perceptual skew characteristic of psychotics: they continue to perceive reality much as normal people do, though they do not react to it in the same way. Third, neurosis produces a phenomenon known as secondary gain; that is, the neurotic incapacity delivers something needed by the personality; it spares the personality confrontation with a stress area. A classic example is hysterical blindness in air force pilots before dangerous missions; another is writer's cramp.

Neurotic behavior is recognizable by some or all of the following characteristics. Neurotic persons have such basic feelings of inferiority and inadequacy that facing ordinary problems produces considerable anxiety. They avoid stressful situations rather than cope with them. Though they know that their

---

33. In *DSM-III*, the new term for neuroses is neurotic disorders, and the description of them is distributed in a wide variety of sub-categories. The basic understanding of the concept is fundamentally unchanged. The manual itself admits much resistance to the change (p. 9): "Throughout the development of *DSM-III*, the omission of the *DSM-II* diagnostic class of Neuroses has been a matter of great concern to many clinicians." A new textbook echoes the reservations of many of these clinicians on the new terminology: "Ingrained patterns of usage will be slow to change, however, the most current research and treatment personnel will likely continue to use the term *neurosis* for some time to come." Coleman et al., *Abnormal Psychology*, p. 205. The most recent edition of Kolb and Brodie, *Modern Clinical Psychiatry*, continues to use the term *neurosis*.

34. *DSM-II*, p. 39.

behavior is not normal, they lack insight into it, for fear drives out understanding. They become self-centered, dealing constantly with their anxieties, and thus unnaturally with other people; and they experience much dissatisfaction with their way of life and anxiety over their inability to deal with their problems.[35]

Neurotic behavior has quite a variety of manifestations. Anxiety neurosis is defined by free-floating and diffuse fear and panic. Hysterical neurosis, conversion type, is psychogenic loss of sensory capacity, sight, feeling, hearing, with a suspicious indifference (*la belle indifférence*) to the incapacity. Hysterical neurosis, dissociative type, is the alteration of consciousness to produce amnesia, somnambulism, fugue, and multiple personality. Phobic neurosis is the intense fear of a thing or a situation, such as to produce nausea, tremors, or panic. Neurasthenic neurosis is chronic psychogenic fatigue, weakness, or exhaustion. Depressive neurosis and hypochondriacal neurosis are well known and self-evident. Depersonalization neurosis "is dominated by a feeling of unreality and of estrangement from the self, body, or surroundings."[36] These do not describe Paul's behavior.

Only one category of neurosis is worth exploring in Paul's case: obsessive-compulsive neurosis. Such behavior is suggested in Paul by his taste for drilling his troops and by his passion for perfect order in their drill exercises as in other areas of his life. Personalities with obsessive tendencies are easily recognized: "they are excessively cleanly, orderly, and conscientious, sticklers for precision; they have inconclusive ways of thinking and acting; they are given to needless repetition. Those who have shown such traits since childhood are often morose, obstinate, irritable people; others are vacillating, uncertain of themselves and submissive."[37]

These characteristics are, however, fairly common in the population at large, and to some extent, in some cultures, they are even advantageous. "Most of us have obsessional traits and lead an obsessional way of life; we are preoccupied with clock time and with problems of order and orderliness in our paper

---

35. Coleman et al., *Abnormal Psychology*, pp. 205-207. Kolb and Brodie, *Modern Clinical Psychiatry*, pp. 463-464.

36. *DSM-II*, pp. 39-41.

37. A. J. Lewis and E. Mapother, "Obsessional Disorder," in Sir Ronald Bodley Scott, ed., *Price's Textbook of the Practice of Medicine*, 11th ed. (London: Oxford, 1973), p. 1379.

subculture. In a sublimated way, obsessional values are part of our middle-class social character. At their best, the operation of these values gets things done, particularly the routine ones, makes the world move more smoothly--so to speak, the trains run on time."[38]

The incidence and epidemiology of obsessive problems are unknown. "Scattered anecdotal evidence indicates that it has occurred throughout history. . . . It is known that persons with obsessive-compulsive disorders tend to be secretive about their symptoms and to avoid disclosing them to physicians. . . . Furthermore, since people with obsessive-compulsive symptoms are frequently able to work and earn a living despite marked limitations in their social and emotional life, their disorder may never be known except to their closest associates."[39]

In fact, there is more than anecdotal historical evidence of the disorder. It was, oddly enough, not the subject of comment in the works of the eighteenth-century physicians whose schemes of classification of mental disorders we have previously cited, but it is abundantly documented in a more informal genre of literature on madness throughout early modern Europe. In 1658, Richard Flecknoe described such a personality in his curious book *Enigmaticall Characters* (London): "he hovers in his choice, like an empty Ballance with no waight of Judgement to incline him to either scale . . . every thing he thinks on, is matter of deliberation . . . and he does nothing readily, but what he thinks not on . . . when he begins to deliberate, never makes an end. . . . Has some dull *demon* cryes, *do not, do not* still, when hee's on point of doing any thing. . . . He plays at *shall I, shall I?* so long, till opportunity be past . . . and then repents at leisure."[40]

A common variation of this behavior in the mid-seventeenth century was religious in nature. "William of Oseney was a devout man, and read two or three Books of Religion and devotion very often, and being pleased with the entertainment of his time, resolved to spend so many hours every day in reading them, as he had read over those books several times;

---

38. Rose Spiegel, "Psychotherapy with Obsessive-Compulsive Patients," in Max Hamner, ed., *The Theory and Practice of Psychotherapy with Specific Disorders* (Springfield, Ill.: Charles C. Thomas, 1972), p. 99.

39. John C. Nemiah, "Obsessive-Compulsive Disorder (Obsessive-Compulsive Neurosis)," in Kaplan et al., *Comprehensive Textbook of Psychiatry*, 2nd ed., 2:1505.

40. Hunter and Macalpine, *Three Hundred Years of Psychiatry*, pp. 116.

that is, three hours every day. In a short time he had read over the books three times more," and this compelled him, according to his scheme, to spend six hours per day reading his devotional books. He soon realized that by following this principle, he would shortly be using all his time in this manner. This realization disturbed him, both because he would soon have no time for any other business and because his increasing familiarity with the books that he was reading diminished the profit of reading them further. But resistance was useless: he was the victim of obsession.[41]

John Moore described in 1692 men of pious character who were overwhelmed by salacious and blasphemous thoughts: "the more they struggle with them, the more they encrease."[42] Bernard de Mandeville, a Dutch physician renowned for his influential polemical rhyme *The Fable of the Bees* (1714, 1723, 1728), took an interest in the problem and especially in the manifestation of it known as syphilophobia.[43] In fact, this was one of the most common presenting symptoms of the obsessive disorder in the early eighteenth century. In Daniel Turner's *Syphilis: a Practical Dissertation on the Venereal Disease* (London, 1724), syphilophobia, syphilomania, and venereophobia are prominent problems.[44] David Hartley in 1749 described obsessives in whom there was "frequent Recurrency of the same Ideas."[45]

A variety of well-known authors exhibit similar traits from the seventeenth through the nineteenth centuries. "Samuel Johnson, John Bunyan, and Charles Darwin all had obsessional traits and at one time or another suffered from an obsessional disorder. It is interesting too that in each case their work bears the marks of their obsessional tendencies--systematically ordering and organizing, making increas-

---

41. Jeremy Taylor, *Ductor dubitantium, or the Rule of Conscience* (London: 1660), quoted in Hunter and Macalpine, *Three Hundred Years of Psychiatry*, pp. 163-165.

42. John Moore, *Of Religious Melancholy* (London: 1692), quoted in Hunter and Macalpine, *Three Hundred Years of Psychiatry*, pp. 252-253.

43. Bernard de Mandeville, *A Treatise on the Hypochondriack and Hysterick Passions* (London: 1711), quoted in Hunter and Macalpine, *Three Hundred Years of Psychiatry*, p. 296.

44. Cited in ibid., pp. 315-318.

45. *Observations on Man, his Frame, his Duty, and his Expectations* (London: 1749), cited in Hunter and Macalpine, *Three Hundred Years of Psychiatry*, pp. 379-382.

ingly fine distinctions, struggling with unacceptable thoughts, and so on."[46]   Bunyan described how "both day and night" he would "tremble at the thoughts of the fearful torments of Hell-fire; still fearing that it would be my lot to be found at last among those Devils and Hellish Fiends, who are there bound down with the chains and bonds of eternal darkness."   Such thoughts bothered him even as a child of nine or ten years as he played games with other children, and he would during such games "despair of Life and Heaven."   Later, "would the Tempter so provoke me to desire to sin [by blaspheming], that I was as if I could not, must not, neither should be quiet until I had committed that; now no sin would serve but that: if it were to be committed by speaking of such a word, then I have been as if my mouth would have spoken that word whether I would or not; and in so strong a measure was this temptation upon me, that often I have been ready to clap my hand under my chin, to hold my mouth from opening; and to that end also I have had thoughts at other times to leap with my head downward, into some Muckhil-hole or other, to keep my mouth from opening."[47]

Johnson's "inner tensions expressed themselves in a number of compulsive habits.   Going along a street in which there were posts, he would carefully lay his hand on each one as he passed, and if inadvertently he missed one he would go back a considerable distance in order to touch it.   He also . . . made a ritual of entering or leaving a door or passage in such a way as to take a certain number of steps to reach a certain point."[48]   In the spring of 1761, Johnson wrote down a resolution most of the contents of which Paul himself might have written.   He "resolved, I hope not presumptuously . . . hoping in God . . . to lead a new life. . . .   My purpose is

1. To repel vain and corrupt imaginations.
2. To avoid idleness.
To regulate my sleep as to length and choice of hours.
To set down every day what shall be done the day following.
To keep a journal.
3. To worship God more diligently.
To go to church every Sunday.

---

46. Stanley J. Rachman and R. J. Hodgson, *Obsessions and Compulsions* (Englewood Cliffs, N.J.: Prentice-Hall, 1980), p. 25.

47. John Bunyan, *Grace Abounding* (London: Oxford, 1966), pp. 8, 35.

48. John Wain, *Samuel Johnson* (New York: Viking, 1974), p. 253.

4. To study the Scriptures.
To read a certain portion every week."[49]

Charles Darwin's case is more complicated and problematical. It is widely agreed that he had obsessive characteristics,[50] but Darwin exhibited a rich and massive variety of illness, and the particulars on his obsessive behavior are none too clear.[51]

In summary, obsessive disorders were by no means uncommon in Europe in the seventeenth and eighteenth centuries--though they were not considered so serious then as now--and modern psychology and psychiatry have not been hesitant to identify them. It is, then, plausible and practical to raise the question whether obsessive-compulsive neurosis was at work in the personality of Paul.

"This disorder is characterized by the persistent intrusion of unwanted thoughts, urges, or actions that the patient is unable to stop. The thoughts may consist of single words or ideas, ruminations, or trains of thought often perceived by the patient as nonsensical. The actions vary from simple movements to complex rituals such as repeated handwashing. Anxiety and distress are often present either if the patient is prevented from completing his compulsive ritual or if he is concerned about being unable to control it himself."[52]

The obsessive-compulsive person is concerned to control both his environment and his own personality and impulses. He wants to render his experiences as planned and predictable as possible, and he wants to eliminate the spontaneous and accidental. Obsessive people "tend to increase the predictability of life events by ensuring that their room is always the same from day to day, that clothes are taken off in the same order and that the daily constitutional is taken at the same time and along the circumscribed routes. By doing this they are reducing the chances of being caught unawares by an event which may present difficulties of interpretation. . . . If the world ceases to be orderly, if prized possessions are moved, then chaos throughout

---

49. Quoted in James L. Clifford, *Dictionary Johnson: Samuel Johnson's Middle Years* (New York: McGraw-Hill, 1979), p. 240.

50. Hunter and Macalpine, *Three Hundred Years of Psychiatry*, p. 417. Ralph Colp, *To Be an Invalid: The Illness of Charles Darwin* (Chicago: University of Chicago Press, 1977), p. 143.

51. The most authoritative work, though somewhat inconclusive, on Darwin's medical problems, is ibid.

52. *DSM-II*, p. 40.

their whole environment is a possibility."[53] If the things in their environment depart even slightly from their preconceived notion of proper and secure order, obsessive persons experience considerable consternation and frustration.[54] In an increasingly self-centered and eccentric fashion, "Obsessional thinking is concerned more and more with less and less."[55]

Obsessional thinking absorbs attention and relieves tension. It also precludes threatening thoughts, and it diminishes the capacity to observe spontaneous or accidental developments which might disturb a person given to perfect order.[56]

Obsession and compulsion, though related in this syndrome of behavior, are not identical, and it is useful to distinguish between them. Purely obsessional behavior is simply a thought pattern, internal and private, "which forces itself insistently into consciousness and recurs against the conscious desires of the person concerned."[57] It cannot be observed, and it is detected only through the confession of it. These obsessional phenomena may be words, phrases, often nonsensical or obscene, or images of violence or repugnance. They may include idle rumination on philosophical or religious questions. They may be personally or socially unacceptable impulses, such as the impulse to jump out of a high window or to shout obscenities in church. They may be obsessional fears, especially the fear of dirt, danger, or contamination.[58] Obsessive thoughts in patients produce strange complaints: a young woman came to her doctor to get rid of the thought of her father and herself in intercourse; a mother was plagued every time her young daughter left the house with the thought of the child's being killed by a car; a law student, whenever he turned on the light in

---

53. Fay Fransella, "Thinking of the Obsessional," in H. R. Beech, ed., *Obsessional States* (London: Methuen, 1974), p. 179.

54. H. R. Beech and J. Perigault, "Toward a Theory of Obsessional Disorder," in Beech, *Obsessional States*, p. 114.

55. Fransella, "Thinking of the Obsessional," in Beech, *Obsessional States*, p. 194.

56. Henry P. Laughlin, *The Neuroses* (Washington, D.C.: Butterworth's, 1967), p. 311.

57. Joseph Sandler and Anandi Hazari, "The Obsessional; on the Psychological Classification of Obsessional Character Traits and Symptoms," *British Journal of Medical Psychology* 33:113 (1960).

58. Donald W. Goodwin, Samuel B. Guze, and Eli Robins. "Follow-up Studies in Obsessional Neurosis," *Archives of General Psychiatry* 20:183-184 (1969).

his room, always thought, "my father will die"; a young man was anguished whenever he left his house by the thought that he had left a cigarette burning.[59]

Compulsion is an impulse expressed in action, an impulse carried out. It is eccentric behavior ritualized. It is hanging up one's clothes a certain way, just so, before going to bed. A workman on an assembly line was compelled, before soldering one piece to another, to tap three times on his workbench with his left hand, then with his right, then with each foot. Later the rituals grew more complex and so slowed his work that he lost his job.[60] The classic case of compulsive behavior is that of repeated hand-washing. Milder examples include stepping over cracks in the sidewalk, running a finger around the collar repeatedly. A rather troublesome example is *folie du doute*, in which the sufferer rechecks himself. He locks the door before going to bed at night but upon reaching bed wonders if the door really is secured. He goes back, checks it, returns to bed, doubts again, rechecks the door, and so on.[61] When this type of behavior is well developed, it incapacitates the victim and becomes a considerable burden on others in his environment.[62]

A wide variety of research in the past two decades has shown something of considerable interest for Paul's behavior that was scarcely suspected in his lifetime: obsessives have stronger feelings of ambiguity about many things than other people do. They also have a stronger need for certainty and therefore a stronger need to avoid ambiguity. For example, in tests for the hearing of faint auditory signals, obsessive-compulsives asked for the repetition of the signals much more frequently than the controls and left many fewer answers marked "not sure." The researchers concluded that obsessive rituals and ruminations are "the result of an overpowering need for certainty in decisions to terminate quite ordinary activities."[63]

---

59. John C. Nemiah, "Obsessive-Compulsive Disorder," in Kaplan et al., *Comprehensive Textbook of Psychiatry*, 3rd ed., 2:1511.

60. Nemiah, "Obsessive-Compulsive Reaction," in Freedman et al., *Comprehensive Textbook of Psychiatry*, 1st ed., pp. 916-917.

61. Coleman et al., *Abnormal Psychology*, pp. 214-215. Kolb and Brodie, *Modern Clinical Psychiatry*, pp. 476-477.

62. For other examples, see Peter G. Mellett, "The Clinical Problem," in Beech, *Obsessional States*, p. 58.

63. A. D. Milner, H. R. Beech, and V. J. Walker, "Decision Processes and Obsessional Behavior," *British Journal of Social and Clinical Psychology* 10:88-89 (1971).

Other studies show that obsessives repeat this pattern of avoiding ambiguity in tests discriminating for differences in weight, length, block shapes, and so forth. "By avoiding ambiguity, the Neurotic person, and the Conversion Hysteric and Obsessional in particular, would appear to avoid both subjective uncertainty and conflictful situations. By avoiding uncertainty and conflict, the individual would appear to avoid further anxiety."[64] Tests show that obsessive-compulsives also err in the direction of symmetry in response to visual stimuli more than other people do.[65]

The obsessive's behavior is driven and full of effort; it lacks spontaneity. There is a "trend toward the replacement of 'I want to' or 'I enjoy' with 'I ought to' or 'I should'. . . . Tragically, he often does things for or with others mainly because he feels *required* to do so."[66] Marital life is more than usually difficult for obsessives, as it is for paranoids, and celibacy is common among them.[67]

Superficially, Paul fits into the concept developed here. He liked order, and he was a stickler for precision and punctuality, especially in the military. But he fits in the popular sense of the terms obsessive and compulsive, not in the scientific sense. To find a genuine obsessive-compulsive neurosis requires the demonstration of obsessive thinking, compulsive actions, and feelings of ambiguity.

As for obsessive thinking, it may be credible that Paul thought in this fashion, but we have no evidence of it. Obsessive thinking is entirely internal and private, and most persons experiencing it, at least with a neurotic degree of intensity, are embarrassed about it and reluctant to admit it. It is identifiable only by confession. Paul did not confess it in any known material that survives him. Hence, for lack of evidence, we must rule out all but the possibility of it.

Compulsive behavior is not so obscure, for it has outward manifestations. Paul was devoted to ceremony. The ceremonies of the Maltese Knights are perhaps the best example.

---

64. Vernon Hamilton, "Perceptual and Personality Dynamisms in Reactions to Ambiguity," *British Journal of Psychology* 48:200-215 (1957).

65. B. G. Rosenberg, "Compulsiveness as a Determinant in Selected Cognitive-Perceptual Performances," *Journal of Personality* 21:506-516 (1953).

66. Laughlin, *The Neuroses*, pp. 326-329.

67. Alan Black, "The Natural History of Obsessional Neurosis," in Beech, *Obsessional States*, p. 30.

But they were not the kind of personal, private rituals that qualify as obsessive disorder, and they cannot, in this instance, be demonstrated to have relieved anxiety in him.

Neurotics who practice private rituals are embarrassed about them, and hence the practice is known only to themselves and a few intimates. If Paul carried on compulsive rituals, they would probably be known, if at all, only to Mariia Fedorovna, Nelidova, or Kutaisov. Kutaisov left no written record of his association with Paul, and there is nothing in the correspondence of Mariia Fedorovna and Nelidova about compulsive rituals. Mariia Fedorovna's most intimate record of her life with Paul was a voluminous set of diaries. They would have been an invaluable historical source, perhaps the best record of Paul's life. Unfortunately, upon her death, Nicholas I followed her order to destroy them.

There is some evidence of ambiguity and the struggle to overcome it. Paul observed that those who are engaged in a conflict between reason and passion are happier when won by reason. He saw a conflict endemic in the relationship of these two forces and avoided prizing them equally. Paul's well-documented impetuosity may simply have reflected the momentum of resolution necessary to break away from paralyzing indecision. He must have had a desperate need to make up his mind instantly, and this feature of his personality was likely abnormal. The whole impetus of his writings is to establish an unambiguous order of things as they should be. The surest guarantee of making things what they should be was autocratic power, his own power. His attitude toward Russians was ambiguous. He both scorned and revered them, saying that if they were governed properly, they would be the awe of their neighbors. Of the three essential symptoms, a case can be made for only one, and, as will appear later, feelings of ambiguity (and an aversion to them) are not specific to obsessive neurosis alone.

To summarize the assessment of Paul to this point, we have found some plausible, or at least intriguing, evidence of both paranoid dynamisms and obsessive dynamisms, but not enough in either case to justify the use of labels designating such serious problems as paranoid psychosis or obsessive neurosis.

The last category of functional psychological disorders to be considered is that of the personality disorders. This is an especially fruitful concept for the study of Paul, though not without its problems. This particular terminology was introduced by *DSM-II* in 1968. Understandably, several years passed before it began to be reflected significantly in the literature. It is still slighted in some of the standard textbooks--for example, Coleman et al., *Abnormal Psychology* (6th ed., 1980), and Kolb and Brodie, *Modern Clinical Psychiatry* (10th ed., 1982). This state of affairs is recognized by the editor of one of the most important contributions to the subject: "This book is designed to fill a void in the literature regarding personality disorders and their clinical care. As a teacher and therapist I have become aware of deficits in both psychiatric training and treatment of this very large group of patients about whom much less has been studied than neurotic and psychotic disorders [sic]."[68]

Personality disorders, according to *DSM-II*, are characterized by "deeply ingrained maladaptive patterns of behavior that are perceptibly different in quality from psychotic and neurotic symptoms. Generally, these are life-long patterns, often recognizable by the time of adolescence or earlier."[69] They are perceptibly different from other disorders in that they are, in the opinion of most specialists, less severe than neuroses and psychoses. They are different, too, in that although in many cases they display the same style of abnormal behavior as is sometimes found in psychoses and neuroses--perceptual skew or strident anxiety, respectively--they do not do so to the same degree.

DSM-III's definition is similar and also interesting: "Personality *traits* are enduring patterns of perceiving, relating to, and thinking about the environment and oneself, and are exhibited in a wide range of important social and personal contexts. It is only when *personality traits* are inflexible and maladaptive and cause either significant impairment in social or occupational functioning or subjective distress that they constitute *Personality Disorders*. The manifestations of Personality Disorders are generally recognizable by adolescence or earlier and continue throughout most of adult life, though they often become less obvious in middle or old age."[70]

The schizoid personality, for example, is markedly shy and withdrawn. The schizotypal resembles a low order of schizophrenia. The antisocial personality has criminal tendencies. The passive-aggressive personality expresses aggression in a passive mode, for example, by obstruction, pouting, procrasti-

---

68. John R. Lion, ed., *Personality Disorders: Diagnosis and Management* (Baltimore: Williams & Wilkins, 1974), p. v.

69. *DSM-II*, p. 41.

70. *DSM-III*, p. 305.

nation, intentional inefficiency, or stubbornness.[71]   There are other varieties, but let us look at the three varieties which are of special interest in Paul's case.

The hysterical personality is also known as the histrionic personality, and this latter name better suggests why it requires attention in reference to Paul.   "These behavior patterns are characterized   by   excitability,   emotional   instability, over-reactivity, and self-dramatization.   This self-dramatization is always attention-seeking and often seductive, whether or not the patient is aware of its purpose.   These personalities are also immature, self-centered, often vain, and usually dependent on others."[72]   Paul was histrionic, excitable, unstable.   He was not seductive--at least not in any conventional sense.   He was self-centered, vain, and dependent.   Hence he fits enough of the definition to make the matter worth pursuing.

The recognition of hysteria and the use of the term are both very old.   The problem was known to the ancient Egyptians and, of course, to Hippocrates and the Greeks.   The condition was familiar throughout early modern Europe.   Both William Cullen and Philippe Pinel were conversant with it.[73]

The hysterical personality is defined by the less conspicuous features of the hysterical neurotic.   The more obvious symptoms of the hysterical neurotic, either conversion or dissociative type, are medical complaints and physical disabilities. The histrionic features are present, too, but they are overshadowed by the more dramatic evidence of, perhaps, blindness or altered consciousness.   In the hysterical personality, the physical complaints are not indicated, and the histrionic disposition is thus more noticeable.

Hysterical personalities "are vain, egocentric individuals displaying labile and excitable but shallow affectivity.   Their dramatic, attention-seeking, and histrionic behavior may encompass lying and *pseudologia phantastica.*   They are quite conscious of sex and appear provocative, but they may be frigid and

---

71. I am using here the typology of *DSM-III*, pp. 306-330.

72. *DSM-II*, p. 43.

73. Ilza Veith, "Four Thousand Years of Hysteria," in M. J. Horowitz, ed., *Hysterical Personality* (New York: Aronson, 1977), pp. 10-14, 32-39. Hunter and Macalpine, *Three Hundred Years of Psychiatry,* pp. 68-75, 143-147, 221-224, 319-324.

are dependently demanding in interpersonal relations."[74]   Patterns of expression are symptomatic: "Language patterns reflect a heavy use of superlatives; emphatic phrases may be used so repetitively that they acquire a stereotyped quality."[75]   The hysterical personality has a characteristic style of intellectual operations.   Mental functions are simplistic and impressionistic, given to romance and fantasy, and showing little power of concentration.   Such people tend to be gifted in *savoir faire* and deficient in factual knowledge.   They are rare among scientists, scholars, and professional people.

Much of this describes Paul.   His behavior on the parade ground can be interpreted as attention-seeking and self-dramatization.   His use of the Knights of Malta suggests dramatization of himself.[76]   His outbursts of violent dissatisfaction fit the same pattern, as do his efforts to mediate a general pacification of Europe and, more trivially, his wish not to have the audience in the theater applaud before he did.

As for seductiveness, so far as I am aware, it never characterized him.   He could be charming, as several people have attested, but he was not in any sense seductive.

His mental mode of operations, as manifested in his writings, was simplistic and impressionistic.   Witness the outlawing of words reminiscent of the French Revolution.   His political testament shows that he thought autocracy, properly conducted, might remedy all the evils of society.   But the memorandum entirely lacked realistic detail on the institutions that might be appropriate for a better-governed country.   He would have stopped the French Revolution with cannon.   The evils of Russia he ascribed to *ces gens-là*, a perverse people, especially the nobility, who preferred to be ruled by women and their favorites.   His moralism was conspicuously vague but strident.   He assumed that his several pages of political principles were sufficient to govern the kingdom.

The qualities of repetition and emphasis are quite tiring in his writing.   Over and over again he wrote of the "well-being of

74. E. Brody and S. Lindbergh, "Personality Disorders, I: Traits and Pattern Disturbance," in Freedman et al., *Comprehensive Textbook of Psychiatry*, 2nd ed., 1:942. See also ibid., 2:1284-1285.

75. Roger A. MacKinnon and Robert Michels, *The Psychiatric Interview in Clinical Practice* (Philadelphia: Saunders, 1971), p. 112.

76. A joke circulated after Paul's death to the effect that he had asked his assassins for a short postponement of their purpose while he drew up plans for the funeral ceremony. August Kotzebue, "Zapiski," in *Tsareubiistvo*, p. 368.

each and of all," of the power of the laws and the need for laws, of the virtue of autocracy as a guarantee of the impartiality of the laws.

He did not exhibit *savoir faire*, but he was full of romance and fantasy. He admired Peter I, Henry IV, Frederick II. He aspired to be like them. He preferred, he said, to be hated for doing good rather than loved for doing bad. He looked forward to the day when everything in the state would be in proper order and harmony, when the well-being of each and all would have been achieved, and when all his work would be blessed by God's heavenly hand.

There are, however, serious problems in the application of the criteria of hysteria to Paul. Perhaps the primary feature of this style of behavior, self-dramatization, was an adaptive and virtually prerequisite quality of being the emperor of all the Russias. Paul *was* the center of attention, he was expected to be the center of attention, to take the leading role in court ceremony and in political life in general. It would have been extremely awkward and unnatural for him to find a means of avoiding a kind of behavior that in the man in the street would have been called self-dramatizing.

A second problem concerns the sexual distribution of hysteria. Hippocrates named the phenomenon for the wandering of the uterus in women, and since his time, it has been regarded as exclusively or predominantly characteristic of women. This was clearly the case through the seventeenth and eighteenth centuries. Cullen and Pinel considered hysteria a sexual disorder of women, usually related to nymphomania. The similar thinking of Breuer and Freud (*Studies on Hysteria*) in the 1890s is well known. This idea has come under attack; yet it remains true even in our own time that diagnoses of hysteria are applied predominantly to women.[77] One study of hysterical types "was confined to women because the number of men so diagnosed was insufficient to obtain even a small representative

---

77. Veith, "Four Thousand Years of Hysteria," in Horowitz, *Hysterical Personality*, pp. 10-14, 32-39, and passim. Hunter and Macalpine, *Three Hundred Years of Psychiatry*, pp. 68-75, 143-147, 221-224, 319-324. Robert A. Woodruff, Jr., Donald W. Goodwin, and Samuel B. Guze, "Hysteria (Briquet's Syndrome)," in Alec Roy, ed., *Hysteria* (New York: John Wiley, 1982), p. 120. Lydia Temoshok and C. Clifford Attkisson, "Epidemiology of Hysterical Phenomena," in Horowitz, *Hysterical Personality*, pp. 145-211, passim. David Shapiro, *Neurotic Styles* (New York: Basic Books, 1965), p. 180.

sample."[78] Other studies are even more categorical: "criteria for the diagnosis of hysteria are probably never or only rarely met in civilian males."[79]   According to Arkonac and Guze, "it occurs primarily if not exclusively in women."[80]   Guze, Woodruff, and Clayton state that "no more than two or three percent of hysterics have been men."[81] A type of hysterical personality that is mentioned among men is the "Don Juan" type, and this does not conceivably approximate Paul.[82]

One of the few places where diagnoses of hysteria for males are found is in military hospitals. In most cases, men so diagnosed have "compensation prospects."   The term means "that the patient had immediate prospect of tangible, material reward accruing from his illness, i.e., collecting money from pension or insurance sources, getting out of military service or avoiding arrest and prosecution."[83] There were no such compensation prospects or secondary gain available to Paul in his position.

DSM-III is helpful with this problem. It is more explicit and restrictive than its predecessor, and several of its criteria do not apply to Paul. "Individuals with this disorder . . . are apt to be overly trusting of others, . . . frequent complaints of poor health, such as weakness or headaches, or subjective feelings of depersonalization may be present. During periods of extreme stress, there may be transient psychotic symptoms of insufficient severity or duration to warrant an additional diagnosis." Finally, "the disorder is apparently common, and diagnosed far more frequently in females than in males."[84]

---

78. Martin G. Blinder, "The Hysterical Personality," *Psychiatry* 29:229 (1966).

79. Michael J. Perley and Samuel B. Guze, "Hysteria--the Stability and Usefulness of Clinical Criteria," *New England Journal of Medicine* 266:423 (1962).

80. Oguz Arkonac and Samuel B. Guze, "A Family of Hysteria," *New England Journal of Medicine* 268:239 (1963).

81. Samuel B. Guze, Robert A. Woodruff, and Paula J. Clayton, "Sex, Age, and the Diagnosis of Hysteria," *American Journal of Psychiatry* 129:745 (1972).

82. Kolb and Brodie, *Modern Clinical Psychiatry*, p. 602.

83. James J. Purtell, Eli Robins, and Mandel E. Cohen, "Observations on Clinical Aspects of Hysteria," *Journal of the American Medical Association* 146:903 (1951).

84. *DSM-III*, p. 314.

The case for obsessive-compulsive personality is more richly suggestive. According to *DSM-II*, "this behavior pattern is characterized by excessive concern with conformity and adherence to standards of conscience. Consequently, individuals in this group may be rigid, over-inhibited, over-conscientious, over-dutiful, and unable to relax easily."[85] *DSM-III* designates this problem compulsive personality disorder: "The essential feature is a Personality Disorder in which there generally are restricted ability to express warm and tender emotions; perfectionism that interferes with the ability to grasp 'the big picture'; insistence that others submit to his or her way of doing things; excessive devotion to work and productivity to the exclusion of pleasure; and indecisiveness. . . . Preoccupation with rules, efficiency, trivial details, procedures, or form interferes with the ability to take a broad view of things. . . . Individuals with this disorder tend to be excessively conscientious, moralistic, scrupulous, and judgmental of self and others."[86]

This disorder is distinguished from obsessive-compulsive neurosis by the absence of obsessive thinking or impulses and compulsive rituals. The label is usually applied to persons driven by the need for orderliness and perfection. Like obsessive-compulsive neurotics, they cannot tolerate ambiguity. "An obligatory quality pervades much of their life experience. When forced to work under circumstances over which he has no control and which may vary unpredictably, the compulsive personality may become anxious and disorganized. . . . As a supervisor, he is one who breathes down the necks of his subordinates and drives them to distraction by his attention to petty detail and his insistence on following the letter of the law. His need for perfection and order always carries with it the potential for conflict with others who may view him as obstructionistic, petty, inordinately scrupulous, and irascible."[87]

This type of personality is highly controlling, of himself, of his environment, and, if possible, of others. He maintains a hyperalert vigilance, for he is consumed by doubt whether other people and the world in general are friendly or hostile. To con-

---

85. *DSM-II*, p. 43.

86. *DSM-III*, pp. 326-327.

87. Brody and Lindbergh, "Personality Disorders," in Freedman et al., *Comprehensive Textbook of Psychiatry*, 2nd ed., 1:944.

struct a confident relationship between himself and others, he is constantly in search of the "right rules."[88]

Obsessive traits are common among normal people and have adaptive value in many situations. The distinction between the traits and the disorder is determined by the degree of disability and by character rigidity. "If fear of closeness and a need to control others keeps the compulsive at a distance from family and prevents him from forming close friendships, it is reasonable to consider his behavior as deviant." Such a personality may divert attention from people onto "activities and areas related to maintaining physical integrity and cleanliness, such as exercise, sleep, skin care, and dental hygiene. In short, this pattern of obligatory attention, rigidly applied to minutiae, control of which is essential for the maintenance of a high degree of order and predictability, implies a narcissism that can preclude the development of sustained, warm human relationships free of nagging doubts, suspicions, and irritations."

Scandinavian research has provided key bits of evidence that apply to Paul's personality. Hojer-Pedersen found that his obsessive patients tended to regard themselves as altruistic and yet behaved in a narcissistic manner. They reflected the same ironic paradox with respect to generosity and stinginess. Even more interestingly, all of them were ambiguously dependent and independent.[91]

Paul adhered rigidly to standards of conscience and sought the imposition of his own conscience on others. He was dutiful in the extreme, and he admired monarchs who were known for devotion to duty. His quest for order and perfection prompted contemporaries to speak of a "Gatchina spirit" which pervaded his military concerns and other affairs of state. He dreaded the French Revolution in part for its threat to the good order of Europe. His note to Mariia Fedorovna acquainting her with her new homeland and the imposing duties that she would have to assume there dwelled emphatically on order in their

---

88. Walter Weintraub, "Obsessive-Compulsive and Paranoid Personalities," in Lion, *Personality Disorders*, p. 87. Ernest G. Schachtel, "On Attention, Selective Inattention and Experience; an Inquiry into Attention as an Attitude," *Menninger Clinic Bulletin* 33:65-91 (1969).

89. Weintraub, "Obsessive-Compulsive and Paranoid Personalities," in Lion, *Personality Disorders*, p. 87.

90. Brody and Lindbergh, "Personality Disorders," in Freedman et al., *Comprehensive Textbook of Psychiatry*, 2nd ed., 2:944.

91. Willy Hojer-Pedersen, "The Compulsive Personality Type," *Acta Psychiatrica Scandinavica* 44:166-167 (1968).

monetary accounts and their schedule. The "right rules" were the burden of the remainder of that document. If it all seemed too much to bear, she should consider that the rules themselves would, if adhered to, provide the refuge which they could not otherwise have. The new army field manual, the new field maneuvers, the new law on succession--all represent salvation by rules. This is not to say that they were useless or inappropriate. Rather, they represent the extreme degree of service which Paul expected of right rules.

No one would deny that Paul was vigilant and hyperalert, that he was a mobilized personality. Witness Rostopchin's comment on his sense of being slighted. Paul scanned the environment intently for signs of disrespect, as well as for signs of disorder. Reading the environment for those signals in particular, he often misread what was really there.

There was a conspicuous dearth of close relationships in Paul's life. Of course, this is not surprising or perhaps unnatural for a person in his position, for a Russian emperor. It is likely a characteristic of persons in general who dispose of enormous authority which others want to influence or use.

If we consider his schedule, it is easy to believe that he arranged his life so as to pre-empt personal spontaneity. He was demonstrably afraid of his inner impulses and kept them under tight rein. "Our manner of life must be strictly regulated. . . . Subjecting ourselves to well-known rules, *we protect ourselves from our own fantasies*, which frequently become caprices, and together with this, we give an example to other people, *who are obliged to subject themselves to the same rules.*"[92]   All must be arranged just so, "without changes, because any change in these things appears in the eyes of the public as a caprice." Paul did not want to be capricious or, worse, to appear to be capricious. "While we hold to the established rules, we spare ourselves much, including tedium, one of the chief enemies of man."

The findings of Hojer-Pedersen are especially interesting for Paul's case. Paul's own expression is full of intentions of generosity and self-sacrifice and of the ideal of service on his part to the suffering nation. He was, he thought, an altruist. This pose was accepted by the common people, who rarely came into contact with him. It was repudiated in morbid fashion by those who dealt with him daily. For them, his touchy narcissism was only too apparent. The ceremonies that he loved, the

---

92. Emphasis added.

care that he lavished on them, the fanfare of the Maltese Order, all of these manifested a wounded vanity seeking compensation.

Even more telling is Hojer-Pedersen's observation on ambiguous dependency. Paul was childishly dependent, so much so, and so much in need of being demonstratively independent, that he was putty in the hands of clever intriguers about him. He required Panin's support against Catherine, the support of religion and principle against his evil enemies, and finally the support of his barber-lackey Kutaisov against those persons, Mariia Fedorovna, Nelidova, and the Kurakins, whose support had been essential to him until he was required to recognize it.[93]

A variant of personality disorder often associated with the obsessive is the paranoid. "This behavioral pattern is characterized by hypersensitivity, rigidity, unwarranted suspicion, jealousy, envy, excessive self-importance, and a tendency to blame others and ascribe evil motives to them. These characteristics often interfere with the patient's ability to maintain satisfactory inter-personal relations. Of course, the presence of suspicion of itself does not justify this diagnosis, since the suspicion may be warranted in some instances."[94]

The behavior characteristic of the paranoid personality is similar to that characteristic of the paranoid psychotic. The most significant difference is the absence of delusions in paranoid personalities. The paranoid personality takes a defensive position against the world. He is sensitive and easily slighted. "These individuals fear and simultaneously desire close meaningful relationships with others but seem unable to admit and accept these affective needs."[95] They are intense and serious,

---

93. It is the need for independence that provokes the anger of the obsessive at minor frustrations. The car, or the coach, must work right, just as the troops on the drill field must. Such frustrations limit the aspirations of this personality type, keep him dependent, form a barrier to his expectations, not to mention the fact that they intrude the unexpected and spoil predictability. It is similarly characteristic of the type to enjoy the conveniences of home life and yet to resent the dependence implied by this pleasure provided by others. There is, therefore, latent hostility present in the apparently stable and satisfactory family situation. "It is not long before the obsessional begins to feel that those he is dependent upon are malevolent exploiters while he is a generous benefactor." Leon Salzman, *The Obsessive Personality* (New York: Science House, 1968), pp. 63-64.

94. *DSM-II*, p. 42. *DSM-III*, p. 307, is compatible.

95. Brody and Lindbergh, "Personality Disorders," in Freedman et al., *Comprehensive Textbook of Psychiatry*, 2nd ed., 2:943.

loners, and they frequently do not marry.[96] Their main weapons against the world are suspicion and aggression.[97]

As we have previously seen, Paul had in low degree some of the symptoms of the paranoid mechanism. The basic ingredient of paranoid psychoses that was missing in Paul was the delusional system. Most of the other symptoms characteristic of paranoid behavior were at least possibly present in him: a sense of inferiority, alert observation of a hostile world, grandiosity, and the creation of a paranoid pseudo-community.

Here we must deal with one essential symptom, a troublesome one that is as essentially characteristic of the paranoid personality as it is of the paranoid psychotic: projection. To demonstrate in Paul the use of this defense mechanism, we must be able to show that he attributed to others thoughts, characteristics, or impulses that he found it uncomfortable to recognize in himself.

There were two fundamental criticisms that he directed against his chief enemies, Catherine and the Russian nobility. The first was that Catherine had illegitimately denied him his rightful place on the throne. While Paul undoubtedly harbored the wish to supplant his mother as she had done him, the conflict was initiated not by his imagination, but by her actual usurpation. His own respectable and superior claims to the throne presumably precluded any feeling of embarrassment or discomfort in him about the rivalry. It would have been plainly impossible for him to feel any sense of guilt about a usurpation on his part which he had in no way realized. Hence this part of his thought process was not projection.

The second criticism was that Catherine, her government, and the nobility were negligent, corrupt, and not mindful of their duty, and that the nation suffered the consequences. It is hard to judge this criticism objectively. Perhaps it was true, perhaps the situation described was not much better or much worse than was typical in eighteenth-century Russia. What is more important is the issue whether Paul privately felt or even feared that he himself was negligent, corrupt, and undutiful. This question is impossible to answer directly: there is no evidence from the inner reaches of Paul's mind on the point, and given the likelihood of at least residual paranoid and/or obsessive processes in him, had he had such feelings, those processes

---

96. Weintraub, "Obsessive-Compulsive and Paranoid Personalities," in Lion, *Personality Disorders*, p. 93.

97. Swanson et al., *The Paranoid*, p. 66.

would have acted to conceal them. Still, the indirect evidence is interesting and not altogether obscure. The burden of Panin's teaching was that Paul should be almost inhumanly conscientious, dutiful, and virtuous in the Stoic mode and that he should serve the nation accordingly. Poroshin tells us that as a student, Paul fell far short of these standards and that he was reproached by Panin not infrequently. During much of his adulthood, he filled his life, while waiting for the grandeur of his destiny, with a surfeit of unproductive busywork. We may infer, then, that Paul was taught a standard that he felt that he failed to exemplify, and consequently that he experienced feelings of guilt from this source. That the burden of his criticism of his mother and her favorites singled out precisely the absence of those characteristics which he admired but perhaps did not exemplify produces a strong presumption of projection.

It seems inescapable that certain societies as a whole function by more paranoid impulses than do other societies; for example, samurai society, the police and the military, fascist societies, certain religious groups, especially the sectarian and millenarian. In addition, it seems likely that persons in authority adopt more paranoid dynamics than do others and that this is more likely to characterize authority the more exclusive it is.

There are two behavioral styles in Paul, then, for which the evidence seems strong, those of the obsessive and the paranoid personality. These two, as it happens, are commonly associated together in the same individual. Both disorders rely heavily on the use of reason for defensive purposes. Both types are characteristically verbally explosive. Both have severe consciences. They are both "loners" and "tend to deal with strongly dependent needs by the reactive development of an 'inner directed,' autonomous way of life." Both are very controlling and combative.[98] There is considerable agreement among the authorities that the two disorders are complementary. "Here are two styles, each of which is characterized by rigid and tense hypertrophy of normal functions and subjective experiences of autonomy. Each style, in its typical manifestation, includes a special and touchy mindfulness of the right of self-determination; each is peculiarly uninfluenceable and marked by special wilfulness and tense, unrelenting purposiveness and self-direction; and, yet, each involves the special expe-

---

98. Weintraub, "Obsessive-Compulsive and Paranoid Personalities," in Lion, *Personality Disorders*, p. 85.

rience of living in the company of some external or quasi-external, superior, and/or threatening voice."[99]

Paul would probably be properly classified by our contemporary standards of mental illness *in our contemporary society* as a borderline case of obsessive-compulsive personality and perhaps of paranoid personality as well. The looser and grosser criteria of mental illness characteristic of his time do not allow us to identify abnormality in him. In addition, we must admit that the milder mental disorders, such as the personality disorders, are defined principally by whatever is culturally conversant in any given environment. Given the currency and the strength of the ideas of natural law, autocratic duty, and the *Polizeistaat* of Paul's time, it is very likely that the kind of character that we would classify as obsessive-compulsive or paranoid personality disorders was not only acceptable and normal but requisite for a person in Paul's station. It was the kind of character that the tutors of young princes of the day aspired to inculcate in their pupils. We must admit that Paul was irascible, unpredictable, abrasive, volatile, the whole unlovable spectrum of things which his contemporaries perfectly plausibly accused him of being. But, given the considerations that we have reviewed, it is at best difficult to sustain an argument that Paul was, either by the standards of his time or by those of ours, in any formal, scientific, medical sense mad.

---

99. Shapiro, *Neurotic Styles*, p. 107.

Conclusion

Paul was born into an unusually threatening and insecure situation. As a child, he exhibited a good deal of impatient,
restless, and fearful behavior, and he was given to sudden impulses of wrath. As a young adult, he turned his estate at
Gatchina into a kind of refuge, a retreat from the world. He
made it, in the opinion of one observer, into something like a
foreign country, specifically Prussia. Before his accession to the
throne, there was a relatively common opinion that he was
mentally ill. He was regarded as a "dear sick person . . . in
need . . . of supervision," one whose "disorder of faculties" and
lack of self-control made him at times so hated as to provoke
"shuddering and pity" in natives and dread in foreigners and to
lead to the opinion that "his mind is deranged."

He was given a careful education in a slightly warped
and outmoded variant of authentic Enlightenment
neo-classicism, and his tutors effectively communicated to him
their own--and the age's--wonderfully exaggerated conception of
the power of education to transform state and society into a
happy and orderly whole. Paul's head was as full of beautiful
ideas and good intentions as were those of Alexander I and the
Decembrists and other "superfluous men" of a slightly later time.

Unlike them, however, he was morally literal-minded, he never shrank from attempting (in the Soviet phrase) "to translate into life" the abstractions that fermented in his head, and this fact was the central feature of his reign. Judged in terms of moral courage, he must be given high marks for the stubbornness with which he tried to implement through legislation the convictions that he had been taught. It was otherwise with his intelligence. He was evidently, as Joseph II commented, clever and mentally quick, but, as Frederick II suggested, he was woefully lacking in judgment of human relations. After 1796, he quickly got himself into serious trouble. The connection which he tried to establish between the ideas that he cherished and the state and society that he governed was naive. On the other hand, his naïveté was by no means unique among his peers, the other proud and presumptuous enlightened princes of the age.

In pursuit of one of the chief aims of this study, the resolution of the question whether Paul was mad, several considerations seem more important than all others. First is the fact that both on the eve of his reign and during the last year of his reign, a respectable variety of responsible observers, who were neither implicated in opposition to him nor damaged or disgraced by him, reported that he was mad. On the other side of the ledger, however, the evidence is written somewhat larger. He does not conform plausibly to any of the medical criteria of madness current in his time. Moreover, all of the clearly and authentically mad monarchs of the age were treated mercifully and humanely by the conventional medical standards of the time (George III of Great Britain, Maria I of Portugal) or were allowed a regime of more or less benign neglect (Christian VII of Denmark, Felipe V and Fernando VI of Spain). On the other hand, those monarchs and ministers who aspired to implement in policy the political programs that Paul took so seriously invariably encountered the same kind of desperate opposition that he provoked, though it did not always lead to regicide. Lastly, although few of the particulars that comprise the suspicion that Paul was framed with a case of madness by Pahlen and his co-conspirators can be documented beyond a doubt, still the very abundance of such particulars makes it hard to resist the idea that Paul was quite deliberately made to appear more mad than in fact he was.

The evidence of what the politically active people of the age did, as distinct from what they said, strongly suggests that Paul was not mad. If he had been genuinely and demonstrably mad, he would have been sufficiently harmless as to obviate the conspirators' need to kill him. Still, there is no denying that the man was bizarre and that his conduct was radically imprudent.

If Paul was sane, he did not enjoy that elementary, robust sanity that manifests itself in middle-of-the-road qualities of personality and shuns the extremes of histrionic posturing and self-effacing withdrawal. The most provocative insight on this point is that of Kliuchevskii, who thought Paul not mentally, but "morally abnormal." His eccentricities derived from the fact that he neither knew the habits of human society nor wanted to know them because he did not want to be constrained by them. "In Paul, this moral solitude became a kind of timorous asylum."[1] Pierre Morane has elaborated on this theme. Paul presumed "to reach too high, to dream of the inaccessible, the impossible, the sublime. . . . There is never to be found in him a firm purpose, a brave resolution to make modest efforts, to practice common virtues. . . . But he exhausts himself in chimerical quests of unmixed blessings."[2] It was only in a chimerical world of unmixed blessings, a fantasized, moral world, that Paul felt safe because, to rephrase Karamzin, he frightened others in great part in order not to be the most frightened of all. And so, he presumed to exploit his own superior moral truth and sovereign power to achieve a degree of social and political beatitude that was quite beyond human reach. In this way, he would catch the human flux and its disposition to err in a net of the right rules to make it live happily--and hence innocuously, and thus himself, safely--ever after.

Paul's predicament was, ironically, like that of the Marquis de Sade's Justine, whose experience illustrates, in the words of Norman Hampson, that "to try to regulate one's life by a moral principle is to set one's self athwart the rhythm of nature, so that one's suffering is likely to be proportionate to one's disinterestedness."[3] The Bavarian diplomat, the Chevalier de Bray, explained Paul's frustrations in much the same way: "If Paul I had been better acquainted with men and his century, he would not have made the strange mistake of supposing them without passions and without interests other than those of justice. He would have joined the powers not in order to do good

1. Vasilii O. Kliuchevskii, *Sochineniia*, 8 vols. (Moscow: Sotsekizdat, 1958), 5:189-190, 439-440.

2. Morane, *Paul I de Russie*, pp. 336, 441, 349.

3. Norman Hampson, *A Cultural History of the Enlightenment* (New York: Pantheon, 1968), p. 123.

absolutely but to do what good he could."4   In fact, Paul was probably trying unconsciously to use moral principles to serve his own interests. If he could have constrained his contemporaries sufficiently in a straitjacket of natural law and good morals, he would thereby have served his own interests because the ultimate aim beyond the extravagant collage of paradox and idiosyncrasy that passed for his policy was really desperately simple. It was to make the world safe for an eccentric Russian autocrat.

So much for questions of Paul's mental condition. Now, what of the role of psychology in the study of history?   David Stannard, in a work called *Shrinking History*, has concluded that "psychohistory does not work and cannot work."5   That, in my opinion, depends on what is meant by the term psychohistory. If it means, as it apparently does both in Stannard's work and in most of the writing that goes by that name, Freudian theory in historical literature, then I agree with him entirely for reasons set out in Appendices A and B of this study. But I see no reason to declare a comprehensive condemnation of all use of psychology in the study of history.   Its usefulness depends, not surprisingly, on the intelligence with which it is used, and intelligent uses of it are possible.

If we begin with a plausible portrait of Paul as an obsessive person, then we can use the clinical literature for biographical details and insights into his behavior that our conventional historical sources do not allow us. For example, we can in this way appreciate quite plausibly, perhaps not quite demonstrably, the inner ambiguity, the deep uncertainties, of his character. We can thus easily believe that the vehement resolution, the often violent outbursts, the notorious impulsiveness to which he was often roused were perhaps not merely what they seemed, but the development of sufficient momentum of resolution to enable him to break away from the nearly paralytic irresolution that afflicted him. On the outside a posturing, tyrranical monster, on the inside he was a cowering, frightened child. To my knowledge, there were no contemporary observations on the ambiguity in his character, and yet the pursuit of certainty is a flight from ambiguity, especially in the obsessive character. Hojer-Pedersen's description of the conflict over dependent-independent relations with other persons in the case of the

---

4. François-Gabriel de Bray, "La Russie sous Paul Ier," *Revue d'histoire diplomatique* 25:595-596 (1911).

5. David Stannard, *Shrinking History: On Freud and the Failure of Psychohistory* (New York: Oxford University Press, 1980), p. 156.

obsessive character explains a great deal in Paul's relations with Mariia Fedorovna and Nelidova. Here is an insight that is plausible on other grounds, yet helps to illuminate the grounds that make it plausible.

It is very likely that the study of abnormal psychology is useful for the study of historical biography in general. Admittedly, there is nothing in the corpus of psychological or psychiatric literature that is remotely so articulate or illuminating on the etiology or development of the normal personality as is the literature on the abnormal personality, and this, we must recognize, is a considerable weakness inherent in the whole idea of using psychology in the study of history. On the other hand, taken in sufficiently large samples, normal personality exhibits in lesser degree all of the dynamics of abnormal personality, and hence there is something to be learned about it in the light of psychiatric literature.

From either the historical or the psychological point of view, much of the key to understanding Paul, as well as to understanding Russia both in that age and throughout its modern history, lies in the conception of the *Polizeistaat*. Paul took refuge from his fears in psychic dynamics of an obsessive and a paranoid style, and the theory of the *Polizeistaat* at once exemplified and facilitated both of these styles. This is a particularly important point. His own psychic needs and habits found an especially comfortable intellectual milieu in a prestigious political theory much like themselves. Having done so, and having felt the relief that defense mechanisms by definition bring, he clung to this mode of cerebration with all of the passion of someone nearly in possession of security and with all of the unbending rigor which the obsessive and the paranoid style exemplify. This kind of behavior, however, deceived him and led him into error, for Paul and his theories did not allow for those ordinary derogations from the high-flown principles of the Enlightenment that are so universally human.

In this respect, there was much that he could have learned from Catherine, as a couple of stories illustrating her outlook demonstrate. Catherine had invited Diderot to St. Petersburg. She spent a good deal of time with him three days a week in conversation about politics and other matters of mutual interest, and she eventually became convinced that Diderot's ambitious plans for political reform were, in Isabel de Madariaga's words, "more fitted for the study than for real life." As Catherine told him, "you only work on paper, which will tolerate anything, while I, poor empress, I work on the human skin, which is on the contrary so delicate and touchy (*irritable et chatouilleuse*)."⁶   This idea evidently never entered Paul's consciousness.

V. S. Popov relates a similar incident. He had spoken to Catherine "of the surprise I felt at the blind obedience with which her will was fulfilled everywhere, of the eagerness and zeal with which all tried to please her." Catherine's response puts the matter in perfect perspective. "It is not as easy as you think. . . . In the first place my orders would not be carried out unless they were the kind of orders which could be carried out; you know with what prudence and circumspection I act in the promulgation of my laws. I examine the circumstances, I take advice, I consult the enlightened part of the people, and in this way I find out what sort of effect my law will have. And when I am already convinced in advance of general approval, then I issue my orders, and have the pleasure of observing what you call blind obedience. *And that is the foundation of unlimited power.* But believe me, they will not obey blindly when orders are not adapted to the customs, to the opinion of the people, and if I were to follow only my own wishes not thinking of the consequences."⁷ In other words, law will not achieve what custom will not endure, and no power available in the age of absolutism sufficed to make it do so.

But there is another, a social and cultural dimension of Paul's tragedy. He attempted to turn his Russians, *ces gens-là,* as he called them--dedicated as they were to pleasure-loving habits of relaxation and indulgence, to the principles of "perhaps, somehow, never mind," as a proverb puts it--into the virtuous, well-ordered automatons that the Germans of the *Polizeistaat* allegedly were, and the culture rebelled. The obsessive qualities of the political theory of the *Polizeistaat* were far more normal in Paul's time than they are in our own politically liberal milieu, but it was not normative in the Russian environment to attempt to apply a theory which the servants of the state regarded as so aversive. In this sense, too, because as Kant said, the "only general characteristic of insanity is the loss of a sense for ideas peculiar to ourselves (*sensus privatus*)," Paul was less than perfectly sane. He had embraced an ambitious version of an abstract theory that was never literally applicable even in the society and culture that generated it; and he set out to apply

---

6. Isabel de Madariaga, *Russia in the Age of Catherine the Great* (New Haven, Conn.: Yale University Press, 1981), p. 339.

7. Ibid., p. 580.

it to a society and culture far less hospitable to it than that from which it was taken.

And yet the *Polizeistaat* was as essential to Russia as it was to Paul, and its presence there was at least a hundred years old at the time of his reign. It was the most widely distributed vehicle of modernization and of political efficiency in eastern and central Europe in the eighteenth century. No state, at least in eastern and central Europe, which failed to embrace this presumptuous model of policy could remain viable and secure in an order of international affairs as competitive, aggressive, and predatory as the European state system of that time--Poland is a dramatic counter-example. Russia was deficient in those cultural and psychological dynamisms, restless, meddlesome curiosity and demonic enterprise, from which modernization and both economic and political mobilization draw so much strength. The *Polizeistaat* provided the Russians an important *part* of a short-cut remedy for their environmental, cultural, and political deficiencies. It is a model which has served them severely but in some respects well for nearly three hundred years now. It is, however, a tricky one, and as the experience of Paul and several of his successors shows--down to our own time--it leads as easily to great failures as to great successes, depending upon the force and aptitude with which the power is wielded.

APPENDIX A:
PAUL IN THE PERSPECTIVE
OF PSYCHOANALYSIS

There is an element of unfinished business here. It has to do with the methodology which we call psychohistory, the application of the richly historical viewpoint of Freudian theory of personality to individuals and social groups of the past in search of a better understanding of the motives of their behavior or the development of their personalities and values. The historian writing, as I am, of history and psychology together is obliged by the methodological conventions of his discipline to take into account one of the important lines of inquiry of the day.

I am concerned here, then, to do two things: first, to explain by Freudian theory those characteristic dynamics of Paul's personality that were identified in Chapter 7; and, second, to evaluate the probable reliability of those aspects of the theory that are applicable to Paul's case.

Paul developed what is currently regarded as two distinct styles of behavior, the obsessive-compulsive and the paranoid. The first appropriate question to raise, then, is whether Freud understood the term obsessive-compulsive to mean what modern clinicians understand it to mean. The pertinent passage is from his paper on "Character and Anal Erotism": "The people I am about to describe are noteworthy for a regular combination of the three following characteristics. They are especially *orderly, parsimonious*, and *obstinate*. Each of these words actually covers a small group or series of interrelated character-traits. 'Orderly' covers the notion of bodily cleanliness, as well as of conscientiousness in carrying out small duties and trustworthiness. Its opposite would be 'untidy' and 'neglectful.' Parsimony may appear in the exaggerated form of avarice; and obstinacy can go over into defiance, to which rage and revengefulness are easily joined. The two latter qualities--parsimony and obstinacy--are linked with each other more closely than they are with the first--with orderliness. They are, also, the more constant element of the whole complex. Yet it seems to me incontestable that all three in some ways belong together."[1] The translator notes that the meaning of Freud's German word *ordentlich* has "become greatly extended in use. It can be the equivalent of such English terms as 'correct,' 'tidy,' 'cleanly,' 'trustworthy,' as well as 'regular,' 'decent,' and 'proper,' in the more colloquial senses of those words."

Here we have a definition of what Freud calls the anal personality, and it fits in all essentials the clinical description of the obsessive-compulsive style.[2] Freud and contemporary clinicians agree in the main about what obsessive-compulsive behavior is. "The majority of the psychiatric writers . . . recognize an obsessional personality, which, if not precisely the same as the anal character, inasmuch as there is usually no mention of parsimony, is certainly very similar."[3]

Like other phenomena that Freud observed, obsessive-compulsive behavior was explicable. He believed that it stemmed from fixation in the anal phase of psychosexual devel-

---

1. James Strachey et al., tr. and ed., *The Standard Edition of the Complete Psychological Works of Sigmund Freud*, 24 vols. (London: Hogarth Press and the Institute of Psychoanalysis, 1953-1974), 9:169. Hereafter cited as Freud, *Standard Edition*.

2. For an elaboration, see "The Disposition of Obsessional Neurosis," Freud, *Standard Edition*, 12, "Notes upon a Case of Obsessional Neurosis," ibid., 10, and Otto M. Fenichel, *The Psychoanalytic Theory of Neurosis* (New York: W. W. Norton, 1945), ch. 14, "Obsession and Compulsion," pp. 268-310. Of course, these three works, unlike "Character and Anal Erotism," are specifically about neuroses as distinct from personality disorders or personality styles, but the difference is one of degree, and the characters of the two phenomena have much in common.

3. Paul Kline, "Obsessional Traits, Obsessional Symptoms, and Anal Erotism," *British Journal of Medical Psychology* 41:299 (1968).

opment, approximately the second year of life. Persons who at that time failed to accommodate gracefully the stress of toilet training would later show clear signs of disturbance. Such a failure would be caused by the interaction of a constitution possessing exceptional sensitivity in the anal area and the enforcement of exceptional standards of cleanliness in toilet training.[4] As he explained it, "it is easy to gather from these people's early childhood history that they took a comparatively long time to overcome their infantile *incontinentia alvi* [fecal incontinence], and that even in later childhood they suffered from isolated failures of this function . . . we infer that such people are born with a sexual constitution in which the erotogenicity of the anal zone is exceptionally strong. . . . Now anal erotism is one of the components of the [sexual] instinct which, in the course of development and in accordance with the education demanded by our present civilization, have become unserviceable for sexual aims. It is therefore plausible to suppose that these character-traits of orderliness, parsimony and obstinacy, which are so often prominent in people who were formerly anal erotics, are to be regarded as the first and most constant results of the sublimation of anal erotism."[5]

In scattered places throughout his work, Freud tells us that orderliness is an elaboration of the need to be obedient to the demands of cleanliness. Parsimony represents the displacement onto other objects of the wish for anal retention. Obstinacy represents rebellion against the strict control of toilet training.[6]

What use can the historian make of the theory of the anal personality? If he knows enough about the historical personality in question, then the biography itself will serve as evidence of the relative accuracy of the theory. This is, in fact, rarely the case, as the demonstration of the theory depends on an extraordinary knowledge of intimate biographical details usually regarded as insignificant or embarrassing or both. In any event, it is not the case in the biography of Paul. As we have seen, except for the eighteen months during which Poroshin's diary recorded such an extraordinary amount of ma-

---

4. "Character and Anal Erotism"; also "Three Essays on the Theory of Sexuality," Freud, *Standard Edition*, 7.

5. "Character and Anal Erotism," ibid., 9:170. The brackets are the editor's.

6. For a convenient summary, see Fenichel, *Psychoanalytic Theory*, ch. 14.

terial, we have only a scant knowledge of his childhood, and even Poroshin did not take an interest in such matters as Freud demanded.

Another possibility is a reversal of the first. If the theory of the anal personality could be verified on grounds other than historical personality, then it could be employed deductively to reconstruct details of the biography--perhaps details more intrinsically interesting than those of toilet training--lost to the conventional process of historical research.

Finally, if we can develop a sound etiology of the personality profile in question, one in which we have confidence, then we have important clues to the less manifest, and perhaps more fundamental, features of the personality. We can thus develop a more insightful, coherent, and cogent understanding of his motivations and goals. We have seen that this approach did yield some not insignificant results when we looked at the psychodynamics of the obsessive personality. We were able to conceive Paul's somewhat disturbing impulsiveness as an effort to break out of the detested mold of ambiguity and uncertainty. Perhaps psychoanalytic theory can yield similar insight on his behavior.

We must look first to the relative reliability of the theory. It is immediately apparent that the heuristic problems are large. Freud did not explain, for example, how to identify either of the two elements that allegedly produce the obsessive personality, the anally sensitive constitution or exceptional standards of toilet training. His only reference to standards was a warning that obsessional traits are produced by training that is too early, too late, too severe, or too "libidinous." Errors of this kind in training might encourage the development of a style of behavior that is hostile, rebellious, and "anally expulsive." On the other hand, they might encourage the development of an "anally retentive" personality, one given to hoarding and to scrupulous cleanliness. Freud failed to specify what kind of errors in training lead to which kind of personality, whether it is too little or too much toilet training that produces the anally expulsive personality, or vice versa. Furthermore, if either style of behavior were sufficiently punished, the theory allows the intervention of the defense mechanism of reaction formation, which simply reverses the natural inclination of behavior and produces its polar opposite.

These very instances of vagueness and ambiguity that render the theory so tricky to apply to a historical personality have also bedeviled clinical and experimental attempts to verify it. In spite of that, there is a long history of robust efforts to do so. Experimental studies of this kind are numerous; a recent bibliography listed more than 2,000.[7]   Not even their conclusions can be digested here.   Moreover, it is difficult to evaluate the technical methodology--as distinct from the logic--of such studies.   Fortunately other experts come to our assistance by providing something like critical inventories of these experimental studies.

Robert R. Sears, in his *Survey of Objective Studies of Psychoanalytic Concepts*, notes only the most tangential evidence of the anal quality of the obsessive-compulsive.   He observes that there is some evidence of a correlation between nervous disorders, constipation, and other bowel disorders.[8]   There is, however, no compelling reason to believe that psychoanalytic theory alone is capable of accounting for that correlation.

Harold Orlansky, in "Infant Care and Personality," thinks that cleanliness and orderliness are primarily the consequences of social demands, that they represent forms of obedience.   They come naturally to children of middle-class parents.   He is skeptical of Freud's theory of the anal personality and says flatly, "the more economical theory would appear to be to explain 'anal' personality traits in terms of the cultural universe which gives rise to them."[9]

Paul Kline, in Fact and Fantasy in Freudian Theory, says that there "is no strong evidence relating . . . anal characteristics in children . . . to pot training. . . .   There is good evidence for the existence of personality dimensions resembling the anal . . . but these have not been linked to repressed pre-genital erotism nor to infant-rearing procedures."   Elsewhere, in an experimental study of his own, he says, "If it is admitted that there is some objective support for the existence of a syndrome [of anality], there is practically none for the psychoanalytic aetiology."[10]

The most comprehensive work of this kind is the most recent, *The Scientific Credibility of Freud's Theories and Therapy* (1974) by Seymour Fisher and Roger P. Greenberg.   Fisher and

---

7. See Seymour Fisher and Roger P. Greenberg, *The Scientific Credibility of Freud's Theories and Therapy* (New York: Basic Books, 1977).

8. Robert R. Sears, *Survey of Objective Studies of Psychoanalytic Concepts* (New York: Social Science Research Council, 1943), p. 14.   Sears is a psychologist.

9. Harold Orlansky, "Infant Care and Personality," *Psychological Bulletin* 46:20 (1949).   Orlansky is an anthropologist.

10. Paul Kline, *Fact and Fantasy in Freudian Theory* (London: Methuen, 1972), pp. 79, 94.   Kline is a psychologist.

Greenberg have addressed themselves chiefly to two problems that concern us here: the etiology of the anal personality and the anal nature of Freud's triad of traits. Clinical and experimental studies of the etiology of the personality have compared the nature of the child's toilet training and the features of his personality. Information on his toilet training comes largely from interviews with the mothers. Information on personality features comes from personality inventory tests. "Sifting through the disparate findings, one is forced to conclude that there is little support for the hypothesis that a child's toilet training determines whether he will manifest the three traits (orderliness, obstinacy, parsimony) Freud linked with anality." On the other hand, what the experimental studies reviewed do show is that there is likely to be a direct cultural imprint of the mother's personality. "While the search for a simple connection between an individual's anality and his toilet training experiences does not seem promising, there are observations in the literature suggesting a connection between his anality and the existence of anal traits in his mother . . . since there are indications that a mother with an anal orientation is often rigid about other training procedures besides those having to do with anal sphincter control, it may be that her impact on her child will also register importantly during non-anal developmental phases." Finally, they conclude that the "only thing we can state with even moderate assurance is that a mother with anal character traits will tend to raise an offspring with analogous traits."[11]

As was suggested earlier, it would seem that if there is no evidence that Freud's theory of the origins of the obsessive-compulsive personality is sound, there is little reason to continue to call it an anal personality. Evidently the experts do

---

11. Seymour Fisher and Roger P. Greenberg, "Obsessional Traits, Obsessional Symptoms and Anal Erotism," in *Scientific Credibility of Freud's Theories*, pp. 300, 146-148, 164-165. Fisher and Greenberg are psychiatrists. I have also consulted Fisher and Greenberg, eds., *The Scientific Evaluation of Freud's Theories and Therapy: A Book of Readings* (Hassocks, England: Harvester Press, 1978). I have decided not to use it here for two reasons. First, to use a book of readings by authors whose evaluations of other research reports I have already used extensively would skew the balance of expert opinion excessively in favor of these two authors among various others. Second, the authors admit a bias in the selection of material: "No claim is made that the papers are scientifically the 'best'. . . . It should be acknowledged that there is a definite trend for a majority of the papers presented here to be at least partially supportive of Freud, and this does reflect our judgment concerning what is true." Sic, p. x. A dash of Strunk and White is needed here.

not agree. Fisher and Greenberg give much attention to the question, "Is there an anal trait constellation?" In their opinion, "there is no question but that past studies have almost unanimously found it possible to isolate recognizable clusters of anal traits and attitudes. . . . Orderly and parsimonious traits are, indeed, among the most frequently cited in the anal clusters. While the third member of Freud's anal triad, stubbornness, is relatively infrequently directly mentioned,[12] there are parallel qualities such as perseverance and rigidity that often appear. Traits related to being clean and avoiding dirt are also referred to relatively often. It is rare to find qualities included in the anal clusters that are totally alien to the spirit of Freud's formulation."[13]

But there is a serious practical problem involved in detecting what is anally inspired in personality traits. The average adult male does not overtly practice anal eroticism. His anal eroticism is repressed because it is taboo. It is, in Freud's conception, unconscious. Hence it cannot be identified by any direct form of inquiry, but must be ferreted out by subtle means. The most common method is the projective personality test: the Rorschach Inkblot Test (1922), the Thematic Apperception Test (1935), the Blacky Pictures Test (1949), and many others. The Blacky Test was devised by Gerald S. Blum for the express purpose of examining Freud's ideas about psychosexual stages of development. It seems to be the most widely used of the projective tests concerned with verifying Freudian theory.

Blum's own research design has been characteristic of the approach to the problem. He submitted his subjects to two instruments of measurement, the projective one and a personality inventory. He then tried to match indications of the prevalence of unconscious fixations from one or more of the psychosexual stages alleged by Freud with the quite conscious character traits that these fixations were said to give rise to. It is a fascinating procedure.

In constructing the projective test, Blum devised a series of twelve cartoons featuring a dog named Blacky and its mother, father, and a sibling. Various cartoons were designed around explicitly Freudian crises of personality development, for example, Blacky being nursed by his mother (oral eroticism), Blacky's sibling about to have his/her *tail* cut off (castration anxiety).

---

12. Note the disagreement with Kline. See note 3 above.

13. Fisher and Greenberg, *Scientific Credibility of Freud's Theories*, pp. 144-145.

The subjects being tested were asked to write two-minute stories explaining the situation depicted in the cartoons.[14] The cogent interpretation of the results of this test presents some difficulty. One cartoon pictures Blacky defecating near his parents' doghouse. If the subject writing the story about this cartoon included prominently anal themes, Blum scored him strong in anality. If the subject's story was conspicuous for the absence of anal themes, his response was interpreted as the product of reaction formation, and he was also scored strong in anality. It's a case of "Heads, I win; tails, you lose."

In addition to this feature of the procedure, there is a question whether defecating is erotic. In the words of two of the critics of this experiment, "one . . . point is likely to occur to any researcher who approaches [these] results without Freudian blinders firmly fixed. [The researcher] assumes throughout that the picture of Blacky defecating is a measure of 'anal erotism' (also called the 'anal stamp'). Indirectly, we suppose it could be referred to as 'anal,' but where is the justification for assuming that it is also 'erotic.'   In English, this word refers to love (particularly of a sexual kind); exactly what it means to Freud is not made clear . . . , and [the projectionists] do not appear to feel any responsibility for specifying in what way the Blacky pictures should be regarded as an 'objective measure of anal erotism.' To the non-Freudian it remains nothing more than a rough index of attitudes toward shitting dogs."[15]

Cautious psychologists have reservations about the validity of projective personality tests.[16] These reservations were shared by the designer of the Blacky Test itself. Blum wrote that he hoped for the "future validation of the Blacky Test. If it can be demonstrated clinically that the test actually measures psychoanalytic dimensions, the data will increase in stature. . . . To accomplish such validation is not an easy task."[17] Unfortunately much of the experimental evidence for the validity of Freud's concept of an anal constellation of personality traits is based on such tests.

---

14. Gerald S. Blum, "A Study of the Psychoanalytic Theory of Psychosexual Development," *Genetic Psychology Monographs* 39:3-99 (1949).

15. Hans J. Eysenck and Glenn D. Wilson, *The Experimental Study of Freudian Theories* (London: Methuen, 1973), p. 98.

16. See F. Schumer and J. Zubin, "Projective Techniques," *Encyclopedia of Psychology,* 3 vols. (New York: Herder and Herder, 1972), 3:47-51.

17. Blum, "Theory of Psychosexual Development," *Genetic Psychology Monographs* 39:73 (1949).

In a more recent study of the anal question, Kline has demonstrated a relationship between reactions to the picture of Blacky defecating and a general concern with cleanliness (for example, "When eating out, do you wonder what the kitchens are like?" "Do you regard the keeping of household dogs as unhygienic?"). Kline then suggests that the link between the positive responses to questions of cleanliness and negative responses to the picture of Blacky defecating is the theory advanced by Freud.[18] As Eysenck and Wilson point out, a more parsimonious explanation of the relationship would be a common concern for cleanliness.[19]

In summary, experimental studies of the theory of the anal personality point to two conclusions. First, personalities exemplifying the combination of traits to which Freud gave the name anal are in fact relatively common, i.e., traits of orderliness and stubbornness, at least, are often found together in the same personality, though clinicians and experimenters tend to substitute the trait of punctuality for Freud's suggested trait of parsimony. Second, there is no evidence that these personality traits come from toilet training (and hence deserve the name anal) and much evidence that they come from cultural conditioning.

These experimental findings point to a conclusion in Paul's case that is vastly more economical and more persuasive than Freud's suggestions; that Paul learned his characteristic behavior and values from the teachings of the Panins, from the theory of the *Polizeistaat*, from the claims of natural law, and from the neo-Stoic morality prevalent in his day, which is to say, from the ideas that were normative and culturally imperative in his environment. Perhaps the only surprising thing here is the obstinacy with which psychohistorians cling to a more obscure style of explanation.

Some of the features of Paul's personality, and of the obsessive-compulsive style in general, are derived in Freudian theory not from the anal phase alone, but from the preceding one as well, the oral phase. These features, in Paul's case, have to do with ambiguous attitudes toward independence and with an apprehensively pessimistic outlook. The basic elements of psychoanalytic theory of oral fixations are laid down in Freud's

---

18. Kline, "Obsessional Traits," *British Journal of Medical Psychology* 41:299-305 (1968).

19. Eysenck and Wilson, *Experimental Study*, p. 98.

"Three Essays on the Theory of Sexuality."[20]   The subject is somewhat amplified in "New Introductory Lectures on Psychoanalysis," and there are pertinent remarks on it in "The Instincts and Their Vicissitudes."[21]   But Freud did not devote a paper to anything so specific as an "oral character."   The details of this concept were spelled out by followers building on his work, the most important contribution being that of his close collaborator Karl Abraham in "The Influence of Oral Erotism on Character-Formation" (1924).[22]

There can be little doubt that Freud regarded Abraham's work on the subject as authoritative. He referred to Abraham soon after the latter's death as one of his two closest collaborators, and he especially recommended Abraham's work on the oral personality to Marie Bonaparte.[23] Even so, the whole concept remains less satisfactorily defined than does the anal style of fixation and behavior, as Abraham himself admitted: "I cannot offer a picture comparable in completeness to that of the anal character."[24]

One of the problems in dealing with oral fixations is that they are, at least by implication, less distinct than their anal cousins. Abraham says that residual manifestations of infantile oral eroticism--grimacing, chewing, eating, drinking, speaking--are more acceptable for adults in our civilization than is the case with manifestations of anal eroticism.[25] As such, they are less subject to repression, and hence they presumably produce less distinct pathology.

---

20. Especially in the second essay, "Infantile Sexuality," Freud, *Standard Edition*, 7:173-206.

21. Ibid., 22:122ff.; 14:117-140.

22. Karl Abraham, *Selected Papers on Psychoanalysis* (London: Hogarth, 1965), pp. 313-406. In addition, there are two papers by Edward Glover on the oral syndrome in personality development, "The Significance of the Mouth in Psycho-Analysis" (1924) and "Notes on Oral Character Formation" (1924) in his *On the Early Development of Mind* (New York: International Universities Press, 1956), pp. 2-24, 25-46. They are turgid and obscure. See also Fenichel, *Psychoanalytic Theory*, pp. 62-66, 460-492.

23. "Karl Abraham," Freud, *Standard Edition*, 20:277. Freud to Marie Bonaparte, 26 April 1926, in Ernest Jones, *The Life and Work of Sigmund Freud*, 3 vols. (New York: Basic Books, 1953-1957), 3:445. Jones was, of course, instrumental in the psychoanalytic movement and was a close friend of Freud for forty years. His biography of the master, though not uncritical, is friendly.

24. Abraham, *Selected Papers*, p. 394.

25. Ibid.

Paul exhibited, as we have seen, symptoms of what psychoanalysis calls unconscious orality (dependency, ambiguity, pessimism). He showed, so far as we know, no signs of manifest orality, and presumably, if he were fixated at the oral level, he should have.

Another problem that complicates the clear identification of behavior of oral origin is that it seldom stands alone. According to Abraham, any regression in behavior that proceeds backwards through the phallic and the anal as far as the oral stage will inevitably mix that style with contaminants from the other stages, especially the anal. Hence it will be harder to isolate and identify.[26] This mixture of symptoms is encouraged by a process that occurs on the borderline between the oral and the anal phase of personality. As the irruption of teeth and the onset of toilet training occur about the same time, and the teething spoils some of the infant's pleasure in sucking, that pleasure consequently "migrates" to another area, the anus, where the action of the sphincter muscles--and here is a hypothesis to test the imagination of research design--"is the same as that of the lips in sucking, and is obviously modelled on it."[27] Whatever we might think of the suggestion of the sphincter learning to love from the lips, the theory has the nice advantage of accounting for some of the notably oral features that appear in Paul's variation of the obsessive-compulsive personality.

The arrival of the infant's teeth has another important influence on the development of personality. Initially his relation to his mother (object relations, in psychoanalytic terminology) was strictly one of dependent sucking. This was his primary source of (erotic) pleasure. The possession of teeth provides another source of pleasure in the form of chewing and biting. A personality that relates to others as the child did to his mother before teething is known as oral incorporative or oral dependent. The contrary style is oral sadistic.[28] It is most important whether the personality "is the expression of an unconscious tendency to suck or to bite. In the latter case we shall find in connection with such a character-trait the most marked symptoms of ambivalence."[29] Just what this last sentence means is not quite clear. How are we to determine, except by looking at the mature personality, which oral style formed it?

---

26. Ibid., pp. 394-395.

27. Ibid., p. 396.

28. Ibid., pp. 395-396.

29. Ibid., p. 402.

And, in that case, how are we to test the theory? At one point Abraham suggests that it is the development of biting that compensates for the decline of pleasure in sucking; elsewhere, he says it is the migration of pleasure to the sphincter. The theory would demand that the first of these processes produce an oral-sadistic personality and the second an anal-retentive, two very different creatures, but Abraham did not pursue the matter.

One of the more immediately plausible of the psychoanalytic theories of orality is the idea that abundance at the breast encourages an optimistic outlook and deprivation, a pessimistic outlook. "Whether in this early period of life the child has had to go without pleasure or has been indulged with an excess of it, the effect is the same. It takes leave of the sucking stage under difficulties." As Abraham goes on to point out, the effect is not precisely the same, for the nature of the difficulties is different. In some cases, "the person's entire character is under oral influence . . . we are here concerned with persons in whom the sucking was "undisturbed and highly pleasurable. They have brought with them from this happy period a deeply-rooted conviction that everything will always be well with them. They face life with an imperturbable optimism which often does in fact help them to achieve their aims."[30] Obviously this is not Paul.

Some persons do not react in so happy a fashion, however, to the good fortune of abundance at the breast. Such people "are dominated by the belief that there will always be some kind person--a representative of the mother, of course--to take care of them and to give them everything they need. This optimistic belief condemns them to inactivity. We again recognize in them individuals who have been over-indulged in the sucking period. Their whole attitude towards life shows that they expect the mother's breast to flow for them eternally, as it were."[31] This characterization is not entirely inapplicable to Paul. He did seek emotional sustenance from a variety of people, ironically, in opposition to his mother. It is questionable whether he was characterized by inactivity prior to his accession to the throne or by a plethora of spurious and trivial activity that amounted to much the same thing. But there are the practical difficulties here that we encountered in the theory of the anal personality: How and why does lactic luxury form a productive individual in one case and a derelict in another? How do we define abundance at the

---

30. Ibid., pp. 397-399.

31. Ibid.

breast? How is it measured? In addition, it is curious that there is no reference in Abraham's work to a special sensitivity of the lips as there is in Freud's work such a reference to the anus. Is this factor important in one case and not in the other?

There is still another possibility of character formation at the breast, a pessimistic one. Abraham refers to "a melancholy seriousness which passes over into marked pessimism. I must point out, however, that this characteristic is to a great extent not directly of anal origin, but goes back to a disappointment of oral desires in the earliest years. In persons of this type the optimistic belief in the benevolence of fate is completely absent. On the contrary, they consistently show an apprehensive attitude towards life, and have a tendency to make the worst of everything and to find undue difficulties in the simplest undertakings."[32] This characterization is more obviously applicable to Paul than the preceding one, and this fact causes confusion. Was he deprived or over-gratified? "In psycho-analytic work, . . . we observe . . . individuals who are burdened throughout their whole life with the after-effects of an ungratified sucking period. . . . In their social behaviour these people always seem to be asking for something, either in the form of a modest request or of an aggressive demand. The manner in which they put forward their wishes has something in the nature of persistent sucking about it; they are as little to be put off by hard facts as by reasonable arguments, but continue to plead and to insist." Paul constantly complained of having been denied his legitimate rights, and by his mother. "One might almost say that they 'cling like leeches' to other people. They particularly dislike being alone, even for a short time. Impatience is a marked characteristic with them."[33] Paul disliked being alone in spite of his difficult relations with people, and he clung like a leech to one court cabal after another. But which is the real psychoanalytic model of Paul? The theory is not sufficiently exclusive: it is too fluid. That an infant who finds too little milk at the breast is likely to become pessimistic is not hard to believe, but it is not easy to prove.

How do experimenters approach the theory of the oral phase of personality? They can hardly design research techniques to test some of the ideas advanced here. In fact, they have to extrapolate related hypotheses to work with. There has been much research on the influence of breast-feeding on in-

---

32. Ibid., p. 400.

33. Ibid., pp. 400-401.

fants.   The researchers make several assumptions related to
psychoanalytic hypotheses: that the breast is better than the
bottle, that short periods of feeding and early weaning are tantamount to oral deprivation, and that thumb-sucking is an index
of oral deprivation.   These hypotheses are not precisely congruent with the theory of Freud and Abraham, but they are as close
as the nature of the theory and the constraints of behavioral research in the laboratory allow.   Perhaps findings on these questions will tell something about the validity of the psychoanalytic
theory of orality.

Sears, in *A Survey of Objective Studies of Psychoanalytic
Concepts*, finds that the evidence, while meager, supports
Freud's views in the following respects: "Nonnutritional sucking,
either of the food source or of the fingers, seems to be motivated
by some drive other than hunger"; "The degree of independence
of nonnutritional sucking from the hunger drive is unknown";
and "The effects of deprivation are similar to such effects with
other drives."   On the other hand, the evidence is insufficient to
clarify the following points: "Nonnutritional sucking develops as
a consummatory response by virtue of the association between
sucking and eating"; "Nonnutritional sucking has a strong or-
gastic effect"; and "Fingersucking is a preferred form of nonnutritional sucking because of its autoerotic quality."[34]   Sears's
study was one of the earliest, and today more data are available.

Orlansky, in "Infant Care and Personality," concludes
that thumb-sucking is not an unqualified index of oral deprivation.   He observes that there is no measurable difference in the
impact of breast- or bottle-feeding on the infant.   He cites a variety of studies to show that very early or very late weaning appears to be healthier for the infant than weaning at six to eight
months.[35]

Kline, in *Fact and Fantasy in Freudian Theory*, reviews
the type of testing--projective personality tests and a comparison
of their results with data on the infantile feeding of the sub-
jects--at which we looked in respect to the anal personality.   He
concludes that the oral character is less well supported than the
anal.[36]

Fisher and Greenberg approach the problem of orality as
they did that of anality, with the same two questions.   First, "Is

---

34. Sears, *Survey of Objective Studies*, pp. 8-9.

35. Orlansky, "Infant Care and Personality," *Psychological Bulletin*
96:5-12 (1949).

36. Kline, *Fact and Fantasy*, pp. 28-29.

there an identifiable oral character?" The studies which they review are typically "based on administering questionnaires that
inquire about a wide variety of feelings and ways of dealing with
people, and then determining by statistical procedures (usually
factor analysis) whether those facets of behavior theoretically
ascribed to the oral character are significantly linked to each
other." They seek to ascertain whether persons who are notably
dependent are also especially optimistic or pessimistic and exhibit manifest modes of oral gratification. Though the studies
differ somewhat in how they define the traits of orality, most
have looked for dependence, passivity, optimism-pessimism, and
socially affiliative tendencies. "A review of these studies reveals
that they have generally been able to isolate trait aggregations
recognizably resembling the oral character profile. . . . It would
be an exaggeration to declare that [they] strongly support the
existence of an oral character cluster. But they are moderately
supportive." The incidence of alcoholism and smoking is higher
among persons with oral character traits. Obese people exhibit
more oral imagery in Rorschach tests.[37]

"What Abraham and Freud labeled as oral traits do frequently cluster together. The empirical studies do not as yet tell
us in any decipherable fashion about the patterning of these
traits. . . . We can only say that there are trends for certain
traits to show up more frequently in the clusters." Dependency
is first among these and pessimism a close second. Other common ones are passivity, egocentricity, "tendencies to be either
unusually affiliative or withdrawing . . . , and the inclination toward various brands of hostile expression (for example, 'covert
hostility' or 'sadism'). Pessimism is much more common than
optimism. The distinction between oral incorporative (or recep-
tive) and oral sadistic is not demonstrable.[38]

The second question which Fisher and Greenberg raise is
the etiological one, "Can oral traits be traced to experiences in
the oral development phase?" The experimental evidence, they
think, "is fairly persuasive in pointing to a link between pertinent oral experiences in infancy and later adult attributes. . . .
However, that is about all one can say on the positive side.
There is not enough consistency to weigh the relative contributions of under- as compared with over-oral gratification to oral
character development. . . . We have no empirical data to help

---

37. Fisher and Greenberg, *The Scientific Credibility of Freud's Theo-*
ries, pp. 88-91, 128-129.

38. Ibid., pp. 131, 133, 137.

us conceptualize why early maternal nurturance may in one instance be antecedent to strong dependency but in another promote the opposite. In short, we are in the simplistic state of
merely being able to declare the existence of a correlation that is
roughly congruent with a theory." Finally, "the etiological aspect
of the oral character theory is the vaguest and least verified."[39]

The theory of the oral personality is especially pertinent
to Paul's case in one way: he was conspicuous for behavior that
is ambiguously dependent-independent, a trait that the theorists
ascribe to oral fixation. But the theory itself is very complex. It
is inherently ambiguous on the question what factors lead to the
formation of ambiguous dependence. Moreover, it is so subtle
as to be nearly beyond the reach of research. Consequently it
remains largely hypothetical with little support in the research
literature. We must conclude that it is not useful in attempting
to understand Paul.

Thus far we have dealt with two theoretical approaches
to the etiology of the obsessive-compulsive personality. There
remains Paul's other likely dynamic, the paranoid. Freud had a
distinct explanation of paranoid impulses. His classic exposition
was "Psychoanalytic Notes on an Autobiographical Account of a
Case of Paranoia" (1911).[40] Freud never saw the subject of his
study, Daniel Paul Schreber. His analysis was based entirely on
Schreber's memoirs, *Denkenwürdigkeiten eines Nervenkranken*
(Leipzig, 1903).

Schreber was a respected judge who suffered painful
delusions. He imagined that he was being persecuted by his
physician, Dr. P. E. Flechsig, a person for whom Schreber had
formerly shown a high regard. With God's help, Schreber believed, Flechsig aspired to deliver Schreber's body up to "foul
purposes." At the same time, "rays of God" were sent to mock
him, calling him "Miss Schreber." In the face of the formidable
conspiracy represented by Flechsig and God, Schreber had "a
mission to redeem the world and to restore it to its lost state of
bliss. This, however, he could only bring about if he were first
transformed from a man into a woman." He had dreamt "that
after all it really must be very nice to be a woman submitting to
the act of copulation."[41]

---

39. Ibid., pp. 114, 134.

40. Freud, *Standard Edition*, 12:9-82.

41. Ibid., pp. 16, 13.

Freud explained that paranoia was a defensive reaction whereby persons with homosexual impulses drove the painful realization of them out of their consciousness. For the Schreber case, the association of paranoia and homosexuality must be accepted as plausible, but Freud was not disposed to limit the association to one case. "We should be inclined to say that what was paranoic about the illness was the fact that the patient, as a means of warding off a homosexual wishful phantasy, reacted precisely with delusions of persecution of this kind." Freud consulted his fellow psychoanalysts, C. G. Jung and Sandor Ferenczi, whose paranoid patients represented a great variety of social types. "Yet we were astonished to find that in all of these cases a defence against a homosexual wish was clearly recognizable at the very center of the conflict which underlay the disease, and that it was in an attempt to master an unconsciously reinforced current of homosexuality that they had all of them come to grief."[42] It follows--and this is an important point--that the sex of the persecutor in paranoid delusions is always the same as the sex of the victim of the delusions.

Freud's theory of paranoia had been first suggested to him by Wilhelm Fliess (1858-1928), a physician who practiced in Berlin. From the time of their meeting in Vienna in 1887, the two became intimate friends and carried on an extensive correspondence for about twelve years. Though Fliess was two years younger than Freud, it was Freud who played the more junior and deferential role in the relationship.

Fliess was an advocate of notions of numerology and pansexualism. Freud picked up the idea of the basic bisexuality of both sexes from him. "Of those who knew [Fliess], with the exception of the level-headed Karl Abraham, who was not impressed, everyone speaks of his 'fascinating' personality. He was a brilliant and interesting talker on a large variety of subjects. Perhaps his outstanding characteristics were an unrestrained fondness for speculation and . . . a dogmatic refusal to consider any criticism."[43]

Fliess began with two ideas "on which he built an enormous superstructure of hypotheses. They were (1) that menstruation occurs once a month, and (2) that there is a relationship between the mucous membrane of the nose and genital activities; it often swells with genital excitement before or during menstruation." The process of menstruation itself evidently in-

---

42. Ibid., p. 59.

43. Jones, *Life and Work of Sigmund Freud*, 1:289.

trigued Fliess. It was, he thought, an expression of a tendency toward periodicity in the vital activities of both sexes. "He thought he had found the key to this periodicity by the use of two numbers, 28 and 23; the first was evidently derived from menstruation, the second probably from the interval between the close of one menstrual period and the onset of the next."[44]

Jones says that Freud cherished in regard to Fliess a "passionate friendship for someone intellectually his inferior" and "for several years [subordinated] his judgment and opinions" to Fliess. Eventually the relationship embarrassed him; he destroyed all of Fliess's letters and tried unsuccessfully to obtain and destroy his letters to Fliess. Freud had three fainting fits in Munich in a room which he associated with the memory of his relationship with Fliess. Ironically he explained the last of these, in 1912, to Ernest Jones as follows: "There is some piece of unruly homosexual feeling at the root of the matter."[45]

Freud's debt to Fliess in the matter of the etiology of paranoia does little credit to the respectability of the theory, but the detailed working out of the process was evidently Freud's own. There are two steps of defensive reaction against the wishful homosexual fantasy. The first is denial: "I do not *love* him--I *hate* him." The second is projection, the defense mechanism most characteristic of paranoia: "I do not *love* him--I *hate* him, because HE PERSECUTES ME."[46]

Homosexuality, in the psychoanalytic conception, is primarily the consequence of fixation in the third psychosexual stage, the phallic. It is the product of an unresolved Oedipus complex. As this is certainly one of Freud's more widely circulated ideas, it may be summarized here briefly; as we are concerned here with the analysis of Paul, only the male part of the theory will be considered.[47] In the phallic phase (c. 3 to 6

44. Ibid., p. 290.

45. Ibid., pp. 287, 317, and ch. 13, passim. See *The Complete Letters of Sigmund Freud to Wilhelm Fliess*, Jeffrey M. Masson, tr. and ed. (Cambridge, Mass.: Belknap/Harvard, 1985).

46. Freud, "Autobiographical Account of Paranoia," *Standard Edition*, 12:63.

47. "Three Essays on the Theory of Sexuality" (1905), ibid., 7: chs. 2 and 3; "The Dissolution of the Oedipus Complex" (1924), ibid., 19:173-179; "New Introductory Lectures on Psychoanalysis" (1923), ibid., 22: ch. 5; "The Infantile Genital Organization" (1923), ibid., 9:141-145; "The Ego and the Id" (1923), ibid.: ch. 3; "Leonardo da Vinci and a Memory of his Childhood" (1910), ibid., 11:63-137; "Some Neurotic Mechanisms in Jealousy, Paranoia,

years), the male child begins to develop erotic feelings for his mother and thus becomes his father's rival. He soon suspects that if he persists in the pursuit of his mother, his father will eliminate the unwelcome competition by castrating him--this is the castration complex. The reality of this threat is confirmed for him by the sight of a female's genitals, which he interprets as the result of castration. Faced with the prospect of the loss of his penis, the male child might solve the problem, and resolve the Oedipus complex, either by identifying with his mother and accepting a feminine social role, thereby averting the father's hostility, or by identifying with his father and repressing his desire for his mother. The latter is the more normal outcome or dissolution of the Oedipus complex.

Fortunately Freud's theory of paranoia and the Oedipus complex is eminently more suitable to experimentation and clinical study than is the theory of orality. The idea of paranoia as a defensive screen for homosexual impulses is a case in point. If the theory is to be borne out, then investigation should show both that the sex of the persecutor is the same as that of the victim of the delusions and that the subject is not aware of the alleged homosexual significance of this fact.

The first two inventories, or critical reviews, of the clinical and experimental studies of Freudian theory, Sears's *Survey of Objective Studies of Psychoanalytic Concepts* (1943) and Orlansky's "Infant Care and Personality" (1949), were published before the accumulation of a significant quantity of evidence on the question of homosexuality and paranoia. Kline's *Fact and Fantasy in Freudian Theory* (1972) does not deal with it. Fisher and Greenberg, in *Scientific Credibility of Freudian Theories* (1977), are better informed. They find that the theory of the same sex of the persecutor "is probably not tenable."[48]

Fisher and Greenberg review a variety of experiments in which paranoids and controls were subjected to homosexual, heterosexual, and neutral imagery. In some cases the paranoids responded more positively than the control group to homosexual imagery, in some cases more negatively.[49] But such results are problematical. If paranoids respond more positively than con-

---

and Homosexuality" (1922), ibid., 18:221-232. See also Fenichel, *Psychoanalytic Theory*, pp. 74-80, 91-98, 108-109, 328-337, 427-436, 495-496.

48. Fisher and Greenberg, *Scientific Credibility of Freud's Theories*, p. 269.

49. Ibid., pp. 259-267. For a good example of an experiment of this sort, see Harold S. Zamansky, "An Investigation of the Psychoanalytic Theory of Paranoid Delusions," *Journal of Personality* 26:410-425 (1958).

trols to overtly homosexual imagery, it disproves Freud's theory because their condition is supposed to be unconscious; and if they respond less positively, it proves nothing. In order to procure authentic findings, the research design must be able to discriminate between manifest and unconscious impulses.

A more promising line of inquiry consists of observations by psychologists of their own children. For example, the British psychologist C. W. Valentine recorded careful observations on the five children in his own family and reported no evidence of the Oedipus complex. His children preferred their mother prior to the alleged phallic phase. Then the girls preferred their mother more than the boys did. After age two, both boys and girls began to pay more attention to their father, but this was more characteristic of the boys than the girls. Valentine did not see signs of jealousy of himself among the boys. The child who most wanted to sleep with mother was a girl. Valentine cites similar observations, published and unpublished, by other psychologists and friends.[50]

There is evidence that it is not castration anxiety that impels the male child to identify with his father, but rather other things. According to Fisher and Greenberg, "several investigators have mustered evidence that when a boy seems to be identifying with his father, he may to a noteworthy extent be simply identifying with widely accepted masculine values. That is, a part of the similarity between father and himself may reflect coincidental aspects of the culturally current masculine stereotype they have both adopted." Freud's theory of identification, they think, "is in serious error. . . . In general, the empirical results contained in the literature weigh in favor of a boy's identification being facilitated by a nurturant rather than a fear-inspiring stance on the part of the father." The evidence on this point is unanimous.[51]

The laboratory and the clinic offer us reason to doubt the validity of Oedipal theory. Let us, nevertheless, give it the bene-

---

50. Charles Wilfred Valentine, *The Psychology of Early Childhood; a Study of Mental Development in the First Years of Life*, 3rd. ed. (London: Methuen, 1946), pp. 316-323.

51. Fisher and Greenberg, *Scientific Credibility of Freud's Theories*, pp. 186, 203-207. The authors also find no reliable evidence of penis envy in women or of the Freudian ideas that women regard their bodies in a more negative and deprecating fashion than men--rather, just the contrary. They conclude that "most of the formulations concerning the Oedipal process in the female are either uselessly vague or empirically contradicted and therefore need complete rethinking." Ibid., p. 224.

fit of the doubt and try for a moment to apply it to Paul. It may be interesting or titillating to speculate that homosexual impulses lay behind his behavior, but he does not fit the Freudian model. The sex of his chief persecutor was not the same as his own, his chief persecutor, in his conception, being his mother.

It is hard to imagine how Paul might have developed an erotic interest in his mother at age three to five in view of his removal from her vicinity during that part of his childhood. The relations between his parents were not sufficiently harmonious to exhibit a model male approach to a desired female. In addition, he was not with them enough to have learned about relations between the sexes from them even had their relations been better. The role of Peter III as parent was such as to make his part in the irresolution of an Oedipus complex credible, because Freud says that a weak or largely absent father does not threaten a male child sufficiently to force his decision to identify with the father and repress his desire for his mother. But even so, the child must live in his mother's presence to make Freud's idea plausible. Whatever Paul learned about family sexuality must have been learned from tutors and from the women who were his servants and caretakers in childhood. Judging from the childhoods of other royal heirs--for example, that of Louis XIII--there is much that he could have learned, but it was scarcely Oedipal. Poroshin tells us that Paul showed a lively curiosity about sex and developed ideas of love for much older women. But, as he also "had no clear idea of the difference between the sexes," he could not, by Freudian criteria, have conceived the possibility of castration. The social environment in his childhood was so extraordinary--it amounted to institutionalization, and was tantamount to deprivation--and differed so radically from the usual pattern of family life that the idea of the Oedipus complex seems irrelevant to any effort to understand it.

On the other hand, Freud's respected disciple Fenichel develops an idea of an unconventional style of Oedipus complex that might be more useful.[52] "The Oedipus complex with too few participants, is developed in children who grow up either with only one parent or without any parents. . . . If the parent of the same sex has died, this is felt as a fulfillment of the Oedipus wish, and thus creates intense feelings of guilt. . . . In the case

---

52. Fenichel, *Psychoanalytic Theory*, pp. 93-97. It may be worth noting that all of Fenichel's references on this theory are to relatively minor people in the psychoanalytic movement. There is no reference to Freud or to anyone of the stature of Abraham.

of the boy, if the father is missing (or 'weak') this might create a disposition toward femininity."

Family conflict or breakup may have similar results. "If the children themselves are the subject of parental arguments, this circumstance easily creates an intensification of the complete Oedipus complex and a fixation on narcissism which makes them expect that everybody will feel the same exaggerated interest in them that the parents have shown, an expectation doomed to disappointment." This last point applies to Paul only in a skewed sense, as he was no doubt the object of far more fussy attention than most children, though the attention was not that of his parents. For this reason, it does not help us to understand him in terms of the Oedipus complex.

"What has been said about children who did not know one of their parents also holds true for institutional children . . . they never get an opportunity to develop any lasting object relationships and their Oedipus complex remains pure fantasy. In any sort of permanent community there are always adults who serve as substitutes for the parents, but the fact that they were not the real parents will reflect itself in the special form of the Oedipus complex." Panin might well have served as a parental substitute for Paul--he undoubtedly did--but what special form of the Oedipus complex are we to anticipate in such a circumstance? Fenichel did not specify.

In conclusion, the historian studying the personality of Paul with the aid of Freudian theory cannot find in the theory rich and provocative material for speculation about the factors that made Paul what he was and cannot apply the theory to Paul in a persuasive and illuminating fashion. Moreover, he cannot, if he looks at the clinical and experimental literature, find reason to place confidence in those elements of Freudian theory that might help to explain Paul but do not.

Appendix B:
Psychoanalytic
Theory in Other
Historical Biography

The effort to use Freudian psychology to achieve a better understanding of Paul does not work out sufficiently persuasively. Perhaps it works better in other cases. As was pointed out in the Introduction, there are legions of such studies these days. Let us have a quick review of some of them.

Glenn Davis, writing in the *History of Childhood Quarterly*, asserts that Teddy Roosevelt grew a fierce set of teeth as an expression of his "oral rage."[1] Were TR's teeth privy to Freud's secrets? The *History of Childhood Quarterly* is the most enthusiastic of the publications on psychohistory, but more sedate journals, too, beg our credulity. The *American Historical Review* lent its dignity to two articles by Peter Loewenberg, one of which undertook to demonstrate through the use of psychoanalytic concepts that the generation of Germans who marched into the Nazi movement had had an unhappy childhood during

---

1. Glenn Davis, "The Early Years of Theodore Roosevelt," *History of Childhood Quarterly* 2:461-492 (1975).

World War I and afterwards.[2]   The other, a study of Heinrich Himmler, says that "Himmler's adolescent diary, taken as a whole, shows him to have been a schizoid personality who was systematic, rigid, controlled, and restricted in emotional expression in a pattern that is consistent with what psychoanalysis defines as the obsessive-compulsive character."[3]   Neither the term schizoid personality nor the term obsessive-compulsive personality is exclusively the property of psychoanalysis, and the American Psychiatric Association usually makes a distinction between the two.   "The psychodynamics of an obsessional character," Loewenberg continues, "are those of a person whose object relations are intact and whose character has regressed to the anal mode."[4]   All of this is authoritative and pontifical. Never is the question of the validity of the analytic apparatus raised.

One of the chief urges that Himmler was concerned to control, Loewenberg says, was sexuality.   His diary ascribed especially strong sexual urges to young girls.   "Attributing the loss of sexual control to the girls is, of course, a projection of Himmler's own sexual impulses."[5]   This idea is plausible enough, and it may well be true, but the burden of the evidence is borne--or disguised--by the phrase "of course."   Until the advent of the fad for psychohistory, professional historians had not welcomed the writing of history in a style utterly devoid of evidence.   Is there any reason to offer psychohistory a privileged asylum?

One of the psychohistorians' favorite rhetorical devices is to "point out."   "As Richard L. Ruberstein has pointed out, the Nazi death camps were the scene of the acting out of the most primitive fantasies of excremental aggression."[6]   How much forensic force is there in pointing out?   Suppose we pointed out that the French Revolution happened in Harlem or that Stalin was born in Bolivia?   In non-psychoanalytic contexts, unsupported propositions lack credibility.

But perhaps we are reviewing in contemporary publications irresponsible departures from the standards of the master. Let us consider whether the psychoanalyst as historian has been

2. Peter Loewenberg, "The Psychohistorical Origins of the Nazi Youth Cohort," *American Historical Review* 67:1457-1502 (1971).

3. Peter Loewenberg, "The Unsuccessful Adolescence of Heinrich Himmler," ibid. 67:616 (1971).

4. Ibid., pp. 616-617.

5. Ibid., p. 629.

6. Ibid., p. 640.

more effective than the historian as psychoanalyst--whether Freud, in his own work in historical biography, set a better example. The first such study was of Leonardo (1910). The interpretation turns on two key memories from the artist's childhood: "I recall as one of my very earliest memories that while I was in my cradle a vulture came down to me, and opened my mouth with its tail, and struck me many times with its tail against my lips."[7] Freud said that this passage signified homosexuality. "A tail, 'coda,' is one of the most familiar symbols and substitutive expressions for the male organ, in Italian no less than in other languages; the situation in the phantasy, of a vulture opening the child's mouth and beating about inside it vigorously with its tail, corresponds to the idea of an act of *fellatio*.[8] The other key passage is a reference to an ancient Egyptian myth which Freud plausibly shows that Leonardo must have been aware of: "In the hieroglyphics of the ancient Egyptians the mother is represented by a picture of a vulture. The Egyptians also worshipped a Mother Goddess, who was represented as having a vulture's head, or else several heads, of which at least one was a vulture's."[9] Freud relates this pair of associations to Leonardo's illegitimacy and to his early life allegedly alone with his mother--a probability, not a certainty.[10] Leonardo's memory becomes, then, a veiled insight into the Oedipal crisis of father absence which gave rise to Leonardo's homosexuality.

There are two problems with this interpretation. The first is that homosexuality, according to Freud's own theory, is the consequence of castration anxiety, and it would seem impossible to develop castration anxiety without the presence of the father. The second is that Freud's argument is based on a mistake. The word that Leonardo used to describe the bird in his memory was the Italian "nibbio," which means not vulture, but kite. Freud incorporated the mistake into his work from an error in Marie Herzfield's German translation of Leonardo's notebooks (1906). She rendered "nibbio" as "Geier," German for vulture, instead of "Milan," German for kite. In addition, the source for most of Freud's information on Leonardo was Dmitrii Merezhkovsky's novel *The Romance of Leonardo da Vinci.* Though Merezhkovsky used the correct Russian word for kite,

7. "Leonarda da Vinci and a Memory of his Childhood," Freud, *Standard Edition*, 11:82.

8. Ibid., pp. 85-86.

9. Ibid., p. 88.

10. Ibid., pp. 88-92.

"korshun," the German translation which Freud read and heavily annotated renders "nibbio/korshun" as "Geier." If the bird of Leonardo's memory was not a vulture, but a kite, the burden of Freud's argument about the Egyptian myth ceases to be relevant and the whole interpretation breaks down.[11]

In "Dostoevsky and Parricide" (1928), Freud applied psychoanalytic theory to a modest amount of evidence for the sake of amplifying by inference the historical and biographical record of Dostoevsky. The fundamental facts are Dostoevsky's epilepsy and his father's murder. Freud argues that the epilepsy was affective or psychological rather than organic. He interpreted its development in terms of the Oedipus complex. The novelist hated his father but identified with him, too. When he learned of his father's death, in 1839, he both rejoiced and felt guilty. The logic of this explanation leads to the hypothesis that Dostoevksy's epilepsy dates from his father's murder and was self-inflicted punishment to expiate the guilt of the Oedipal wish of parricide. The same logic leads to the implicit expectation that the epilepsy should have ceased in Dostoevsky's Siberian exile, starting in 1849, because that punishment imposed from without should have relieved the unconscious need for self-punishment. In fact, as Freud admitted, the epilepsy did not relent in Siberia.[12]

The whole interpretation has recently been subjected to authoritative criticism. First, it turns out that Dostoevsky's three-year-old son, Alexei, died in May 1878, after a three-hour epileptic attack. This suggests an organic and a hereditary basis for Dostoevsky's own disease. Second, sources unavailable to Freud contain evidence that Dostoevsky's "nervous disease" began no earlier than 1846-1847, that it worsened in his Siberian exile, and that he developed his first genuine epileptic attacks only in the early 1850s.[13] In this instance, psychoanalysis as an instrument of reconstructing history failed.

The last of Freud's historical biographies is the study of Woodrow Wilson, which he did late in his life with William Bul-

---

11. On the mistakes in translations, see the editor's notes, ibid., pp. 60-62 and the original Italian text, p. 83.

12. Freud, *Standard Edition*, 22:177-194.

13. Joseph Frank, *Dostoevsky: The Seeds of Revolt, 1821-1849* (Princeton, N.J.: Princeton University Press, 1976), "Appendix: Freud's Case-History of Dostoevsky," pp. 379-391.

litt.[14] Two experts, emphasizing that the style of writing in the volume is altogether different from Freud's, have declared that only a small portion of the book can be properly attributed to him.[15] It is true that the style is flat and that Freud wrote in a more engaging fashion. However, he put his name to the book, and as we shall see, both the quality of the evidence and the quality of the logic are entirely commensurate with those of Freud's works on Leonardo and Dostoevsky.

Initially the authors entered a disclaimer which might serve as a warning to practitioners of psychohistory. "All the facts we should like to know could be discovered if he [Wilson] were alive and would submit to psychoanalysis. He is dead. No one will ever know those facts. We cannot, therefore, hope to comprehend the decisive events of his psychic life either in all their details or in all their connections. We cannot, consequently, call this work a psychoanalysis of Wilson. It is a psychological study based upon such material as is now available, nothing more."[16] However, the disclaimer is soon forgotten: there are few qualifiers and there is little evidence of modesty in the conclusions.

The book is a curious performance. It would have been logical and consonant with the theory to begin with an account of Wilson's psychosexual stages, but there is no mention of the first two of them. Rather, the bulk of the interpretation turns on the idea of the Oedipus complex. Wilson idolized and feared his father, repressed his desire for his mother, and emerged from the experience with an unresolved Oedipus complex, which is to say that he became a passive, feminine, or inadequately masculine person. He repressed all his Oedipal hostility toward his father and displaced this hostility onto a variety of father substitutes, especially his senior administrative colleagues at Princeton, President Francis L. Patton, Dean Andrew F. West, and later President John Grier Hibben. At the same time he sought out younger men to play supporting roles about him, to serve as his protégés--to take the place formerly occupied by his younger brother Joe. A variety of men at one time or another

---

14. Sigmund Freud and William C. Bullitt, *Thomas Woodrow Wilson, Twenty-Eighth President of the United States: A Psychological Study* (London: Weidenfeld & Nicolson, 1967).

15. The experts in question, both of them Harvard psychiatrists, are Erik H. Erikson, *New York Review of Books*, 9 February 1967, p. 3, and Robert Coles, *New Republic*, 28 January 1967, p. 28.

16. Freud and Bullitt, *Wilson*, p. 31.

assumed this relationship, including Joseph Tumulty, William McAdoo, and Colonel Edward House.

There is nothing inherently implausible about this suggestion. To argue that one learns a paradigm of human relations from the society of the family is credible enough, and it would be strongly supported by learning theory. But to take this view of the matter is to cut away by Occam's razor the fecund jungle of Freudian undergrowth.

Freud and Bullitt maintain that Wilson learned from his father, the Presbyterian minister, to think of himself as the son of God or the Prince of Peace. They say over and over again that Wilson cast himself in the role of Christ. Now, it is clear from Freud's study of the Schreber case that delusions of grandeur of this order are paranoid and must be treated accordingly. Yet, Freud and Bullitt do not pursue the question of paranoia in Wilson.

There are some significant incidentals here as well. The authors say that all of Wilson's pleasures were oral,[17] but they do not raise the question of the origins of these pleasures in the psychosexual stage of orality, nor do they pursue the question of its consequences. In fact, the comment is just one undeveloped aside that would seem not simply incidental to the rest of the analysis, but incompatible with it. Of course, love of oratory is, in Freudian terminology, a classic sign of oral impulses, but the authors have already emphasized in this case that it is to be explained rather by Wilson's passionate imitation of his father.

They raise the question of the strength of Wilson's libido but say that they are "unwilling" to pronounce on the matter. They say that "Wilson at the age of twenty-one was a formed character."[18] But had not Freud long since taught us that it is the first six years of childhood, the years of the psychosexual stages and the Oedipus complex, that largely form the personality? How are we to learn respect for a controversial system of ideas whose leading advocate disregards his own criteria?

Bullitt's letter of resignation from the Inquiry in 1919 is unabashedly introduced, and in it the reader can readily detect much of the source of the animus in the biography: Wilson surrendered at Versailles all the ideals worth pursuing because he lacked sufficient masculine assertiveness to get his way.[19] This

---

17. Ibid., p. 26

18. Ibid., pp. 44-45, 75.

19. Ibid., pp. 234-235.

may also be true, but its credibility is not enhanced by a Vesuvian froth of psychic mystique and jaundice.

Though Wilson's relations with the Germans are explored at great length, what was left out or slighted in the book seems significant: Wilson's capacity for dealing effectively with the professional politicians of New Jersey, especially Colonel George Harvey and Boss James Smith; Wilson's enormous popularity in the classroom at Princeton; his ambiguous relations with William Jennings Bryan; his Mexican policy; and his successful role in mobilizing the nation for war. As one reviewer observed, the biography contains no account of the Victorian nature of the family, nothing of Progressive ideology, nothing on the moralistic tradition of American foreign policy.[20] No attempt was made to set Wilson in his context and view him in historical perspective.

It is instructive to compare the work of Freud and Bullitt with another psychological study of Wilson: Alexander L. George and Juliette L. George, *Woodrow Wilson and Colonel House: A Personality Study.* The Georges' account is much influenced by Freud, but it is superior. They drew heavily on ideas which were initially evolved by Freud or catalyzed by him, but the ideas, handled with delicate sensitivity, have in the Georges' work become independent of the master. The crux of the matter they explain very near the beginning.[21]

"It is by now a generally accepted fact among psychologists that in the process of raising their children, parents inevitably arouse a certain amount of resentment against themselves. For to induce a child to conduct himself in a civilized fashion necessarily involves requiring him to abandon many forms of pleasurable behavior. This the child resents and he experiences anger at the parent who thus thwarts him. Specialists in these matters still are not agreed as to what kinds of parental behavior produce what varieties and degrees of resentment. But it is probably not unreasonable to suggest that a boy like Wilson, upon whom very high demands were made, had to contend with an ample load of anger, which was certainly not mitigated by his father's penchant for ridiculing him.

---

20. Cushing Strout, *Journal of American History* 54:184 (1967). John Lukacs has shown that Bullitt's contribution to the book rested chiefly on the study of Wilson's conscious mind and that it is sounder than the contribution of Freud. See his chapter "William Christian Bullitt, or the Rebel Philadelphian," in *Philadelphia: Patricians and Philistines, 1900-1950* (New York: Farrar, Straus, Giroux, 1981), especially. pp. 204-207.

21. Alexander L. George and Juliette L. George, *Woodrow Wilson and Colonel House: A Personality Study* (New York: John Day, 1965), pp. 9, 12.

"It is also a truism among modern psychologists that the manner in which a child handles his resentment of his parents is of crucial importance in the development of his personality. . . . Sometimes the child is so terrified that he dares not even recognize the existence of such feelings within himself but, rather, seeks constantly to persuade himself of a surpassing devotion to his parent. This seems to have been Wilson's method of handling the anxiety engendered by his hostile feelings."

Wilson never rebelled against his father's authority. Rather, he was throughout his life an extravagantly devoted son. He stood in awe of his father even in his own adulthood. "If ever he was aware of his hostility toward his father, he seems to have banished it from consciousness and to have lived in fear of the possibility of ever stumbling upon the knowledge." He had an aversion for introspection and a devotion to self-control. "He seemed to fear that if he let his thoughts flow freely some nameless danger would overwhelm him. He once remarked that he never dared let himself go because he did not know where he would stop."

Men like Dean West and Senator Lodge "seem to have stirred in him ancient memories of his capitulation to his father and he resisted with ferocity. *He* must dominate, out of fear of being dominated."

The authors admit the necessarily inconclusive nature of their interpretation. "No incontrovertible proof can be offered. Nor can any one incident be relied upon to sustain this or any other theory of Wilson's motivation. It is only when the man's career is viewed as a whole that a repetition of certain basically similar behavior is discernible. Let the reader consider whether these patterns of behavior become more consistently comprehensible in terms of the explanations offered than in terms of other explanations. That will be the best test of their usefulness."

This approach to Wilson's personality is intelligent, flexible, modest, believable, open-minded--all the things that the study by Freud and Bullitt is not.

Appendix C:
Historical Application of
Other Personality Theories

If Freud's theories are of so little help to the historian, are there other personality theories that have more promise? Adler's theory is not of much use, as Paul had little sibling contact. Sullivan's interpersonal theory might well have interesting applications if we knew more of the details of Paul's interpersonal relations in his infancy and childhood. Learning theory, because it seems to have better evidential support than other personality theories, might well be the most promising. But it, too, requires a mastery of biographical detail that is not attainable in Paul's case.

One theory that has interesting applications to Paul is George A. Kelly's *Psychology of Personal Constructs*. Kelly describes a mentality very much like Paul's. His fundamental idea is that an individual's outlook is designed to organize his experience into categories and to render new experience predictable by reference to familiar categories of experience: "A person's processes are psychologically channelized by the ways in which he anticipates events. . . . Like the prototype of the scientist that he is, man seeks prediction. His structured network of pathways leads toward the future so that he can anticipate it." This style of thinking is designed to find relief from the awesome flux of events about us. "Theories are the thinking of men who seek freedom amid swirling events. The theories comprise prior assumptions about certain realms of these events. To the extent that the events may, from these prior assumptions, be construed, predicted, and their relative courses charted, men may exercise control, and gain freedom for themselves in the process." The key mental labor in this process is the devising of constructs. "Constructs are the channels in which one's mental processes run. They are the two-way streets along which one may travel to reach conclusions." It is the individual's collection and organization of constructs that enable him to anticipate experience: "Constructs are the controls that one places upon life--the life within as well as the life which is external to him. Forming constructs may be considered as binding sets of events into convenient bundles which are handy for the person who has to lug them. Events, when so bound, tend to become predictable, manageable, and controlled." Thus do people try to make sense of what happens to them. "Only when man attunes his ear to recurrent themes in the monotonous flow does his universe begin to make sense to him. Like a musician, he must phrase his experience in order to make sense out of it."[1]

Some constructs and systems are flexible, some tend to be rigid. "Constructs . . . remain relatively serene and secure while the events above which they rise rumble and churn in continuous turmoil." Yet they themselves must sometimes change if they do not successfully interpret or organize a new experience. Anxiety is explained by confronting events which are not readily assimilated into one's construct system. "It represents the awareness that one's construction system does not apply to the events at hand."[2] In this case, people can avoid that type of experience, rearrange the construct system to take account of it, or try to force the experience to conform to expectations. Obviously, Paul opted for the last alternative.[3]

---

1. George A. Kelly, *Psychology of Personal Constructs*, 2 vols. (New York: W. W. Norton, 1955), 1:46, 49, 21-11, 126, 52.

2. Ibid., pp. 486, 495.

3. Leon Festinger has developed a theory close to that of Kelly and one that is undoubtedly better known: *The Theory of Cognitive Dissonance* (Evanston, Ill.: Row, Peterson, 1957). The idea is that when there is dissonance between two cognitions or two cognitive relationships, the result is uncomfortable for the personality whose cognitions are in question. He then tries to find ways to enhance cognitive consonance and to reduce dissonance. Another variation on this theme, and a somewhat more elegant one than Festinger's, is Paul McReynolds's theory of perceptual congruence: "Anxiety,

Theories of this kind have been labeled consistency theories.[4] From the point of view of understanding Paul, they have one decided strength. They describe the more or less involuntary process characteristic to one degree or another of almost everyone but exceptionally characteristic of the obsessive-compulsive style. They describe in a specialized and technical terminology much that has been attributed to Paul in more conventional language. Paul was concerned to predict, and the clinical psychologist believes that the value of prediction, especially for the obsessive, consists in its function of controlling. Consistency theory elaborates in a generic and abstract fashion mental processes especially characteristic of Paul. It suggests something that may well have a factual basis in Paul's biography. It suggests that Paul evolved a system of constructs pertinent to his designated role in life as Emperor of Russia, but since he did not have a chance to experience that role until he was forty-two years old, he could not subject his system to the constant process of revision and of constructual permeability that the system is supposed to undergo. Hence his psychological structure was both more rigid and more immature than was usual for a man his age, and it was not equal to the task confronting him when he ascended the throne. The bulk of his problems followed from that one. This is a provocative and plausible idea. Yet to apply it, we must assume that Paul had no experiences in his twenties and thirties that would stimulate him to revise his system and develop a more sophisticated one. Still, it is impressive what a panoply of ideas of fair play and justice, devotion, morality, and service filled the head of Paul the adult.

The consistency theory of Kelly and others is not, however, concretely historical. It does not tell us what, if anything, are the influences that predispose the individual to one kind of construction pattern rather than another. In this respect, it falls far short of doing what Freud's theory presumes to do, and that is the weakness of most of the personality theory that rivals Freud.

Perception, and Schizophrenia," in Don De Avila Jackson, ed., *The Etiology of Schizophrenia* (New York: Basic Books, 1960), pp. 248-294. He defines a percept as data passing into a person's range of awareness. People tend to develop patterns of assimilation of percepts, patterns which McReynolds calls perceptual schemata. McReynolds recognizes the similarity of his views and those of Kelly and Festinger. His theory seems to represent a different semantic approach to the same outlook.

4. Salvatore R. Maddi, *Personality Theories: A Comparative Analysis* (Homewood, Ill.: Dorsey, 1968), chs. 4 and 8.

Perhaps a better way to understand Paul's historical biography lies through clinical etiology. For example, there are a variety of studies of the influence on male children of the father's absence from the home. Two of them that appear to be especially respected, as they are almost universally cited in the literature on the subject, show that children whose fathers are absent a good deal tend to idealize their picture of him, that they develop dependency behavior and exhibit compensatory masculinity.[5]

It is not clear what Paul's image of his father was. His dependency behavior was distinct. And the compensatory elements of his behavior had to do with masculinity perhaps on the drill field, but not elsewhere. It is doubtful how appropriate it is to examine Paul's biography for signs of father-absence in view of the fact that studies of this phenomenon have tried to find situations in which it was the unique pathological variable. In Paul's case, the unique skew of his childhood environment was multiple and massive.

Psychologists would be more likely to characterize his situation as childhood deprivation--a subject on which the literature is prodigious. A great deal of it was prompted by the interest of British psychologists in the effect on children of separation from their families during the London blitz of World War II. Anna Freud and her colleagues began this work during the blitz itself.[6] Still more was sponsored soon after the war by UNICEF. The subject probably owes its earliest comprehensive definition to a variety of works by John Bowlby.[7] The story he tells is, in modern form, like that of *David Copperfield* or *The Way of All Flesh*. In short, being unloved, shunted from family to family, or to an institution and back, is not good for children. In the words of *West Side Story*: "this child is depraved on account of he ain't had a normal home." The literature is more sophisticated than this, but basically what it says has become ac-

---

5. George R. Bach, "Father-Fantasies and Father Typing in Father-Separated Children," *Child Development* 17:63-80 (1946). David B. Lynn and William L. Sawrey, "The Effect of Father Absence on Norwegian Boys and Girls," *Journal of Abnormal and Social Psychology* 59:258-262 (1959).

6. Anna Freud and Dorothy Burlingham, *Infants Without Families* (New York: International Universities Press, 1947).

7. John Bowlby, *Maternal Care and Mental Health* (Geneva: World Health Organization, 1951); *Attachment and Loss, I: Attachment* (New York: Basic Books, 1969); *Attachment and Loss, II: Separation* (New York: Basic Books, 1973). See also the work of his colleague, Mary D. Ainsworth, *Deprivation of Maternal Care* (Geneva: World Health Organization, 1962).

cepted as common knowledge. For example, Bowlby tells us solemnly: "Among the most significant developments in psychiatry during the past quarter of a century has been the steady growth of evidence that the quality of the parental care which a child receives in his earliest years is of vital importance for his future mental health."[8] This is hardly startling.

One of the common forms of deprivation is institutionalization. There are a variety of studies of institutionalized children, and to some extent, as already observed, Paul's own childhood environment conformed to that of institutionalization. Children who spend their infancy in an infant care facility are retarded and disturbed in almost all their capacities. They are socially awkward, emotionally desperate, slow to develop intellectual and language skills, and retarded in muscular coordination.[9]

This approach might throw some light on Paul. But students of institutionalization agree with Bowlby that the most important feature of deprivation in an institution is the absence of a principal "attachment figure." The nurses and employees of the institution come on and go off shift with a perplexing rhythm, and they have far too little time for individual infants. In Paul's case, we do not know whether he had a principal attachment figure as an infant, but he was never merely one of many children in his environment, and one who was neglected. Given his birth and heritage, he was certainly fussed over. As yet there have not been enough studies of deprived children born heirs to enormous empires in the eighteenth century to enable us to throw light on Paul's case from this point of view.

In addition, there is evidence that a deprived childhood does not always lead to disaster and that a fortunate one does not always lead to further good fortune. For example, Macfarland and others made detailed annual studies of 166 children from infancy through age eighteen and did a follow-up study at age thirty. Their findings were contrary to all expectations. Many of the most "successful" children turned into disappointing adults. "Our theoretical expectations were . . . rudely jarred by the adult status of a number of our subjects who early had had easy and confidence-inducing lives. As children and adolescents, they were free of severe strains, showed high abilities

8. Bowlby, *Maternal Care*, p. 11.

9. See Mia Lilly Kellmer Pringle, *Deprivation and Education* (New York: Humanities Press, 1965); Sally A. Provence and Rose C. Lipton, *Infants in Institutions: A Comparison of Their Development with Family-Reared Infants during the First Year of Life* (New York: International Universities Press, 1963).

and/or talents, excelled at academic work and were the adulated images of success. Included among these were boy athlete leaders and good-looking socially skilled girls. One sees among them at age 30 a high proportion of brittle, discontented, and puzzled adults whose high expectations have been seriously disappointed."

Many of the troubled children in the study, on the other hand, became the most successful adults. "We had not appreciated the maturing quality of many painful, strain-producing, and confusing experiences which in time, if lived through, brought sharpened awareness, more complex integrations, better skills in problem solving, clarified goals, and increasing stability. Nor had we been aware that early success might delay or possibly forestall continuing growth, richness, and competence." Finally, they concluded, "much of personality theory based on pathological samples is not useful for prediction for the larger number of persons."[10] The findings of George E. Vaillant's *Adjustment to Life* (1977) are similar.[11] The literature on child development does not provide the promising clues that we need to improve our understanding of the personality development of Paul.

Paul's childhood situation was appalling and suggests that later mental abnormalities could be expected. Rejected by his father, perhaps by his mother, without whom, in any case, he had to live, surrounded by transient females, heir to a legacy so disputed as to put his life in imminent danger, and old enough to understand that this state of affairs had resulted in his father's death--he must have faced a most uncomfortable environment.   Arieti, one of the leading specialists on schizophrenia, is concerned to find out why many people facing a complex of assaults on the integrity of their personality and emotional stability do nevertheless survive intact: "One is often impressed by the fact that schizophrenia has not occurred in certain individuals in spite of what seemed to the psychiatrist the most unfavorable environmental circumstances. . . . We shall use the term *averted schizophrenia* to describe a situation where all the ground seemed to have been prepared psychodynamically for a schizophrenic psychosis, and yet the psychosis never occurred." The capacity to avert it, Arieti thinks, is explained by "fortunate external circumstances" that "have com-

---

10. Jean W. Macfarlane, "Perspectives on Personality Consistency and Change from the Guidance Study," *Vita Humana* 7:121-124 (1964).

11. George B. Vaillant, *Adjustment to Life* (Boston: Little, Brown, 1977).

pensatory or remedial effects valuable enough to prevent the disorder. The presence of a beneficial person may be enough to change the pathogenetic potentiality of the environment." Nikita Panin might have been such a person for Paul. In any case, if someone in Paul's situation is to avoid a schizophrenic breakdown, Arieti thinks, he must find effective protection in the powerful defenses of some sub-psychotic mental disorder, a neurosis or personality disorder.[12]

Paul had a resource of the kind that Arieti describes: his ideological commitment. Attachment to an ideology is very comforting for the dependency needs of the obsessive style. The ideology and its backers provide a community of support and a feeling of power. They provide a securely impersonal style of intimacy for the person whose painful interpersonal experiences have driven him to seek isolation in an obsessive system. "The ideological community promises the answer to isolation. It holds out the hope of a group united by common values, ideals and a common fate. For the insecure and self-doubting, it promises acceptance regardless of personal worth. . . . Dogma--the assertion of unassailable, revealed truth--exerts great appeal to the obsessional's uncertainty, doubt and ambivalence. . . . For some paranoid personalities, ideology serves as a nucleus for the development of a paranoid system."[13]

The most persuasive etiological suggestions about the origins and development of the obsessive outlook are starkly simple. Children learn the behavior from their parents, whose anxiety in the face of disorder or the unexpected teaches the child to fear. Similarly, children of these parents are rewarded and punished according to their conformity to parental preferences.[14] Here is a significant clue to Paul's development. Panin's counsel to Paul was full of prescriptions of good legal order, and Paul's circumstances were enough to teach him the advantages of unassailable legal order for his own security.

The clinical etiology of the paranoid personality is more complex. The precipitating problem is commonly focused during, especially near the end of, the fourth decade of life. "There are, objectively considered, some sources of frustration, conflict,

---

12. Arieti, *Interpretation of Schizophrenia*, pp. 197-199.

13. Joseph Barnett, "On Ideology and the Psycho-Dynamics of the Ideologue," *Journal of the American Academy of Psychoanalysis* 1:381-395 (1973), especially 387-392.

14. Brody and Lindbergh, "Personality Disorders," in Freedman and Kaplan, *Comprehensive Textbook of Psychiatry*, 1st ed., pp. 944-945.

and anxiety which are certainly more characteristic of the fourth decade, and after, than of the second and third decades. Some time toward the middle age, when a person turns thirty, thirty-five, or forty, comes the dawning realization that his life span actually is limited. With this recognition may also come fears that his lifelong hopes, overt or latent, will never be realized. . . . To such threats, frustrations, and restrictions the vulnerable individual may react with aggression and delusional restitution."[15]

Paul does not fit this picture. He obviously did not follow the conventional route of preparing himself for a career and embarking on it when he reached his majority. He anticipated a career as royal autocrat when he reached majority, but he was kept waiting for two additional decades and reached the throne only at age forty-two. His life's dream was fulfilled just when the typical paranoid is experiencing the career stress that often precipitates his psychological crisis. On the other hand, there is a sense in which Paul's expectations of his career were held in abeyance until his forty-second year, after which the shock of reality and cognitive dissonance set in. But any paranoid elements in his personality were probably present long before the experience of governing could skew his outlook.

On balance, rival personality theories are, in some respects, more credible than Freud's, but they do not deliver nearly so much as his promises. The effort to extrapolate hypothetical explanations of personality development, akin to personality theory, from the clinical etiology of particular disorders provides better credibility and is more thoroughly rooted in clinical experience.

---

15. Norman Cameron, "Paranoid Conditions and Paranoia," in Silvano Arieti, ed., *American Handbook of Psychiatry* (New York: Basic Books, 1959), 1:511-512.

SELECT BIBLIOGRAPHY

The archival materials used in this study are cited primarily in the notes of Chapter 4. For additional bibliographic materials, see Ragsdale, "Introduction," and Christian D. Schmidt, "The Further Study of Paul," both in Ragsdale, *Paul I: A Reassessment of His Life and Reign.* I have listed with psychological materials those historical works which pertain primarily to questions of psychology and psychiatry and those which I have exploited chiefly for their pertinence to such questions (e. g., biographies of George III and of other mad sovereigns of the eighteenth century), and I have omitted here the bulk of the psychological and psychiatric periodical literature cited in the notes of Chapter 7 and the Appendices.

I. Historical Materials.

Arkhiv kniazia Vorontsova. Petr Bartenev, ed. 40 vols. Moscow: Universitetskaia tipografiia, 1870-1895.

Atkin, Muriel. "The Pragmatic Diplomacy of Paul I: Russia's Relations with Asia, 1796-1801." *Slavic Review* 38:60-74 (1979).

Ballesteros y Beretta, Antonio. *Historia de España y su influencia en la historia universal.* 9 vols. Barcelona: Salvat, 1918-1941.

Bernard, Paul. *The Limits of Enlightenment: Joseph II and the Law.* Urbana: University of Illinois Press, 1979.

Black, J. L. *Citizens for the Fatherland: Education, Educators, and Pedagogical Ideals in Eighteenth-Century Russia.* Boulder, Colo.: East European Quarterly, 1979.

Blackstone, Sir William. *Commentaries on the Laws of England.* 2 vols. New York: Dean, 1844.

Bogoslovskii, M. M. *Oblastnaia reforma Petra Velikago--provintsiia 1719-1727.* Moscow: Obshchestvo istorii i drevnostei rossiiskikh, 1902.

Brown, A. H. "S. E. Desnitsky, Adam Smith, and the *Nakaz* of Catherine II." *Oxford Slavonic Papers* 7:42-59 (1974).

Catherine II. *Sochineniia.* 3 vols. St. Petersburg: Smirdin, 1849-1850.

Crocker, Lester G. *An Age of Crisis.* Baltimore: The Johns Hopkins University Press, 1959.

Czartoryski, Adam. *Mémoires.* 2 vols. Paris: Plon, 1887.

Daudet, Ernest. *Histoire de l'émigration pendant la Révolution française.* 3 vols. Paris: Hachette, 1904-1907.

Demkov, M. M. *Istoriia russkoi pedagogiki.* 2 vols. St. Petersburg: Stasiulevich, 1886-1897.

Dolgorukov, I. M. "Kapishche moego serdtsa." *Russkaia starina*, 1890, Prilozhenie.

Dorwart, Reinhold August. *The Prussian Welfare State before 1740.* Cambridge, Mass.: Harvard University Press, 1971.

Druzhinin, Nikolai M. *Absoliutizm v Rossii XVII-XVIII vv.* Moscow: Nauka, 1964.

Duffy, Christopher. *Russia's Military Way to the West: Origins and Nature of Russian Military Power, 1700-l800.* London: Routledge & Kegan Paul, 1981.

Eidel'man, Natan Iakovlevich. *Gran' vekov: politicheskaia bor'ba v Rossii, konets XVIII-nachalo XIX stoletiia.* Moscow: Mysl', 1982.

_____. "Obratnoe providenie: istoricheskii ocherk." *Novyi mir,* 1970, No. 5, pp. 226-241.

Feldbaek, Ole. *Danmarks Historie: Tiden 1730-1814*. Copenhagen: Gyldendal, 1982.

_____. "The Foreign Policy of Tsar Paul I, 1800-1801: an Interpretation." *Jahrbücher für Geschichte Osteuropas* 30:16-36 (1982).

Fénelon, François de Salignac de la Mothe-. *Oeuvres complètes*. 10 vols. Lille: Lefort, 1848-1852.

Field, Daniel. *Rebels in the Name of the Tsar*. Boston: Houghton, Mifflin, 1976.

Filonov, A. "Orenburgskii pokhod." *Donskie voiskovye vedomosti*, Nos. 1-2, 7 and 14 January (os) 1859.

Fleischhacker, Hedwig. "Porträt Peters III." *Jahrbücher für Geschichte Osteuropas* 5:127-189 (1957).

Ford, Guy Stanton. *Hanover and Prussia, 1795-1803*. New York: Columbia University Press, 1903.

Franklin, Benjamin. *Autobiographical Writings*. Carl van Doren, ed. New York: Viking, 1945.

Frauendienst, Werner. *Christian Wolff as Staatsdenker*. Berlin: Mathiesen Verlag, 1927.

Frederick II. *Oeuvres historiques*. 7 vols. Berlin: Decker, 1846-1847.

_____. *Oeuvres posthumes*. 15 vols. Berlin: Voss, 1788.

_____. *Die politische Testamente*. Gustav Berthold Volz, ed. Berlin: Reimar Hobbing, 1920.

Fuye, Maurice de la. *Rostoptchine: européen ou slave?* Paris: Plon, 1937.

Gagliardo, John C. *Enlightened Despotism*. New York: Crowell, 1967.

Gay, Peter. *The Enlightenment: an Interpretation*. 2 vols. New York: Alfred A. Knopf, 1966-1969.

Geisman, Platon A., and Aleksandr N. Dubovskii. *Graf Petr Ivanovich Panin, 1721-1789: istoricheskii ocherk voennoi i gosudarstvennoi deiatel'nosti*. St. Petersburg: Vasiliev, 1897.

Gershoy, Leo. *From Despotism to Revolution, 1763-1789*. New York: Harper & Row, 1944.

Gleason, Walter. *Moral Idealists, Bureaucracy, and Catherine the Great.* New Brunswick, N.J.: Rutgers University Press, 1981.

_____. "Political Ideals and Loyalties of Some Russian Writers of the Early 1760s." *Slavic Review* 34:560-575 (1975).

Golovkin, Fedor Gavrilovich. *La cour et le règne de Paul I.* Paris: Plon-Nourrit, 1905.

Gooch, George P. *Catherine the Great and Other Studies.* London: Longmans, Green, 1954.

Hampson, Norman. *A Cultural History of the Enlightenment.* New York: Pantheon, 1968.

Hartung, Fritz. *Enlightened Despotism.* London: Routledge and Paul, 1957.

Hazard, Paul. *European Thought in the Eighteenth Century from Montesquieu to Lessing.* Cleveland: World Publishing, 1963.

Heiking, Baron Karl-Heinrich von. "Imperator Pavel i ego vremia." *Russkaia starina,* 1887, Vol. 56, pp. 365-394, 783-815.

Herr, Richard. *The Eighteenth Century Revolution in Spain.* Princeton, N.J.: Princeton University Press, 1958.

Heuzet, Jean. *Histoires choisies des auteurs profanes, traduites en françois, avec le latin à côté: ou l'en a mêlé divers Préceptes de Morales tirés des mêmes Auteurs.* 2 vols. Lyons: Frères Perisse, 1780.

Histoire des négociations diplomatiques relatives aux traités de Mortefontaine, de Lunéville, et d'Amiens. Albert du Casse, ed. 3 vols. Paris: Dentu, 1855.

Istoriia Pravitel'stvuiushchego senata za dvesti let, 1711-1911 gg. 2 vols. St. Petersburg: Senatskaia tipografiia, 1911.

Iudin, P. "Na Indiiu." *Russkaia starina* 1894, Vol. 82, pp. 231-241.

Joseph II und Leopold von Toskana: Ihr Briefwechsel. Alfred von Arneth, ed. 2 vols. Vienna: Braumüller, 1872.

Kaiserlich-priviligierte Hamburgische neue Zeitung. 1800-1801.

Kartashev, A. N. *Ocherki po istorii russkoi tserkvi.* 2 vols. Paris: YMCA Press, 1959.

Kaznakov, S. "Pavlovskaia Gatchina." *Starye gody,* July-September 1914, pp. 101-188.

Keep, John. "Paul I and the Militarization of Government," pp. 91-103, in Hugh Ragsdale, ed., *Paul I: A Reassessment of his Life and Reign.* (See below.)

Kenney, James J., Jr. "Lord Whitworth and the Conspiracy against Tsar Paul I: the New Evidence of the Kent Archive." *Slavic Review* 36:205-219 (1977).

_____. "The Politics of Assassination," pp. 125-145, in Ragsdale, *Paul I.*

Kliuchevskii, Vasilii O. *Sochineniia.* 8 vols. Moscow: Gospolitizdat, 1956-1959.

Klochkov, M. V. *Ocherki pravitel'stvennoi deiatel'nosti vremeni Pavla I.* St. Petersburg: Senatskaia tipografiia, 1916.

Kobeko, Dmitrii F. *Tsesarevich Pavel Petrovich, 1754-1796.* St. Petersburg: n.p., 1882.

Konstantin Nikolaevich, Grand Duke. "Tsesarevich Pavel Petrovich: istoricheskie materialy, khraniashchiesia v Biblioteke dvortsa goroda Pavlovska." *Russkaia starina,* 1874, No. 9, pp. 667-684.

Kotzebue, August von. *Das merkwürdigste Jahr meines Lebens.* 2 vols. Berlin: Sander, 1801.

Krieger, Leonard. *An Essay on the Theory of Enlightened Despotism.* Chicago: University of Chicago Press, 1975.

Lafuente y Zamalloa, Modesto. *Historia general de España.* 25 vols. Barcelona: Montaner y Simón, 1887-1891.

Lappo-Danilevsky, A. "L'idée de l'état et son évolution en Russie depuis les troubles du XVII siècle jusqu'aux réformes du XVIII," in Paul Vinogradoff, ed., *Essays in Legal History.* London: Oxford University Press, 1913.

Lebedev, Petr S. *Grafy Nikita i Petr Paniny.* St. Petersburg: Obshchestvennaia pol'za, 1863.

Locke, John. *Some Thoughts Concerning Education.* Cambridge, Eng.: Cambridge University Press, 1898.

Lough, John.   *An Introduction to Seventeenth-Century France.* New York: McKay, 1954.

Madariaga, Isabel de.   *Russia in the Age of Catherine the Great.* New Haven, Conn.: Yale University Press, 1981.

Mare, Nicholas de la.   *Traité de la police.* 2nd ed. 4 vols. Amsterdam: "aux depens de la Compagnie," 1729-1738.

Materialy dlia zhizneopisaniia grafa N. P. Panina.   Alexander Brückner, ed. 7 vols.   St. Petersburg: Imperatorskaia Akademiia nauk, 1888-1892.

McGrew, Roderick E.   "Paul I and the Knights of Malta," pp. 44-75, in Ragsdale, *Paul I.*

_____.   "A Political Portrait of Paul I from the Austrian and English Diplomatic Archives." *Jahrbücher für Geschichte Osteuropas* 18:503-529 (1970).

_____.   "The Politics of Absolutism: Paul I and the Bank of Assistance for the Nobility," pp. 104-124, in Ragsdale, *Paul I.*

Mémoires de la Société de l'histoire de Paris et de l'Ile-de-France. 51 vols. Paris: Champion, 1875-1930.

Miliutin, Dmitrii A.   *Istoriia voiny 1799 goda mezhdu Rossiei i Frantsiei v tsarstvovanie Imperatora Pavla I.* 5 vols.   St. Petersburg: Imperatorskaia Akademiia nauk, 1852-1853.

Minto, Gilbert Elliott, first earl.   *Life and Letters of Gilbert Elliott, First Earl Minto.* E. E. Elliott, ed. 3 vols.   London: Longmans, 1874.

Montesquieu, Charles-Louis de Secondat, baron de.   *Considérations sur les causes de la grandeur des Romains et de leur décadence.* Paris: Garnier Frères, 1954.

Morane, Paul.   *Paul I de Russie, avant l'avènement, 1754-1796.* Paris: Plon-Nourrit, 1907.

Moskovskiia vedomosti. 1800-1801.

Napoléon I.   *Correspondance de Napoléon I.* J. P. B. Vaillant et al., eds. 32 vols. Paris: Plon et Dumaine, 1858-1870.

Okun', Semen B.   *Istoriia SSSR: konets XVIII-nachalo XIX veka.* Leningrad: Izdatel'stvo Leningradskogo universiteta, 1974.

Osmnadtsatyi vek. Petr Bartenev, ed.   4 vols.   Moscow: n.p., 1869.

Paget, Sir Arthur. *The Paget Papers: Diplomatic and Other Correspondence.* A. B. Paget, ed. 2 vols. London: Heinemann, 1896.

Papmehl, K. A. *Metropolitan Platon of Moscow.* Newtonville, Mass.: Oriental Research Partners, 1983.

Pavlenko, N. I. *Rossiia v period reform Petra I: sbornik statei.* Moscow: Nauka, 1973.

Pingaud, Léonce. *Un agent secret sous la Révolution et l'Empire: le Comte d'Antraigues.* Paris: Plon, 1884.

Poroshin, Semen Andreevich. *Zapiski.* 2nd ed. St. Petersburg: Balashev, 1882.

Quesnay, François. *Oeuvres économiques et philosophiques.* August Oncken, ed. Paris: Geuttiner, 1910.

Racine, Jean. *Complete Plays.* New York: Random House, 1967.

Radishchev, Alexander. *Journey from St. Petersburg to Moscow.* Leo Wiener, tr. R. P. Thaler, ed. Cambridge, Mass.: Harvard University Press, 1966.

Raeff, Marc. *The Origins of the Russian Intelligentsia.* New York: Harcourt, Brace, 1961.

_____, ed. *Plans for Political Reform in Imperial Russia, 1730-1905.* Englewood Cliffs, N.J.: Prentice-Hall, 1966.

_____. "The Well-Ordered Police State and the Development of Modernity in Seventeenth- and Eighteenth-Century Europe: An Attempt at a Comparative Approach." *American Historical Review* 80:1221-1243 (1975).

Ragsdale, Hugh. "Was Paul Bonaparte's Fool? The Evidence of Neglected Archives," pp. 76-90, in Ragsdale, *Paul I.*

_____. *Détente in the Napoleonic Era: Bonaparte and the Russians.* Lawrence: Regents Press of Kansas, 1980.

_____, ed. *Paul I: A Reassessment of His Life and Reign.* Pittsburgh: University of Pittsburgh Center for International Studies, 1979.

_____. "Russia, Prussia, and Europe in the Policy of Paul I." *Jahrbücher für Geschichte Osteuropas* 31:81-118 (1983).

Ransel, David L. "An Ambivalent Legacy: The Education of the Grand Duke Paul," pp. 1-16, in Ragsdale, *Paul I*.

_____. *The Politics of Catherinian Russia: the Panin Party*. New Haven, Conn.: Yale University Press, 1975.

Reutskii, N. V. *Liudi bozh'i i skoptsy*. Moscow: Grakov, 1872.

Reverdil, Elie Salomon François. *Struensée et la cour de Copenhague, 1760-1772*. Paris: Meyrueis, 1858.

Ritter, Gerhard. *Frederick the Great: A Historical Profile*. Peter Paret, ed. Berkeley: University of California Press, 1968.

Rodríguez Casado, Vicente. *La política y los políticos en el reinado de Carlos III*. Madrid: Ediciones Rialp, 1962.

Rollin, Charles. *Histoire ancienne*. 12 vols. Paris: Etienne, 1780.

Rozhdestvenskii, S. V. *Stoletie goroda Gatchiny, 1796-1896*. Gatchina: Gatchinskoe dvortsovoe upravlenie, 1896.

Ruff, Marcel. *L'esprit du mal et l'esthétique baudelairienne*. Geneva: Slatkine, 1972.

Sablukov, Nikolai A. *Zapiski o vremenakh Imperatora Pavla I i o konchine etogo gosudaria*. Berlin: Ladyschnikow, n.d.

Safonov, M. M. "Konstitutsionnye proekty N. I. Panina--D. I. Fonvizina." *Vspomogatel'nye istoricheskie distsipliny*, 1977, No. 6, pp. 261-280.

Jacques Saint-Germain. *La Reynie et la police au grand siècle*. Paris: Hachette, 1962.

Sankt-Peterburgische Zeitung. 1800-1801.

Sankt-Peterburgskiia vedomosti. 1800-1801.

Sbornik geograficheskikh, topograficheskikh, i statisticheskikh materialov po Azii. 85 vols. Moscow: Voennoe ministerstvo, 1883-1914.

Sbornik imperatorskago russkago istoricheskago obshchestva. 148 vols. St. Petersburg: Stasiulevich, 1867-1916.

Scharf, Claus. "Staatsauffassung und Regierungsprogramm eines aufgeklärten Selbstherrschers, Die Instruktion des Grossfürsten Paul von 1788," in Ernst Schulin, ed., *Gedenkschrift Martin Goehring*. Wiesbaden: Studien zur europäischen Geschichte, 1968, pp. 91-106.

Schilder, Nikolai K. *Imperator Aleksandr I: ego zhizn' i tsarstvovanie.* 4 vols. St. Petersburg: Suvorin, 1897-1898.

Schilder, Nikolai K. *Imperator Pavel I: istoriko-biograficheskii ocherk.* St. Petersburg: Suvorin, 1901.

Schroeder, Paul. "The Collapse of the Second Coalition." *Journal of Modern History* 59:244-290 (1987).

Segel, Harold B. *The Literature of Eighteenth-Century Russia.* 2 vols. New York: E. P. Dutton, 1967.

Ségur, Louis Philippe, comte de. *Mémoires.* 3 vols. Paris: Alexis Eymery, 1824-1827.

Semevskii, Mikhail I., ed. "Materialy k russkoi istorii XVIII veka (1788)." *Viestnik Evropy* 1:297-330 (1867).

Shumigorskii, Evgenii S. *Ekaterina Ivanovna Nelidova (1758-1839).* St. Petersburg: Obshchestvennaia pol'za, 1898.

_____. *Imperator Pavel Pervyi: zhizn' i tsarstvovanie.* St. Petersburg: Smirnov, 1907.

_____. *Imperatritsa Mariia Fedorovna, 1759-1828.* St. Petersburg: Skorokhod, 1892.

_____. "Instruktsiia Velikago Kniazia Pavla Petrovicha Kniagine Marii Fedorovne (1776)." *Russkaia starina,* 1898, No. 93, pp. 247-261.

Small, Albion W. *The Cameralists.* Chicago: University of Chicago Press, 1909.

Solov'ev, Sergei M. *Istoriia Rossii s drevneishikh vremen.* 15 vols. Moscow: Mysl', 1959-1966.

Stedingk, Curt Bogislaus Ludwig Kristoffer von. *Mémoires posthumes.* 3 vols. Paris: Bertrand, 1844-1847.

Sully, Maximilien de Béthune, duc de. *Mémoires.* 10 vols. London: n.p., 1778.

Tessin, Carl Gustav. *Letters to a Young Prince.* London: Reeves, 1755.

Thiers, Adolphe. *Histoire du Consulat et de l'Empire.* 21 vols. Paris: Paulin, 1845-1874.

Trudoliubivaia pchela. 1759.

Tsareubiistvo 11 marta 1801 goda: zapiski uchastnikov i sovre-mennikov. 2nd ed. St. Petersburg: n.p., 1908.

Vattel, Emmerich de. *Le droit de gens: ou principes de la loi na-turelle, appliquée à la conduite & aux affaires des Nations & des Souverains.* Washington, D.C.: Carnegie Institution, 1916.

"Velikii kniaz Pavel Petrovich: perepiska v. k. Pavla Petrovicha s gr. Petrom Paninym." *Russkii arkhiv,* 1882, No. 33, pp. 403-418, 739-764.

Verbitskii, E. D. *Russko-frantsuzskie otnosheniia v 1800-1803 gg.* Kandidatskaia dissertatsiia, Khersonskii pedagogich-eskii institut, 1950.

Voltaire, François-Marie Arouet. *Oeuvres complètes.* 52 vols. Paris: Garnier Frères, 1877-1885.

Waliszewski, Kazimierz. *Paul the First of Russia.* Philadelphia: J. B. Lippincott, 1913.

Willey, Basil. *The Eighteenth-Century Background: Studies on the Idea of Nature in the Thought of the Period.* New York: Columbia University Press, 1940.

Wittram, Reinhard. *Peter I, Czar und Kaiser: Zur Geschichte Pe-ters des Grossen in seiner Zeit.* 2 vols. Göttingen: Van-denhoek und Ruprecht, 1964.

Wolff, Christian. *Jus gentium methodo scientifica pertractatum.* 2 vols. Oxford: Clarendon, 1934.

_____. *The Real Happiness of the People Under a Philosophical King.* London: Cooper, 1750.

Wolzendorff, Kurt. *Die Polizeigedanke des modernen Staats.* Breslau: Marcus, 1918.

II. Psychological/Psychiatric Materials.

Abraham, Karl. *Selected Papers on Psychoanalysis.* London: Hogarth, 1965.

Arieti, Silvano. *The Interpretation of Schizophrenia.* 2nd ed. New York: Basic Books, 1974.

Arnold, Thomas. *Observations on the Nature, Kinds, Causes and Prevention of Insanity.* 2 vols. London: Phillips, 1806.

Bain, R. Nisbet. *Gustavus III and His Contemporaries.* 2 vols. New York: Bergman, 1970.

Barzun, Jacques. *Clio and the Doctors: Psycho-History, Quanto-History.* Chicago: University of Chicago Press, 1974.

Beech, H. R., ed. *Obsessional States.* London: Methuen, 1974.

Beiro, Caetano. *D. Maria I, 1772-1792.* 4th ed. Lisbon: Empresa nacional de publicidade, 1944.

Boissier de Sauvages, François. *Nosologie méthodique.* 3 vols. Paris: Hérissant, 1770-1771.

Bowlby, John. *Attachment and Loss.* 2 vols. New York: Basic Books, 1969-1973.

_____. *Maternal Care and Mental Health.* Geneva: World Health Organization, 1951.

Brooke, John. *King George III.* New York: McGraw-Hill, 1972.

Chistovich, Ia. A. *Istoriia pervykh meditsinskikh shkol v Rossii.* St. Petersburg: Trei, 1883.

Chizh, Vladimir F. "Imperator Pavel I: psikhologicheskii analiz." *Voprosy filosofii i psikhologii* 1907, pp. 222-290, 391-468, 585-678.

Christiansen, Viggo. *Christian den VII's Sindssygdom.* Odense: Odense Universitetsforlag, 1978.

Clifford, James L. *Dictionary Johnson: Samuel Johnson's Middle Years.* New York: McGraw-Hill, 1979.

Coleman, James C., James N. Butcher, and Robert C. Carson. *Abnormal Psychology and Modern Life.* 6th ed. Glenview, Ill.: Scott, Foresman, 1980.

Colp, Ralph. *To Be an Invalid: The Illness of Charles Darwin.* Chicago: University of Chicago Press, 1977.

Cullen, William. *First Lines of the Practice of Physic.* 4 vols. Edinburgh: Elliott, 1784.

Davis, Glenn. "The Early Years of Theodore Roosevelt." *History of Childhood Quarterly* 2:461-492 (1975).

Deporte, Michael. *Nightmares and Hobby Horses: Swift, Sterne and Augustan Ideas of Madness.* San Marino: Huntington Library, 1974.

Diagnostic and Statistical Manual of Mental Disorders. 2nd ed. Washington, D.C.: American Psychiatric Association, 1968. 3rd ed. 1980.

Dix, Kenneth S. *Madness in Russia, 1775-1864: Official Attitudes and Institutions for its Care.* Ph. D. dissertation, University of California, Los Angeles. 1977.

Doppet, François Amédée. *Vrach filosof.* Moscow: Universitetskaia tipografiia, 1792.

Eysenck, Hans J., and Glenn D. Wilson. *The Experimental Study of Freudian Theories.* London: Methuen, 1973.

Fenichel, Otto M. *The Psychoanalytic Theory of Neurosis.* New York: W. W. Norton, 1945.

Festinger, Leon. *The Theory of Cognitive Dissonance.* Evanston, Ill.: Row, Peterson, 1957.

Fisher, Seymour, and Roger P. Greenberg. *The Scientific Credibility of Freud's Theories and Therapy.* New York: Basic Books, 1977.

Foucault, Michel. *Madness and Civilization: A History of Insanity in the Age of Reason.* Richard Howard, tr. New York: Pantheon, 1965.

Frank, Joseph. *Dostoevsky: The Seeds of Revolt, 1821-1849.* Princeton, N.J.: Princeton University Press, 1976.

Freedman, Alfred M., and Harold I. Kaplan, eds. *Comprehensive Textbook of Psychiatry.* Baltimore: Williams & Wilkins, 1967.

Freud, Anna, and Dorothy Burlingham. *Infants Without Families.* New York: International Universities Press, 1947.

Freud, Sigmund. *The Complete Letters of Sigmund Freud to Wilhelm Fliess.* Jeffrey M. Masson, tr. and ed. Cambridge, Mass.: Harvard/Belknap, 1985.

_____. *The Standard Edition of the Complete Psychological Works of Sigmund Freud.* James Strachey et al., trs. and eds. 24 vols. London: Hogarth Press and the Institute of Psychoanalysis, 1953-1974.

_____, and William C. Bullitt. *Thomas Woodrow Wilson, Twenty-Eighth President of the United States: A Psychological Study.* London: Weidenfeld & Nicolson, 1967.

George, Alexander L., and Juliette L. George. *Woodrow Wilson and Colonel House: A Personality Study.* New York: John Day, 1965.

Haslam, John. *Considerations on the Moral Management of Insane Persons.* London: Hunter, 1817.

Horowitz, M. J., ed. *Hysterical Personality.* New York: Aronson, 1977.

Hunter, Richard A. and Ida Macalpine, eds. *Three Hundred Years of Psychiatry.* London: Oxford University Press, 1963.

Jackson, Don De Avila, ed. *Etiology of Schizophrenia.* New York: Basic Books, 1960.

Jones, Ernest. *The Life and Work of Sigmund Freud.* 3 vols. New York: Basic Books, 1953-1957.

Kant, Immanuel. *Anthropology from a Pragmatic Point of View.* Victor Lyle Dowdell, tr. Hans H. Rudnick, ed. Carbondale, Ill.: Southern Illinois University Press, 1978.

Kaplan, Harold I., Alfred M. Freedman, and Benjamin J. Sadock, eds. *Comprehensive Textbook of Psychiatry.* 3rd ed. 3 vols. Baltimore: Williams & Wilkins, 1980.

Kelly, George A. *Psychology of Personal Constructs.* 2 vols. New York: W. W. Norton, 1955.

King, Lester S. *The Medical World of the Eighteenth Century.* Chicago: University of Chicago Press, 1958.

Kline, Paul. *Fact and Fantasy in Freudian Theory.* London: Methuen, 1972.

Kolb, Lawrence C., and H. Keith H. Brodie. *Modern Clinical Psychiatry.* 10th ed. Philadelphia: W. B. Saunders, 1982.

Kovalevskii, Pavel I. *Imperator Petr III, Imperator Pavel I: psikhiatricheskie eskizy iz istorii.* St. Petersburg: Akinfiev, 1909.

Laughlin, Henry P. *The Neuroses.* Washington, D.C.: Butterworth's, 1967.

Lion, John R., ed. *Personality Disorders: Diagnosis and Management.* Baltimore: Williams & Wilkins, 1974.

Loewenberg, Peter. "The Psychohistorical Origins of the Nazi Youth Cohort." *American Historical Review* 67:1457-1502 (1971).

Loewenberg, Peter. "The Unsuccessful Adolescence of Heinrich Himmler." *American Historical Review* 76:612-641 (1971).

Lukacs, John. *Philadelphia: Patricians and Philistines, 1900-1950.* New York: Farrar, Straus, Giroux, 1981.

Macalpine, Ida, and Richard Hunter. *George III and the Mad Business.* New York: Pantheon, 1969.

Maddi, Salvatore R. *Personality Theories: a Comparative Analysis.* Homewood, Ill.: Dorsey, 1968.

Metzger, Johann Daniel. *Nachal'nyia osnovaniia vseobshchikh chastei vrachebnyia nauki.* St. Petersburg: Gosudarstvennyi meditsinskii kolledzh, 1799.

Meyer, Georg Friedrich. *Opyt o lunatikakh, sochinennoi publichnago ucheniia filosofii, i Korolevskoi Akademii nauk v Berline chlenom Georg Friedrich Meyer.* Moscow: Universitetskaia tipografiia, 1764.

Müller-Dietz, Heinz. *Aertze in Russland des achtzehnten Jahrhunderts.* Esslinger: Neckar, 1973.

Orlansky, Harold. "Infant Care and Personality." *Psychological Bulletin* 46:1-47 (1949).

Peken, Matvei Khristianovich. *Nachal'nyia osnovaniia deiatel'nyia vrachebnyia nauki.* St. Petersburg: Sukhoputnyi kadetskii korpus, 1790.

Pinel, Philippe. *Nosographie philosophique.* 3rd ed. 3 vols. Paris: Brosson, 1807.

_____. *Traité médico-philosophique sur l'aliénation mentale.* 2nd ed. Paris: Brosson, 1809.

Porter, Roy. *Mind-Forg'd Manacles: A History of Madness in England from the Restoration to the Regency.* London: Athlone, 1987.

Pringle, Mia Lilly Kellmer. *Deprivation and Education.* New York: Humanities Press, 1965.

Provence, Sally A., and Rose C. Lipton. *Infants in Institutions: A Comparison of Their Development with Family-Reared Infants during the First Year of Life.* New York: International Universities Press, 1963.

Rachman, Stanley J., and R. J. Hodgson. *Obsessions and Compulsions.* Englewood Cliffs, N.J.: Prentice-Hall, 1980.

Reddaway, J. F. "Struensée and the Fall of Bernstorff." *English Historical Review* 27:274-286 (1912).

_____. "Don Sebastiano de Llano and the Danish Revolution." *English Historical Review* 41:78-90 (1926).

Richter, August Gottlieb. *Nachal'nyia osnovaniia rukovoditel'nyia vrachebnyia nauki.* 3 vols. St. Petersburg: Sukhoputnyi kadetskii korpus, 1791-1795.

Roy, Alec. *Hysteria.* New York: John Wiley, 1982.

Salzman, Leon. *The Obsessive Personality.* New York: Science House, 1968.

Scott, Sir Ronald Bodley, ed. *Price's Textbook of the Practice of Medicine.* 11th ed. London: Oxford University Press, 1973.

Sears, Robert R. *Survey of Objective Studies of Psychoanalytic Concepts.* New York: Social Science Research Council, 1943.

Shapiro, David. *Neurotic Styles.* New York: Basic Books, 1965.

Stannard, David. *Shrinking History: On Freud and the Failure of Psychohistory.* Oxford: Oxford University Press, 1980.

Sullivan, Harry Stack. *Clinical Studies in Psychiatry.* New York: W. W. Norton, 1965.

Swanson, David W., Philip J. Bohnert, and Jackson A. Smith. *The Paranoid.* Boston: Little, Brown, 1970.

Szasz, Thomas S. *The Myth of Mental Illness: Foundations of a Theory of Personal Conduct.* New York: Hoeber-Harper, 1961.

Taxonera, Luciano de. *Felipe V, fundador de una dinastía y dos veces rey de España.* Barcelona: Juventud, 1942.

Tissot, Simon André. *Vrach svetskikh liudei.* Moscow: Tipografiia kompanii tipograficheskoi, 1792.

Tuke, Samuel. *Description of the Retreat: An Institution near York for Insane Persons of the Society of Friends.* Richard Hunter and Ida Macalpine, eds. Reprint of first 1813 edition. London: Dawsons, 1964.

Vaillant, George B. *Adjustment to Life.* Boston: Little, Brown, 1977.

Valentine, Charles W.. *The Psychology of Early Childhood: A Study of Mental Development in the First Years of Life*. 3rd ed. London: Methuen, 1946.

Wain, John. *Samuel Johnson*. New York: Viking, 1974.

INDEX

About the Author

HUGH RAGSDALE, Professor of History at the University of Alabama, is the author of *Paul I: A Reassessment of His Life and Reign;* and *Detente in the Napoleonic Era: Bonaparte and the Russians.* His articles on Russian and French history have appeared in scholarly journals and other publications.